THE SIMPLE FAITH OF
FRANKLIN DELANO ROOSEVELT

Franklin Delano Roosevelt giving a speech from the rear platform of the "Roosevelt Special."

IMAGE COURTESY OF THE FRANKLIN DELANO ROOSEVELT PRESIDENTIAL LIBRARY

THE SIMPLE FAITH OF FRANKLIN DELANO ROOSEVELT

RELIGION'S ROLE IN THE FDR PRESIDENCY

CHRISTINE WICKER

SMITHSONIAN BOOKS

WASHINGTON, DC

This book may be purchased for educational, business, or sales promotional use. For information, please write: Special Markets Department, Smithsonian Books, P.O. Box 37012, MRC 513, Washington, DC 20013

Published by Smithsonian Books
Director: Carolyn Gleason
Senior Editor: Christina Wiginton
Art Director: Jody Billert
Editorial Assistant: Jaime Schwender

Edited by Carla Borden
Typeset by Blue Heron

Library of Congress Cataloging-in-Publication Data

Names: Wicker, Christine, author.
Title: The simple faith of Franklin Delano Roosevelt : religion's role in the
    FDR presidency / Christine Wicker.
Description: Washington, DC : Smithsonian Books, 2017. | Includes
    bibliographical references and index.
Identifiers: LCCN 2017004086 | ISBN 9781588345240
Subjects: LCSH: Roosevelt, Franklin D. (Franklin Delano),
    1882-1945—Religion. | Presidents—United States—Religion. | Religion and
    politics—United States—History—20th century.
Classification: LCC E807 .W56 2017 | DDC 973.917092—dc23
LC record available at https://lccn.loc.gov/2017004086

Manufactured in the United States of America
21 20 19 18 17   5 4 3 2 1

CONTENTS

Franklin D. Roosevelt, with daughter-in-law Betsey and eldest son James, visiting Fort Worth, Texas, in 1938.

Author's Preface

My mother was among those whom Franklin D. Roosevelt helped keep alive with programs created during the Great Depression.

In 1940 my grandfather was working the oil fields of Illinois, while my grandmother tended to seven kids, the oldest one a lanky deaf boy who was not able to communicate with anyone. When she wanted him, she had to chase after him until he wore out and let her catch up. My mother was the youngest. Her birth certificate lists her as a blue baby, meaning her chances weren't the best. But she hung on, big-eyed and skinny.

In 1942, before my mother was old enough to remember her father, he collapsed and died of what seemed to be a heart attack. No reason for an autopsy; whatever he died of didn't matter. What did matter was that he could help the living no more. The oil company bought train tickets to take the family back to Oklahoma, where they'd come from. President Roosevelt's programs for the poor provided eleven dollars a month for each of my grandmother's children. It wasn't enough to keep them adequately fed or clothed. They were hungry, their shoes were too small, and in winter they didn't have coats. By 1949, when my mother was in junior high, the country was enjoying a postwar economic boom that my mother's family had no part of. That year my mother dropped out of school, unable to bear the smell of lunches that more fortunate children threw away. She and her siblings were scorned, shunned, and shamed, as poor children often are, but none of them starved to death, thanks to FDR.

My grandfather on my father's side was a Kentucky coal miner in a part of the country where people so revered FDR that they had his picture displayed in their homes. When the president died, my dad was a teenager. What he remembers of those days was the fear. "Everyone was scared of what would happen to us without him," he told me. "He was the only president a lot of people had ever known."

I began writing about Roosevelt and his great faith—religious and otherwise—after Ken Burns's *The Dust Bowl* documentary showed a hundred thousand people gathering in July of 1938 to see FDR in Amarillo. I live in Texas, which is a far different place today than it was in 1938, more prosperous and far more conservative. I doubt a liberal president could attract half that many people to an Amarillo speech today. The state's most famous megachurch evangelical ministers would certainly not support such a president.

The television documentary featured a photo of the president looking jaunty as he rode in an open car. It rained a gully washer the day FDR came to Amarillo, and the drenched president smiled even more. That it would rain that day he visited the Dust Bowl seemed just too perfect. It was as if even God was giving the president a big welcome. Like many Americans, I didn't think of FDR as a particularly religious man, but I love a good coincidence. Lots of people see the hand of God in what others call no more than coincidence. My interest was piqued.

It is not a coincidence that I should write a book delving into Franklin Roosevelt's faith and how it played out in his politics and policies. My own religious roots are deep and have held fast despite my many attempts to sever them. My great-grandfather was an Alabama preacher who moved his family to Oklahoma's Indian Territory to pastor a church there. I was an infant when my grandmother carried me the half mile it took to reach the nearest Baptist church so that I could be dedicated to the Lord. At nine, I was saved and baptized in an Oklahoma City Southern Baptist church. As a reporter, I've covered religion in the press and in books for most of my adult life. I was not a practicing Christian for much of that time. But as I only recently realized, there has hardly been a day that I haven't thought of Jesus and what he expects of me. Having admitted that, I can't help remembering a verse I heard often in my childhood, "Train up a child in the way he should go: and when he is old, he will not depart from it."[1] Baptists are big on memorizing scripture. A lot of it comes to me still. But as I've grown older, those verses have taken on different meanings. "The way" has come to seem more complicated than it did when I was a child.

The Christianity I grew up with required that we read the Bible, pray, go to church, tithe, win others to Christ, and not have sex outside of marriage. And, oh, yes, not drink alcohol, not do drugs, and not curse. We were expected to love sinners but not to accept their behavior, and if that meant rejecting them, we did. We were obliged to help those who needed it, but the best help we could give them was to tell them about salvation. I was in my early twenties before I ever heard another Christian say that Jesus expected us to work for social justice. I didn't believe it and said so.

As I studied Christianity through the years, I began to see it differently, and I began to think that Jesus's commands regarding brotherhood, love, and humans' responsibility for one another were directly reflected in policies like those of FDR's New Deal.[2] The evangelical Christians who are most often in the news and have dominated the public square for almost four decades do not commonly laud Roosevelt for his Christian influence on government, even though many of his policies came directly out of their core religious values. White Christians, at least, have widely supported Republican policies that favor business, low taxes, and restricting aid to the poor. Reagan, not FDR, has been their favorite modern president.

The main focus of this book is to show the importance of Franklin Roosevelt's profoundly Christian vision in making America a country with more equality and justice for all. I believe the thrust of FDR's faith will resonate with many people's ideas about what Christian faith ought to be. Implementing that faith into federal policy was and still is controversial. Good people can disagree. But knowing that there was a time when one man's Christianity was bold and powerful enough to inspire a much different course than government usually follows today is an important part of our country's history.

As I researched and wrote, I also wondered how FDR's life might inform my own spirituality. His kind of literal, unreflective Christianity was ridiculed even in his day. Looking at his life caused me to wonder if knowing what is and isn't literally true in the Bible matters as much as many of us think. Roosevelt, a man who famously didn't overthink anything, didn't seem to care, and his faith paid big personal dividends. It helped make him and his life better. Just as important, it didn't make him worse. It didn't make him mean. It didn't cause him to be narrow minded. It didn't cut him off from other people. It didn't keep him from having fun.

It also didn't make him perfect. There is a lot to criticize about FDR, but all the ways he failed to be a good Christian didn't keep him from being an effective Christian. In that realization, there's hope for all of us, no matter what kind of faith we try to follow.

Roosevelt as governor of New York, 1931.

INTRODUCTION

In March of 1933, Franklin Delano Roosevelt and Adolf Hitler, two men of extraordinary persuasiveness and compelling vision, came into elective power. The entire world was being crushed by economic depression. Country after country was abandoning democracy, believing it was too weak to solve the crises at hand. Fear of starvation was keen in Germany, where British blockades had caused great hunger during World War I and peace terms had left the country crippled and in debt. At the same time, hunger riots were breaking out in the United States. Farmers were losing their land; small-town families were being turned onto the streets. Upstanding, hardworking people had become bums queuing up for bread.

Both countries demanded strong leaders. Both got them. Almost nine years would pass before the two countries would go to war against each other, but Roosevelt and Hitler would be engaged in a battle for the soul of humanity from the moment they took power.[1] If religion is defined as that which asks life's deepest questions, their conflict was religious in the truest sense. Between them stood the Jews: anathema to Hitler, divine inspiration for Roosevelt.

Both men needed to restore and energize their people. Hitler took the surer route, inciting fear and violently squashing dissent. It was a reasonable choice for a man who wanted total power. The idea that Hitler was a madman whose irrationality inflamed his countrymen toward unspeakable acts is popular, but some emerging research presents a different picture. Although the acts he inspired were vile, his aims were entirely logical once his founding premise was accepted.

"Hitler's basic critique was not the usual one [made by virulent anti-Semites] that human beings were good but had been corrupted by an overly Jewish civilization. It was rather that humans were animals and that any exercise of ethical deliberation was in itself a sign of Jewish corruption," according to Yale University historian Timothy Snyder. The strong, pure Aryan race must destroy inferior races and weak people in the same way that strong animals destroy the weak ones in the wild, according to Hitler's thinking. Jewish ideas of mercy would cause all humanity to perish, as inferior humans were allowed to live, breed, and take up more of the world's resources, the Führer preached. Once the two parts of his philosophy—survival of the fittest and destruction of Jews to end the influence of Jewish teachings—were accepted, all else could follow. Hitler gave Germans a rationale that allowed their darker selves to flourish under a cover of practicality and even nobility.

On the other side of the Atlantic, Roosevelt was following precisely those Jewish-inspired ideas that Hitler so despised. Eschewing fear by specifically counseling Americans that "all we have to fear is fear itself," FDR breathed his own great faith into America. To him, preserving American democracy, furthering equality, and following God's will were inextricably linked, as he believed they had been for the country's founders. A lifelong Christian who believed that God expected his servants to help those in need, Roosevelt treated America as if it were the beloved community.[2] Drawing upon scripture again and again throughout his administration, he sought to unify Americans and to amplify their highest, most sacred values.

Early in his first term, he announced that he was plotting his course straight out of Jesus's teachings: "The Great Teacher said 'come that ye may have life and that ye may have it more abundantly.' The object of all our striving should be to realize that 'abundant life.'"[3] He meant "abundant life" in the same way it is used scripturally: for everyone.

Roosevelt espoused brotherhood, justice, and faith—faith in God, faith in one another, and faith in a better future. From his first presidential address and for twelve years afterward, he infused his own simple, literal faith so powerfully into the spirit of the American public that many believed he had been sent by God. They looked for signs that God's hand was on him, and sometimes—in his escape from assassination, in his luck, in his care for their welfare—they found such signs.

Germans found the same signs of God's blessing in their leader. His own luck was phenomenal. He escaped multiple assassination attempts. When he militarized the Rhineland, brought Austria under his sway, and moved troops into Czechoslovakia, Europe violated its own treaties by standing completely aside—luck beyond even what Hitler dared hope for. The Führer also used scriptural phrases. In justifying his takeover of other countries, he said Germans must have more land to grow crops for their "daily bread," a resonant phrase from the Lord's Prayer in which

Jesus asks God to "give us this day our daily bread." Rousing their fear was easy; sanctifying his actions with Jesus's words was a master stroke. He claimed God's blessing far more directly than FDR was wont to do. He wrote in *Mein Kampf*, "Therefore, I believe today that I am acting in the sense of the Almighty Creator. By warding off the Jews I am fighting for the Lord's work."[4]

But beneath the exploitation of scripture by both men is a great difference in their methods and their aims. Roosevelt's dependence on scripture and faith is consistent from before his election as president through his terms of office. Hitler's biblical references twist their meanings to justify a philosophy never presented in scripture and belied by his expressed contempt for Jewish and Christian ideals. Hitler targeted the weak and those who opposed him.[5] FDR chose the rich and powerful for denunciation, as the Jewish prophets had before him. Hitler destroyed German democracy; FDR ignored calls for dictatorship, listening to the voice of the people and seeking the guidance of God. Hitler yearned to rule colonies as Great Britain did; FDR eschewed imperialism, speaking against it even with his friend and ally Winston Churchill. Hitler incited violence in his own country and in other countries as a way of undermining the protection of the state; FDR relied on rule of law, bowing to Congress and the Supreme Court even as they blocked his proposals.

Roosevelt's worldview and much of his personality were shaped by the strength and vibrancy of his Episcopal faith, which was fed by his sense of a continuing relationship with God. Amid the millions of words written about the thirty-second president, only a relatively small number have dealt with his faith. Some scholars have seemed hardly aware of it. Others have scoffed at the very idea that he might have been a man of faith.

It's easy to see why. He was far from a holy man in so many ways. He cheated on his wife with her former secretary Lucy Mercer and repeatedly broke his promise to Eleanor never to see Lucy again. Some believe he had numerous affairs, although evidence is scant. He was canny, sometimes ruthless. He was deceitful. He held grudges, was sometimes petty, and could be vindictive.

He tried to pack the Supreme Court and to purge the Democratic

Party of those who weren't progressive enough for him. When he ran for his third and fourth terms as president, he broke the revered two-term custom that was set by George Washington and followed by every other president since.[6] The United States was moving toward war during his third election and engaged in a world war during his fourth. Many believed that duty alone pushed him to run in 1940 and 1944. But did it? Some believed ambition was to blame. He loved being president, and once, after having said so, asked, "Wouldn't anybody?" He was a man of tremendous ego who thrived on power. Even those who loved him most could hardly describe him as selfless.

And yet his public words were filled with images, stories, and quotations from scripture. When author William Federer combed FDR's public papers for references to religious faith, he found enough to fill a four-hundred-page book.[7] Many believed then and now that his words were political strategy, written by speechwriters. Some claimed that he wouldn't have known enough Bible to compose so many references himself. But his speechwriters denied that. They called him the controlling spirit, often the primary writer, behind every speech.[8]

"No American politician has given so many speeches that were essentially sermons rather than statements of policy," wrote historian James MacGregor Burns. "Like a preacher, he wanted and expected his sermons to serve as practical moral guides to his people. Roosevelt was so theatrical that his moral preachments were often dismissed with a smile. Actually he was deadly serious."[9] His faith was so evident to his family that his son James called him a frustrated clergyman.[10]

His actions were devoted to one aim from beginning to end, said Eleanor: "Throughout the whole of Franklin's career there never was any deviation from his original objective—to help make life better for the average man, woman and child. A thousand and one means were used, difficulties arose, changes took place, but his objective always was the motive for what had to be done."[11]

Roosevelt changed American life in countless ways that have endured. Perhaps most importantly and controversially, he made the federal government a powerful instrument of social justice and equality. His New

Deal, which recognized rights never before granted African Americans, was the true beginning of the civil rights movement, according to some scholars. He made the American dream more possible for all Americans. At the same time, however, by inserting elements of social gospel thinking into federal legislation, many believe he created a culture of dependence and victimology that plagues the country still.

Roosevelt's labor legislation changed America from a country where employers could legally work men, women, and children for any wage they liked for as long as they liked and in conditions as inhumane and dangerous as they liked. He passed the first national minimum wage and restricted child labor. With the Social Security Act, he gave Americans security in old age. Unemployment insurance from that act gave them succor during periods of unemployment. The Glass-Steagall Act created the Federal Deposit Insurance Corporation, providing federal protection for Americans' savings. His administration set up the Securities and Exchange Commission to regulate Wall Street. He gave veterans the G.I. Bill, a guarantee to pay war veterans' way through college. That act alone moved millions of Americans from poverty and has been credited by some with creating the American middle class.

The Rural Electrification Act gave lights and heat to rural America. The Tennessee Valley Authority helped bring prosperity to rural areas in seven states through flood control and electricity. He set aside vast tracts of land for the public use: 140 national wildlife refuges and 58 national forests, national parks, and monuments.

Some called FDR's motivation noblesse oblige. Others put it down to progressivism mixed with social gospel. Those are good explanations, but they hardly suffice. This extraordinarily worldly man had a vision for America that was completely, some would say ludicrously, otherworldly. He outlined it in bits and pieces many times. One of his most complete presentations was voiced in a speech after his second election: "We are beginning to wipe out the line that divides the practical from the ideal; and in so doing we are fashioning an instrument of unimagined power for the establishment of a morally better world," he said.

This new understanding undermines the old admiration of worldly success as such. We are beginning to abandon our tolerance of the abuse of power by those who betray for profit the elementary decencies of life. In this process evil things formerly accepted will not be so easily condoned. Hard-headedness will not so easily excuse hardheartedness.

This passage is so impregnated with startling ideas that it needs to be read several times just to be absorbed. Line after line, he is "claiming the promises of God," as the church people would say.

This is not noblesse oblige. This is not social gospel or progressivism. This is social and economic revolution. He wasn't saying, "Let's be nice to the poor." Or even "Let's right the wrongs society has imposed." Like Jesus in the Sermon on the Mount, he was overturning all the old truths about what matters, about what has value, about how life ought to be lived.

Ideas this profoundly religious are rarely heard even inside churches and almost never in the public square. America would wait decades before again hearing such holy boldness from a leader. That leader, the Reverend Dr. Martin Luther King Jr., would hold no office and command no great resources. But the power of his words and his actions changed the nation, as did FDR's.

Roosevelt's unquestioning beliefs were based on scripture, and as far as anyone knows, he took them as literal truth. He believed God communicated with human beings, himself in particular. He believed God expected those who served him to serve others. By interpreting his own immense suffering from polio as a test from God, he was able to transcend severe disability. His optimism, his utter confidence when making hard decisions, and his complete serenity in the face of dire circumstances were all outgrowths of his faith, according to those who knew him best.

That faith was deeply rooted from the very beginning of his life.

Sara Roosevelt in 1893 with a young Franklin.

1

"Plump, Pink, and Nice"

Franklin Roosevelt's belief in the goodness and abundance of life was solidly established before he was old enough to know anything about formal religion. The first pillar supporting the faith that guided his life was his own excellent temperament. The second was the quality of his upbringing and childhood, which provided almost everything he needed to grow into an emotionally and spiritually secure man.

He was born on January 30, 1882, after more than twenty-four hours of labor and a dose of chloroform given to his mother, Sara, that almost killed them both. The baby was blue and not breathing. The doctor immediately began artificial respiration, which roused Franklin into fierce squalling. For the next nine years, that rough birth would be the worst moment of the little rich boy's life.

Weighing ten pounds at birth, he was robustly healthy, "plump, pink, and nice," as his mother put it. He rarely cried, was easily soothed, and laughed often, the kind of happy baby who makes everyone around him smile. As is sometimes the case, he kept his childhood personality traits throughout his life. He rarely showed anger or discouragement. His laugh became famous, a hearty, full-bodied roar delivered with his head tossed back.

His world in the Hudson River valley—Springwood estate in Hyde Park, New York—was a warm, loving place full of delight and approval, a baronial fiefdom that was utterly divided between landed gentry, whose large estates were on some of the loveliest land in America, and the people who served them. The Roosevelts were old money and plenty of it. Their name was one of the most distinguished in America. Coming as close as anyone in America could come to being aristocracy, they and their little boy were courted and cosseted everywhere they went. Nature and nurture conspired to form a man of supreme confidence.

His mother so doted on him that for the rest of her life, she loved passing the sunny upstairs bedroom where "my son first saw the light of day." A typical Victorian woman of Sara's class would have given over the care of her child to nurses and nannies. Behaving otherwise was unconventional, which was never commendable in their set. But Sara, who was an extremely self-possessed young lady, did not care. From the moment of his birth to the moment of her death, she was uncommonly involved with her only child. In those early days, she bathed him herself, breastfed him until he was almost one year old, and recorded every accomplishment of his young life in her diary. She saved every letter he ever wrote her and every picture he drew, referring to him as "baby" long after his christening. She spent countless hours reading to him and playing games. As he grew, mother and son maintained a warm, loving relationship. The two of them conducted playful verbal games of teasing that only they fully understood.

He never lost the sense of security that a child gets from such a mother's devotion, and he never lost that love of teasing. As president he delighted in bestowing nicknames. Advisor Thomas Corcoran became "Tommy the Cork." Army Major General Edwin Watson was "Pa" Watson. Practical jokes were welcome occasions for hilarity. His predecessor Herbert Hoover's White House had been a gloomy place; FDR's was filled with laughter. Roosevelt so relished telling and listening to humorous stories that being with him usually meant a good time would be had by all. "You could joke with him about pretty much everything but his family and his religious faith," said writer Robert Sherwood. It was true that Roosevelt took matters of faith as serious business, but his wide-ranging love of play gave him a lightness of spirit that kept his religion from having the stiff-necked and self-righteous quality that so plagued Woodrow Wilson's.

Young Franklin's life was made even more secure by a houseful of servants who "worshipped him blindly," as Sara put it. Once, questioning one of them after having heard some bad reports about his conduct, she said, "Elespie, I heard our boy has been misbehaving." But Elespie was having none of it. She replied, "They tell me he has faults, but I can't see them."

All this privilege might have produced a spoiled brat, and there were times in Franklin's young adulthood when he was taken to be just that. But his parents were united in the determination that their son would be a man of industry and character. Like other wealthy children, he had a pony of his own and a dog, but he was required to care for both of them himself.

One day Sara played Steeplechase with him, a game that included racing toy ponies. When she won the first few games, Franklin demanded that she hand over her horse, because "it's a better horse." She did. Then she rolled the dice again, and again she won. Franklin became sulky and angry. Sara quietly packed up the game and told him that until he learned to take a beating, he would not be allowed to play any games.

He was four years old.

His mother was teaching her strong-willed son a lesson about dealing with emotions that would define him for the rest of his life. Control your feelings. Hide that fierce, angry self. Show people what they want to see. Be gracious. Be amiable. Or the game will stop. The toys will be taken away. And you will be left alone. Years later she was able to brag that no one ever saw bad sportsmanship in Franklin again. Even more valuable, perhaps, his enthusiasm didn't depend on whether he was winning or losing. He just kept trying.

FDR's father, James, was fifty-three when Franklin was born. He already had an adult son, James "Rosy" Roosevelt, and a two-year-old grandson, nicknamed Taddy. James has sometimes been portrayed as a weak or absent father, but the record shows otherwise. He, like his young wife, was intensely involved with their son. Vice president of the Delaware and Hudson Railway and president of the Southern Railway Security Company, James was home more than many fathers. He took his family with him often when he traveled.[1]

James lavished time on the child of his maturity. Father and son were the best of friends, hiking, sailing, and sledding together, as FDR and his own children later would.[2] Franklin was four when he began touring the family's estate every morning with his father. James, known in Hyde Park as Mr. James and sometimes Squire James, sat on his long-legged trotter, Doolittle, and Franklin rode beside him on his fat Welsh pony, Debby. Their laughter often rang out over their holdings on the Hudson River. But James didn't laugh at Franklin's expense. Ridicule and sarcasm were not part of their communication. What Franklin had to say was received by James with great respect and attention. During those critical years of early childhood, Franklin acquired a sense of himself as a lovable person worthy of respect. His father and various tutors helped him gain confidence in his ability to master serious tasks, take reasonable risks, and enjoy skillful play.

James, whose photos make him appear to be such a staid and stodgy member of his class, had his own independent streak. All the other members of the Roosevelt clan were Republicans. James was a Democrat. Even more surprising, James was an avowed Democrat who nevertheless supported Lincoln during the war, according to Roosevelt aide Stanley High. "To have been a Democrat at all among the rich landowners of the Hudson Valley required a good deal of courage," wrote High. "To have been a Lincoln Democrat in 1863 was reckoned even worse than to have been a New Deal Republican in 1936."[3] One result of James's unusual stance was that nobody thought he was politically principled: his Republican neighbors didn't like his politics and neither did the Democrats. Franklin would often sit in just this kind of thorny seat as president.[4]

Religious people often seem to pattern their image of God after the kind of father they have—or the kind they wish for. FDR's relationship with James did resemble his idea of God. He thought of himself as being guided by God's will but in a rather companionable way. God was good and had provided his people, who were generally good, with Earth, a wonderful place to live. It isn't hard to imagine that he saw a parallel with his father, who took Franklin, still a young child, along on his tours of the lovely estate he would someday inherit. Like Squire James, God expected Franklin to be good and to do good, but he wasn't too focused on any of the ways Franklin failed. God gave advice and support when FDR asked, but otherwise he trusted Franklin to be on course. In return the Supreme Power supported FDR's ambitions. FDR's was not a guilt-ridden, groveling relationship with God, but one of peace, security, and willing service.

Among the lessons his parents modeled were extraordinary stoicism and bravery, qualities he would also exhibit. Franklin's earliest memory dates from when he was three and on a ship with his parents headed home from Europe. A great storm damaged the ship, the captain couldn't be found, and passengers below in steerage were screaming when the lights went out.

"We seem to be going down," James said calmly as he prepared to go on deck to discover what was happening.

"It does look like it," Sara replied, equally calm. As the water lapped at her fur coat, which was hanging on a hook, Sara lifted it and wrapped Franklin snugly in it, saying, "Poor little boy. If he must go down, he's going down warm."

Franklin, clasped in his mother's arms, saw a toy floating on the rising water. "Mama! Mama!" he shouted. "Save my jumping jack!" Sara leaned out from her berth and retrieved the toy.

But the ship did not sink. The captain, who had been knocked out by a fall in his cabin, revived and took control, rallying the crew and righting the ship. Franklin told the story many times as an adult, always in high good humor, a testimony to how Roosevelts faced disaster.

When Franklin was nine, the Roosevelts faced real tragedy. James suffered a heart attack, and the boy's carefree childhood abruptly ended. For the next nine years, Sara and Franklin lived by the rule that nothing must upset dear Popsy. Any consternation, excitement, or anxiety might bring on another heart attack. She and James had kept the little boy close before, protecting him from knowing about events that might make him fearful, but they couldn't protect him now. The awareness that misbehavior on his part might kill his father was a heavy responsibility for a little boy, but he seems to have borne it without complaint. Any urge to separate from his parents or to rebel in the ordinary ways teenagers do seems to have been quelled. His mother needed him more than ever, and he did not disappoint her. A single child without many children around, he had often been expected to conform to adult expectations. Now he took on the much bigger burden of comforting her.

Before James's heart attack, he had been his son's active, adventurous playmate. Now their games became sedate and often delayed by illness. The family's travels had been luxurious fun and adventure. Now the Roosevelts began to make repeated pilgrimages to Germany's Bad Nauheim thermal springs, hoping they might improve James's health. Surrounded by sick people, many of them old and dying, Franklin was constrained even more severely. Don't run. Don't play too loudly. Don't disturb anybody.

In addition, Franklin and Sara now had an urgent reason to solicit God's help. Children often believe themselves to be more responsible for bad events than they are. They may also believe they have more power to make things right than they do. The self-induced pressure on Franklin to pray fervently and frequently would have been intense. To have resisted would have seemed like a deliberate neglect of his beloved father—especially since God seemed to be answering.

Even a trip to visit friends could exhaust James to the point that Sara feared he might die. But again and again, he recovered. Sara, who was devout herself, would have been likely to thank God for such deliverance. For Franklin to deny that his father's recovery was evidence of the Almighty's power would have seemed quite dangerous, the kind of unbelief an offended God might punish. Perhaps those desperate years help explain what some have called the childlike character of FDR's religious faith in later life.

Many people feel closer to God when alone in a beautiful natural setting. FDR's later reverence for the natural world, his fierce desire to protect it, and the scripture verses he quoted in defense of conservation support the idea that nature had a spiritual element for him. If, as seems likely, the child prayed for his father to recover while wandering the woods of Springwood, his faith would have been at the magical stage appropriate to his age. At that stage, it would be natural for a child to look for signs that God heard him and was answering. Each time James seemed near death and then rallied, the boy's faith in a God who was in relationship with him and answered his prayers with definite action would have been affirmed. Some believers grow out of the so-called magical phase of belief, but many do not. They merely learn to be circumspect about whom they confide in. FDR's faith deepened and matured over the years, but it always retained the sense that God was in active communication with his people and played an important part in the world.

The Roosevelt family didn't suddenly turn to God when misfortune struck. Religion had been a constant influence in Franklin's life. When at home, the Roosevelts went to church every Sunday at St. James' Episcopal Church in Hyde Park, where Franklin had been christened and James was a trustee and later a senior warden. Franklin wasn't a particularly pious boy. He so often came down with an incapacitating headache on church mornings that James called his ailment a "Sunday headache."[5]

When he did attend church, young Franklin is likely to have heard at least some of what's been called social gospel. The Roosevelts' Hyde Park ministers would have been well aware of the conservative social views the landed gentry of Hudson Valley held, and they are unlikely to have wanted to offend those families, but because the Episcopal Church was a foremost leader in social gospel teachings during those years, some of those new religious ideas could hardly have been avoided.

The social gospel movement was a brand of Christian thinking that's widely criticized today as a failed doctrine, but its central tenets have nevertheless spread throughout society, radically changing how many citizens view themselves, their neighbors, and the responsibility of government. Social gospel moved the blame for human failure, misfortune, and sometimes even sin away from the idea of original sin. Instead of each individual being a sinner responsible for his own salvation in this world and the next, social gospel said that social factors beyond individual control played a large part in how people's lives played out, even in how they behaved. This new thinking was a tremendous shift that is still being fiercely contested in American politics and religion. It meant that charity alone was no longer an adequate response to human need. It gave a religious imprimatur to the idea that social justice might be a governmental responsibility.

New York parishes were especially subject to social gospel preachings because the bishop of New York, Henry Codman Potter, was one of the social gospel movement's most prominent leaders. He selected those priests who would fill pulpits in his district, and he preached around the state himself, sometimes at St. James'.[6] James and Sara, who kept an apartment in New York City in the Hotel Renaissance at 10 West Forty-Third Street, often stayed in the city for long periods of time. They could have hardly avoided awareness of the bishop's activities and beliefs.

Even before becoming a bishop, Potter had established working-men's clubs, day nurseries, and kindergartens. Long after he became bishop, he worked in missions on the East Side of New York. He was active in promoting labor issues and in settling labor disputes.

Jesus "came to make hateful and odious that cultivated self-love which cares nothing for another's welfare," he said. Bishop Potter called the growth of wealth, the prevalence of luxury, and the massing of large wealth "a standing menace to the freedom and integrity of the individual." He was pained to observe that Americans had come to associate wealth and godliness as though they were the same.[7]

The Roosevelts seem to have performed their Christian duty each in their own way. Sara displayed many outward signs of conventional piety. She believed drinking to be morally suspect and opposed it all her life. She liked having her prayer book near her and would often carry it with her. She took baskets and bouquets to the sick, supplied food and clothing to those in need, paid visits to retired servants, and supervised a sewing class at Hyde Park. She was acting out of noblesse oblige, some might have said, as they later said of her son. Sara, who certainly was the grand lady of all occasions and wouldn't have apologized for it, did construct her life in line with Jesus's parable of the faithful servant in Luke: "For unto whomsoever much is given, of him shall be much required: and to whom men have committed much, of him they will ask the more." She taught her son that his privileges meant he must do well and also do good.

Sara's Christianity was steady and visible all her life, but it did not impress one of her most careful observers, one who accompanied her to church faithfully for many years, her daughter-in-law, Eleanor. After both Sara and Franklin had died, Eleanor described Sara's Christianity as supporting whatever was "customary and respectable." As an example Eleanor remembered that after the death of Helen Astor, the wife of Franklin's half-brother Rosy, he wanted to marry his French mistress of many years. But Sara, as head of the household, would not grant him permission. Franklin, appalled that Rosy would be barred from an honorable action that would give him happiness, protested. His mother responded, "*She* is not of our class." And that was that.[8] It was remarkable, Eleanor told a friend, that Franklin had been able to break free of his mother's standards and find Christian values of his own—ones of which Sara's class decidedly did not approve.

FDR repeatedly and publicly refused to give those in power the reverence they were accustomed to. Jesus had acted likewise, putting Roosevelt on solid Christian ground, but in this case, the powerful whom the American president offended were the very class he had been a seemingly happy part of since birth. His minimum-wage regulations curtailed the prerogatives of the powerful, often business owners, when dealing with the weak, often workers. His Social Security program forced business owners (and workers) to pay into a national retirement fund. He limited laissez-faire capitalism, which posited that unfettered capitalism would result in a fair market, with new agencies and a blizzard of regulations that valued safety, fairness, the environment, and what he called the public good. He blocked industrial attempts to control natural resources such as water. He set aside vast tracts of land as national parks that restricted those who might profit from their natural resources: farmers, ranchers, loggers, or developers.

Sara supported her son, the president, in all his efforts, as of course she would. But in her heart, she preferred the old ways. She would give charity to those who needed it, but unlike her son, she definitely didn't support the minions getting too much above their station. When the presidential library was being built, old Mrs. Roosevelt would sometimes stroll over to see how construction was coming along. Noticing the number of parked cars, she realized that the workmen were driving from Hyde Park village. When she suggested they ought to be walking, they told her that the village was a mile and half away. "When I was your age," she replied tartly, "I was fully capable of walking a mile and a half twice a day, and I did so many times to get the mail." Their profligate ways continued to disturb her so much that she would sometimes shake her head as she eyed their work and grumble, "You're all in clover . . . clover . . . living off the fat of the land!"

Mr. James also did many good works throughout the community. He didn't live long enough for anyone to know how he would have responded to FDR's society-shaking policies, but he seems to have followed Christianity with the mild kindness and tolerance that was his custom throughout life. As an adult, Franklin said of his father, "He was the most generous and kindly of men and always liberal in outlook."[9] How liberal in outlook James could be came out in a speech he once gave before the St. James' Guild. His words show a kind of curiosity, empathy, and responsibility rare among their social set, the kind that his son later embraced even more powerfully.

Entitled "Work," the speech starts off predictably enough. Hard work is the key to success, he tells his audience. "There is not so much to *luck* as some people profess to believe. Indeed, most people *fail* because they do not deserve to succeed." He then goes on to talk of the need to live simply and the importance of saving. It's the kind of rather mindless speech people of wealth sometimes feel themselves entitled to give, seemingly unaware that their own lives are infinitely more lavish than anything their listeners can imagine. But just as Squire James begins to seem utterly unremarkable, he starts to give an entirely different speech, with an entirely different perspective.

He begins to talk of tenements in the cities of New York, Paris, and London that sometimes contain more people than the whole village of Hyde Park. He tells of a day in London's East End when he entered a room in Shepherd's Court that measured just three lengths of his cane one way and four lengths the other. A family of ten lived there, with water running down the walls and dripping from the ceiling. The floor was rotten and full of holes, he says.

In the St. Giles district he peered into cellars where the poor lived, "dozens of them, you can see their open mouths luridly lit by the fire and candle light below. These [cellars] possess no windows, and the only way in which light and ventilation can be conveyed to the inhabitants is through a hole in the pavement." When Mr. James climbed through sewage and gas pipes for a better look, he found "half a dozen nearly nude and hideously dirty children, a man toiling by the flame of a candle, a woman lying ill abed, all in this pestiferous and dingy den." That a man of such privilege would appear in such a dirty, dangerous place was almost unheard of. Even slumlords sent someone else to collect the rent. The poor people Squire James peered at would have been as startled to see him as he was to see them.

What the elder Roosevelt says next to the St. James' Guild is even more unexpected than his stories. He begins to exhort his audience to take action. "Help the helpless!" says Squire James. "Here is work for every man, woman, and child in the audience tonight. . . . Help the poor, the widow, the orphan; help the sick, the fallen man or woman, for the sake of our common humanity. Work for your Lord and Master."

He ends with eloquence quite unlike his dreary beginning. "Man is dear to man . . . for that single cause that we have all of us, one human heart."[10]

Franklin would certainly have absorbed lessons from what his parents said, what they did, and what he heard in church. No great mention of his spiritual ideas is made in his mother's published stories about him, probably because they were either not expressed or in no way exceptional. Chances are good that he had a childlike faith appropriate for his age, denomination, and time. The stories told of him don't include any in which he is particularly sensitive to the suffering of others, or even seemingly aware of it. No acts of extraordinary generosity or selfishness are noted by the ever-vigilant Sara. He seems to have made no protest against the hard work and low station of those who serve him. He is just an ordinary kid.

Religion doesn't always help children. It can scar and pervert them. But there isn't any evidence that Franklin was exposed to such religion, or, if he was, he seems to have shucked it off without much effort. His innate temperament, his wealth, his solid heritage, and the security his parents' care gave him helped Franklin to grow up believing the world was a good, safe place where he would naturally excel.

Just as importantly, his parents anchored his life in the ancient stories and teachings of scripture, which has survived for thousands of years at least partly because it resonates so strongly with the human spirit. The Bible assures believers that life has meaning and purpose. A person whose imagination is fired by such vivid stories and teachings can envision great things that don't yet exist. In the words of St. Paul, such a person is able to have faith in things unseen.

People who are safe and inspired can dare to do great things. People who believe God is working through them can have visions greater than themselves because they see themselves working within God's will, not their own. They interpret what happens as being part of God's plan. If good fortune comes to them, they believe God is in charge. If bad fortune comes, they can take it as a test they must overcome. Whether God is actually with them or not, whether their cause is holy or unholy, they can be tremendously empowered by their belief.

But the great spiritual gift that set Franklin most apart from so many others is that he grew up to be a man who saw the world as a place of abundance. Riches don't seem to protect humans from believing there's not enough to go around. In fact, having great amounts of money and status often seems to make people more afraid. If people see the world as a place of limited good, they naturally fear others will take what they have.

People who are afraid often divide the world into the worthy and the unworthy. Into Christian and Jew. White and black. Winners and losers. Strong and weak. Smart and stupid. Clean and unclean. Hardworking and lazy.

Whether they are religious or not, fearful people give these categories a moral load. They put themselves in the "good" category—the strong, the industrious, the clean, the worthy, the winners. They use religion—whether it's a traditional religion or one they've concocted themselves—to make the boundaries of their categories holy. If they believe in a supreme power or natural law of any kind, that entity or law becomes an enforcer of rules designed to keep some people in and other people out.

But Roosevelt was not afraid. While Hitler was using his master-race ideology to dominate, Roosevelt was infusing the Jesus-based theology of his childhood into politics. Brotherhood, neighborliness, high ideals, compassion: He believed these were the key to survival, the basis for a flourishing society. In his 1932 presidential campaign he said, "Every man has a right to life; and this means he has also a right to make a comfortable living. . . . Our Government . . . owes to everyone an avenue to possess himself of a portion of [America's] plenty sufficient for his needs, through his own work."[11]

Franklin D. Roosevelt at Groton School in 1900.

2

SCHOOL DAYS

When Franklin Roosevelt entered Groton School in Massachusetts at age fourteen, in 1896, his time as the most charming, smartest, best-loved boy in the room ended. If Franklin's parents hadn't wanted to keep him at home for another two years, he would have arrived at school at the age of twelve with the rest of his class. He might have fit in more easily. If he had fit in, he might have grown up to be merely another genial but limited gentleman, living on his estate, adding money to his fortune (or not, as the Roosevelts had enough that it didn't really matter), traveling, tending to his family, safe and happy within the American aristocracy that he was born to. He might very well have been a man with nothing to prove to anybody.

He could easily have resembled a character in Edith Wharton's novels, a typical rich American of the Gilded Age so encased in luxuries that they seemed only his due, completely compliant with the expectations of his class. Young Franklin definitely had a model for living happily in protected idleness. His half-brother Rosy, whose wife was an Astor, hardly ever did anything useful. Like Rosy, Franklin loved to travel. He loved to collect things. He had a beautiful estate to manage. He had plenty of hobbies: golfing, sailing, riding, stamp collecting, buying rare books, acquiring naval prints. He might have become exactly what so many people took him to be for so long: an amiable, privileged man of narrow experience, happy with himself and happy with the world. What a waste that would have been.

Until he entered Groton, Franklin seems to have delighted people he met—his parents, the servants, the farmers and merchants of Hyde Park, the elite travelers who shared first-class accommodations, everyone. But at Groton few of the excellent and well-honed virtues that had made him such a favorite among the adults would endear him to anyone but the teachers.[1] A boy who had always been first-rate in the eyes of everyone who mattered was about to become second-rate, and that was something Franklin would not accede to. Groton gave him something to prove, an excellent spur to ambition.

The idea that the best place for boys to learn how to be men was in a school full of other boys was popular among parents who had become concerned about preserving their sons' masculinity. Industrialization was blurring gender lines, and wealthy parents began to fear their sons might not have the requisite masculinity to flourish. Immigrants were flooding into the cities, increasing crime and crowding. All-male rural schools with male teachers seemed a bracing and healthy antidote to urban temptations. The schools promised to instill what Henry Coit, the headmaster of elite St. Paul's School in New Hampshire, called "high-bred manliness": a combination of discipline, heartiness, and "freedom from the tendency to abnormal precocious vice." Parents were afraid of what Boy Scout cofounder Ernest T. Seton called "degeneracy": the transformation of "a large proportion of our robust, manly, self-reliant boyhood into a lot of flat-chested cigarette-smokers, with shaky nerves and doubtful vitality." For Franklin, whose life had been governed mostly by women, all these ambient fears resulted in him being thrust quite suddenly into an almost totally male, highly competitive environment.

A first shock of every boy's arrival at Groton came as he was required to empty his pockets and hand over all his money except twenty-five cents. The limit on the allowance was meant to create equality in a place where all the students were well off but some boys' families were much wealthier than others. Like the other goals at Groton, this was a worthy one. But limiting the boys to so little money also took away the security that having a small stash might have given them. Forcing a boy to turn out his pockets to show that he had nothing more than allowed was a foreshadowing of the complete control Groton would have over his life while he was there.

The Roosevelts were allowed to go with their son down the long, dark-floored hall of the Hundreds House, a dormitory with twenty-eight cubicles lining each side of a large room. Approximately five by ten feet, each cubicle had a cot and a small window. It had a few hooks for clothes and a small dresser, no closet—extra clothes were sent home because there was no place to put them—and no door separating it from the larger room, just a curtain. The lack of a door and a closet was a deliberate means of keeping the boys from having the privacy that might encourage masturbation, a word Groton headmaster Endicott Peabody would be reluctant to use, certainly in front of ladies.

Things young boys might do when they were alone at night were too disgusting for any man of honor to talk about, he told a teachers' group. Such behavior must always be guarded against, while not being specifically named. As Edith Wharton wrote of her clan, "They all lived in a kind of hieroglyphic world, where the real thing was never said or done or even thought, but only represented by a set of arbitrary signs."

Peabody's straw dog for masturbation and other degenerate practices was loafing. "The curse of American . . . school life is loafing," he once said in a speech.

> The tone of loafers is always low. You can avoid that easily in a school, because you have the great advantage of athletics. . . . To run a school on a high plane of morality without athletics would be a practical impossibility. . . . The best thing for a boy is to work hard . . . to play hard . . . and then, when the end of the day has come, to be so tired that he wants to go to bed and go to sleep. That is the healthy and good way for a boy to live.[2]

When Franklin came to Groton, he was no taller than five foot one and weighed no more than 105 pounds. His first year, he sang soprano in the choir. Other boys his age and older were into puberty or past it. Hairy legged, rough cheeked, and roiling with hormones, their difference from him was humiliatingly evident on the sports field. What transpired in the showers, where comparisons are even more personal, doesn't bear thinking about. The turmoil of adolescence is frightening to those undergoing it, and to a boy not yet there, plunged into closer contact with his peers than he'd ever experienced, it could not have been pleasant.

The boys in Franklin's class had formed their friendships two years ago when they were all new and unsure. The cliques did not part ranks easily to let a new boy in. Franklin met a group of bullies not many days after his parents left him. The bullies demanded that he dance for them as they hit at his legs and feet with sticks. Young Franklin's dancing was so vigorous and good-natured that the bullies soon gave up the game as not being any fun. True to his family's distaste for unpleasantness, Franklin did not mention the episode in letters to his mother.

He did include two methods of punishment that the older boys dealt out to those who were deemed fresh or disrespectful. The first was black booting, which meant that a boy was crammed into a boot box and made to stay there. The second was somewhat like waterboarding. Water was poured down a boy's throat until he almost drowned. Both punishments terrified Franklin, as well they might have.

But it wasn't long before Franklin was writing his mother with some glee about other boys receiving such punishments. Young Franklin was not yet a defender of the underdog; he was too afraid of being one.

On weekday mornings the boys were awakened at 6:55; on Sundays all were allowed an extra half hour in bed. They rushed down the hall to wash their faces and brush their teeth while standing before a trough and individual metal basins. Instead of the big claw-footed tub he had luxuriated in all his life, Franklin now vied with other boys for showers in cold water pumped up from the Nashua River by a windmill. Even when the river water was pumped from beneath thick layers of ice, it was not heated for the boys.

Breakfast was at 7:30. A twenty-minute chapel service came next, with classes starting afterward. Among the classes were studies of scripture, led by Peabody. At midmorning, the boys gathered outside for calisthenics, also led by Peabody, who was known to all as the "Rector." He presided over grace and a brief midday meal as he sat on a raised platform with his wife, Fanny, and the senior prefects. Then came more classes. Team sports came right after classes.

Supper was at 6:30. There was Bible reading each night, after which Peabody and his wife stood to say goodnight, and he shook hands with each one of the boys. Then the boys did homework until bed. On Sundays, dressed in high collars and blue suits, they attended yet another church service. On that day they were forbidden to play sports.

The school was an isolated, rarified place where purity and godliness, idealism and honor jousted with the brutal competition of football, the king of all sports in Peabody's view. At Groton, only God was more important than football. One author described the school as "somewhat on the lines of a concentration camp with games."[3] If you weren't a football star or one of the senior prefects, Peabody might address you as "boy" for most of your time at Groton, not quite being able to hold on to your name. Franklin had the heart for football, but he never had the weight or strength he needed.

He played team sports so poorly that he could only make the fourth-string football team. He knew little about the unspoken and all-important rules of team play because he had rarely played on teams. Golf was his game. And sailing. He was a terrific sailor, but at Groton, so far from the ocean, seamanship didn't mean a thing. He tried out for baseball and won the role of team manager, a position that impressed his mother but had no status among the boys. He did excel at one activity—a strange and painful game that involved kicking a tin plate that was held in front of the boy and above his head. The plate was moved higher and higher until no one was able to reach it with their highest kick. Desperate to win at something, Franklin kicked the plate until it was so high that he crashed to the ground after each kick. It hurt, but he didn't stop. And finally he was a winner.

Franklin stumbled again and again as he tried to gain acceptance. This boy who spent much of his life roaming the woods, poring over his stamp collection, and reading books of his own choice now had no free time and no privacy. Boys raised in big families or even in cities would have had much more opportunity to learn the many ways that boys prove themselves to be men. Franklin knew little about the rude humor that boys employ with one another. His elderly father was a kind, gentle man who had never toughened him up as a more competitive father would have done.

He boasted in letters to his mother that he didn't have even one demerit, not having yet figured out that perfect behavior would get him the praise of teachers and only scorn from his fellow students. His goal, he wrote Sara, was to win the punctuality prize. It wouldn't be easy, he wrote, but he was going for it. He did win the prize three times—hardly an achievement that impressed his classmates.

His rather English way of talking caused the other boys to mock him. Franklin also was the only Democrat in the entire school of staunch Republicans. At Groton, as the boys worked on establishing their own identities, there would be much discussion of politics and formal debates on political topics, often conducted with the usual ignorance and prejudice of young people who accepted whatever their parents believed.

Added to all this, his nephew Taddy Roosevelt, the son of his older half-brother Rosy, was at Groton, too. He was two years older than Franklin and not at all the kind of boy who flourished at such a regimented school. Taddy was decidedly odd. Maladjusted. Not a team player. A boy that a newcomer ought to stay far away from. But staying away from Taddy didn't do Franklin any good. The other boys quickly learned that Franklin was Taddy's uncle, and thenceforth he became "Uncle Frank," not a title that won him friends either.

His letters home recorded a number of minor injuries and various illnesses that boys exposed to other children in public school would have contracted earlier. Once when he had scarlet fever, Sara was so alarmed that she and James rushed back from Europe. Sara wasn't allowed in the sickroom, so she put a ladder outside the window next to his bed and spent time reading to him.[4]

Apart from illness and injury, his letters were so relentlessly cheerful that anyone should have been skeptical. His determination to reassure his mother and father that he was doing fine and was quite happy is almost heartbreaking. Franklin had learned the rules of his class well. As Edith Wharton wrote of those rules: "The real loneliness is living among all these kind people who only ask one to pretend!" Franklin's desire to please had given him an early start in being a pretender, and he would hone that skill through the years.

His first demerit came when he was eight months in. He was so jubilant that he wrote to his mother bragging of it.

Groton roughed Roosevelt up. He found out what it was to be an outsider, a social failure even. He learned to be a striver. And he stopped trying to please everyone. He developed "an independent, cocky manner, and at times became very argumentative and sarcastic," remembered one of his classmates. "In argument he always liked to take the side opposite to that maintained by those with whom he was talking. This irritated the other boys considerably."[5]

Groton also gave Roosevelt two other gifts that would shape his life: an infusion of religious and moral teachings, and a relationship with Endicott Peabody[6] that lasted the rest of Peabody's life. Franklin Roosevelt was the boy Peabody had hoped for from the moment he first thought of opening a school, the boy who would devote himself to the highest of Peabody's teachings, who would revere the schoolmaster all his life, who would change the world exactly as the schoolmaster had preached. This boy would pattern his own spiritual beliefs and goals closely enough on Peabody's example that the schoolmaster's core religious convictions could be applied to America's thirty-second president with hardly a changed word. If Peabody had encountered only Franklin, and no other boys at all, the mission of his life would have been fulfilled. His influence on Franklin was great, and FDR's influence in the world was enormous.

But such are the inscrutable ways of fate that, if such predictions had been made to either of them during the years they first knew each other, they would have been highly doubtful. Peabody wouldn't discover their affinity until after FDR was elected president of the United States. Then, as FDR hyper-charged his parents' and his schoolmaster's scriptural teachings, taking them further than any ever expected or some ever would have wanted, Peabody would find himself in many gatherings of former students and friends where he was the sole defender of FDR's presidential performance and character.

As examples of American masculinity, Peabody and the slightly built youngster could hardly have been more different. Peabody was called the "Sun God" by his schoolmates in the English boarding school he attended.[7] He was a joyous boy, full of fun, but even then of staunch character. "Right and wrong were always on his young mind," wrote his friend Sir Walter Lawrence in a letter to Peabody's wife. "He was very outspoken and emphatic. If he thought a thing was wrong, he would fight against it and never give up."

Peabody had grown from an earnest boy into a massive force for righteousness, so fearsome that corporal punishment was rarely needed at Groton. The threat of a visit with the "Rector" was enough. He would greet those unfortunates who were sent to him by bellowing, "Are you looking for trouble, boy?" Then answering himself in the same shout, "You have found it."

He was not only a big man but had enormous hands, sausage-fingered and wide-palmed. The boys liked to compare his powerful mitts with a cast of Abraham Lincoln's bony hand kept in Peabody's office. His eyes were a blue that could chill to piercing, glassy gray in an instant. At six feet, his posture was unbending; his walk was a confident, long-limbed stride. But it was the force of his personality that caused parents who ruled industrial empires to nod meekly when he spoke, and boys to liken him to God. A man of some charm, he was also the man in control. One graduate wrote, "He must have been exactly like God, or God must have been exactly like him."[8]

Peabody knew the Roosevelts, of course. His family, the Peabodys of Salem, Massachusetts, was equally eminent. It was said that in Salem you were either a Peabody or a nobody. He'd asked his friend Theodore Roosevelt to become one of Groton's first teachers. Theodore, twenty-four years older than Franklin, had other ambitions. But he and Peabody agreed on many concepts regarding how boys should be handled.

Both believed in the value of muscular Christianity, "a belief that Christian faith could be revitalized and made a living force in a new generation of young men if sports and outdoor activity became like a spiritual practice and a means to combat sin."[9] The older Roosevelt was a strong influence on Groton and visited the school. During one of those visits, Franklin was present and was as thrilled as the other boys with his kinsman's stories of crime and justice when he was police commissioner of New York City. His tales of police on bicycles stopping runaway horses, police on foot chasing thieves, police dropping down manholes to trap fleeing suspects and rescuing the drowning amply demonstrated the wisdom he passed to the boys: "To be a man merely good is not enough, he must be shrewd and he must be courageous."

In the English boarding schools, the British upper class was encouraged and prepared to serve its country in civil and political positions. Peabody wanted to do the same with boys from America's best families. "If our boys don't take places in government service, it won't be because they haven't been encouraged to," he said. The great majority of his graduates entered business, which left Peabody bitterly disappointed. From his pulpit, he condemned the "eager greed for money which has been growing upon the country during the last twenty years" and which "has fixed itself with [a] terrible grip upon the rising generation so that they are unwilling to contribute toward anything which is not material."

Although he employed seven servants and enjoyed extensive summer travel, the ideas he conveyed to the boys about wealth were utterly linked to performing good deeds. "The finest outcome of a man's financial success," Peabody told Grotties, is "that it makes it easily possible for his children to give themselves to the service of others or without being hampered by the fear of poverty." Those words echoed Bishop Potter's teachings and to lesser degree James's words during his Hyde Park speech.

Peabody was rigid. He was stubborn. But he was also the real deal. His focus was on God and on the boys. He liked to think of Groton as a big family with himself as the father. In this family, everything must be done for the good of the boys. The teachers he employed must be willing to give over all of their lives to serve the boys' needs during the school year. He aspired to be the father figure that he believed they needed— someone stalwart, reliable, unbending, someone they could count on to lead them. For the rest of their lives, he would be there for them. He would keep up with their successes. He would remember their birthdays with a card for as long as he lived. Following the idea that they were a family, Grotties would come to refer to themselves as the Brethren.

The impregnable, always-confident facade Peabody presented to his students was not all that he was. If it had been, he might never have had the influence on them that he did. He was as hard on himself as he was on them and as honest about his failures as he wanted them to be about their own. These parts of himself he revealed in letters to his closest friend, Frank Atwood.

"I am superficial and I fear somewhat cold," he wrote two years before Franklin arrived at Groton.[10] Five years later:

> Blessings have been showered upon me, more and greater than I
> ever expected and far greater than I have deserved and my life has
> been and is full of happiness and yet that real gain in spiritual and

*intellectual life which one has always thought time would bring
in some mysterious way seems as far off as ever. . . . There is so little
of Christ in my life that I fear I can impart but little to others.*[11]

And in February of 1892, when one of the boys, "a most brilliant fellow,
full of promise of mind and character," died at school, he wrote,

> *It is an awful thing to think of the responsibility of preparing
> a boy for eternity. And it was, so far as I am concerned, all so
> superficial and poor. I ought to have got to know him better and
> to have helped him more, but I thought we had plenty of time.
> May God forgive my neglect. I have been trying to write a sermon
> and have now, at 11 p.m., finished a wretched thing, utterly
> unsatisfactory as practically all of my work is.*[12]

Peabody never lost his focus on the boys being confirmed. He "was essentially a simple man with one gigantic preoccupation: his mission
to prepare boys to receive Christ," according to Louis Auchincloss, who
graduated from the school in the 1930s. Peabody didn't force boys to be
confirmed, and if they were too young or not ready, he might refuse
them permission. But he did everything he could to get them ready. His
own method consisted of three parts.

First, he provided the boys with plenty of formal religion—chapel
in the morning, evening prayers, Sunday services, and five-days-a-week
religion classes, which he taught. When communion was given once
a month, everyone who loved Jesus was invited to partake. Peabody
delivered the sacrament with utter absorption and awe. Grotties may
very well have experienced more hours of religion in one year than in
the rest of their lives altogether. But religious teaching wasn't just for
one year, it was every year. By the time he left Groton, Franklin knew
the Bible in a way that only the sincerely devout might rival.

The second part of Peabody's method was to deliver a gospel of purity and gentlemanly conduct, presented several times a day in various
ways. Knowledge was important but not as important as being a Christian gentleman. Everything at Groton was suffused with what Arthur
Schlesinger called "an awful moral significance."[13]

Smoking and drinking had not been any issue. No one did them. No sports at all were allowed on Sunday during the days Franklin was at Groton. Moral offenses were so dangerous to Peabody that he did not allow them to be punished in the way other transgressions were. Such errors must be dealt with firmly and sensitively. Every year when Peabody delivered his annual report to the board, he included an assessment of the moral climate among the boys. Nothing depressed him more than having to report it was not as high as it should be.

The third part of confirmation preparation was a series of lectures to boys intending to be confirmed. The rector also met once a week with those boys in his study. "Burning logs flickered and snapped in the fireplace. Peabody sat behind his desk, a lamp softly illuminating his long earnest face, as he outlined the tenets of his simple, even primitive faith," wrote biographer Geoffrey Ward.[14]

Franklin was confirmed when he was sixteen. At Groton, confirmation was not an emotional experience of overwhelming fervor. "In such a place religious excitement easily spreads, so that school-masters, more than other people, have to be on guard against mere feeling, and have to distinguish true emotions from false," Peabody asserted.[15]

At the center of all this purity stood Peabody himself, a beacon and a model for the Christian life. As adolescents are forming a sense of their own identity, reflecting on their beliefs and values, they are writing a story of the self, sometimes called the personal mythology of the self. This self-written story brings aspects of an individual's personality together to form a sense of self and even of destiny, according to psychologist Erik Erikson.[16] At this developmental stage, humans are looking for someone to model themselves after, a hero to follow. Ideals and religious teachings can be powerful, especially if they are delivered by someone boys admire.

Not all the boys admired or liked Peabody. Sensitive and artistic boys had a hard time with him. Boys with original ideas or great intellectual ability often didn't fare well. The headmaster wasn't a brilliant man or an especially vivid speaker. But for a boy such as Franklin, who had little experience in the hurly-burly of the world, whose nature seems to have been utterly lacking in rebellion, and whose own father was elderly and weakening, the rector was a powerful force.

There's another reason Peabody's religious ideas and personal example might have influenced young Roosevelt more than some of the other boys: Franklin had been almost exclusively tutored at home. His teachers had taught what his parents wanted them to teach, nothing more and nothing less. His parents' rules were explicitly followed throughout the large estate where they lived. He had almost no experience with independent authority. At Groton, his life was utterly controlled by strangers who paid only limited attention to his parents. Having not encountered such authority, Franklin had few defenses against it. He was far behind other boys in beginning to form a sense of himself as separate from his parents.

Peabody gave Franklin a model of rectitude and service that he held up before himself for the rest of his life. Roosevelt was a politician, of course, not a schoolmaster. His transgressions were of an entirely different kind than Peabody's and much more public. But Franklin aspired to be exactly what Peabody was: a strong pillar that would stand firm no matter how the winds of life might swirl. And he did become that pillar. He held the center firm during two of the worst crises in American history. But perhaps more importantly for Roosevelt, Peabody reaffirmed the existence of a God who was always present, always loving his children, a God who could be depended upon. That fatherly God took the place of Franklin's earthly father, "who was retreating into the shadows of age," believed Rexford Tugwell, later one of the president's closest aides.

As Franklin's life at Groton pushed him to doubt himself in ways that he had not before, he experienced "a need for touch with the supreme giver of sympathy which will never again be so great," Tugwell speculated. Luckily, Peabody's confidence helped rout any doubts about God just as Roosevelt was learning to question so much he had once taken for granted as true. The faith of Peabody and the Grotties was influenced by the preaching of Victorian cleric Reverend Frederick W. Robertson, who declared, "We will not say much of the wretchedness of doubt. To believe is to be *strong*. Doubt cramps the energy. Belief is power. Only so far as a man believes strongly, mightily, can he act cheerfully or do anything that is worth the doing."[17]

Peabody himself was completely without doubts concerning the rightness of his faith, and he interpreted the Bible in a completely literal way as the word of God. When a boy seeking confirmation had the temerity to ask why the rector believed in life after death, Peabody replied with astonishment, "Why, the Bible states clearly that Christ assured us of life immortal." It was as simple as that. Parsing subtle theological matters did not interest him. He was all about moving forward to do what God wanted. As for the infallibility of scripture, he appeared not to think about it.[18] All these attitudes would be adopted by Franklin whole cloth, and he would appear not to question them again.

Years later, when Eleanor asked Franklin if he wanted their children to be schooled in the Bible in the same way he and she had been, or left to make up their own minds, he answered her much as Peabody would have answered: The children should attend church and learn as their parents had. When she pressed him about whether much of what they would be taught was actually true, he looked at her with "an amused and quizzical smile." Then he replied, "I really never thought about it. I think it is just as well not to think about things like that too much." His old teacher wouldn't have put it quite that way, perhaps, but his sentiment would have been the same. Don't dabble in doubt; believe and move on.

As stern as Peabody was, however, his God was not a punisher. His favorite sermons were not about God's wrath. One of them could be used as a blueprint for the life that Franklin would eventually lead. It was based on Isaiah 6:8. "Then said I: Here am I. Send me." Duty can get to be tiresome, Peabody admitted to the boys, but religion is quite different. "Religion is all alive with personality. It is God's will for you. He wants you to do this. He does not compel it. You can refuse it if you like, but He desires it mightily in his great love for you."

The only way to please God is to do what He has planned for your life, Peabody said. Then you will have joy and power, and all things will be possible. "There is a reservoir of strength from which a man may draw without limit. One may say with confidence that it has been the source of power for many great men," he told the boys.

The good works that Peabody urged boys toward could start even before they left school, an opportunity Franklin took advantage of. One winter he and another boy helped the African American widow of a Civil War veteran. They would bring her wood and sometimes food. In the summer, Franklin volunteered to work at Groton's fresh air camp for poor city boys. Aspirations for the camp were not particularly praise-worthy by today's standards: It was assumed that poor city boys would just naturally be elevated by associating with boys of a better class, and the Grotties would be made more aware of how blessed they were.

When Franklin graduated, there were still few outward signs to show that he would grow up to be so sensitive to the less fortunate. He appears to be basically a conformist who stirs up argument as a way of making himself stand out. He shows no great courage. No rebellious nature. He's still a regular guy. Peabody's assessment of Franklin was that he was a good enough student, liked well enough, nothing special. It was an opinion he maintained for many years. Even after FDR was elected president, Peabody wrote another old Grottie: "There has been a good deal written about Franklin Roosevelt when he was a boy at Groton, more than I would have thought justified by the impression he left at the school."[19]

Peabody undoubtedly remembered Franklin accurately. Roosevelt would be slow to come into his own for most of his life, which would cause him to be underestimated again and again. For other men, being considered inconsequential might be a weakness, but for Franklin it was just another piece of luck in a life that was already very, very lucky. As an adult and a politician, being consistently underrated enabled him to become a master of the sneak attack. People who should have been watching him closely tended to think that he wouldn't matter much in the big show. They were wrong.

Peabody ranked with FDR's parents as the most important influences in his life, Roosevelt later said. Each Christmas he gathered his family around him and read Dickens's *A Christmas Carol*, just as Peabody had at school. On the eve of the election of 1940 Roosevelt made his usual "non-partisan" speech and ended with an old prayer he remembered from his Groton days. "Bless our land with honorable industry, sound learning, and pure manners. Save us from violence, discord, and confusion; from pride and arrogancy, and from every evil way. Defend our liberties, and fashion into one united people the multitudes brought hither out of many kindreds and tongues."[20]

In the fall of 1944, Peabody collapsed and died while driving a friend on the country roads around Groton. When FDR heard the news, he sent a wire to the Peabody family saying that things would now be a bit different, as he had leaned on the "Rector" far more than anyone realized. Shortly afterward, in his 1945 inaugural speech, Roosevelt reached back forty-five years to quote his "old schoolmaster" as saying that "things in life may not always run smoothly . . . [but that] the great fact to remember is that the trend of civilization itself is forever upward; that a line drawn through the middle of the peaks and valleys of the centuries always has an upward trend."

Franklin D. Roosevelt after nominating Democrat Alfred Smith for president in 1924.

3

UP AND COMER

Believing God intends you to be president of the United States would indicate true megalomania in most people, but maybe not if you were a Roosevelt in the early part of the twentieth century. Being a Roosevelt meant having been born at the top of the heap, no climbing necessary. One Roosevelt had already been president. Why not another?

That FDR might see himself as selected by God for a certain role in life isn't terribly unusual. Spiritual faith is often linked with a sense of destiny, sometimes referred to by the religious as a calling. This sense that humans are part of a plan, a big, glorious plan designed by God, gives people imagination, it gives them guidance, it gives them the will to believe they can do great things and the strength to keep trying. Preachers, missionaries, doctors, teachers, all sorts of religious people talk about receiving the call.

If Roosevelt, with his buttoned-down Episcopalian faith, entertained the baroque notion of being divinely and specifically ordained to be the most powerful man in America, he kept it deeply hidden. He did believe, however, that attaining the greatest office in the land was within his power and that it was what God expected him to do. "He considered himself appointed to be a leader," Rex Tugwell observed, "but that was because there was work to be done which he judged he could do."[1]

In hopes of impressing the family of a girl he was dating in college, he revealed his plan to be president. It was met with laughter. Later Roosevelt told fellow law clerks that he intended to be president.[2] They weren't quite so disrespectful.

From early in his career, many people besides FDR seemed to believe that he would be president of the United States. There was more than his name; people sensed an air of destiny about him. Josephus Daniels, secretary of the Navy while FDR was assistant secretary, knew that "he was dealing with a man marked for preferment even when he seemed to be distressingly brash and immature." From almost the first time journalist and longtime political aide Louis Howe saw Roosevelt on the New York State Senate floor, he was certain FDR was destined to be president. The day after Woodrow Wilson was nominated for president, Howe addressed Roosevelt as "Beloved and Revered Future President."[3] He was joking—maybe. Howe's sense of FDR's destiny had "a burning intensity" that did not waver and was infused into all of the circle around Roosevelt until "their ultimate effort in politics was making FDR president of the United States."[4]

FDR was no great lion of God in the years after he left Groton. He was no fervent friend of the poor, no raging champion of justice, no rebel. He was still a pleaser, a bit of a snob, charming, energetic, ambitious for himself. Like his father, James, his kinsman Theodore, and many Grotties, Franklin enrolled at Harvard. He and Groton chum Lathrop Brown moved into Westmorly Court, the newest and most ornate of the privately owned residence halls that lined the school's "Gold Coast." With diamond-leaded windows and oak wainscoting, the building was new when they moved in in September of 1900. They took a lovely three-room suite on the first floor, where they would live for four years.[5] On Tuesday Franklin unpacked. On Wednesday he prepared for the academic season by purchasing a pair of evening shoes and a derby hat.[6]

Not all of Harvard's students were rich kids. The ones who weren't lived in the shabby dormitories of Harvard Yard, some of which lacked central heating and plumbing above the basement level. They ate cheap and disagreeable food at Table 30 in Memorial Hall, which served twenty-one meals a week for only four dollars and twenty-five cents.[7] Roosevelt and other Groton graduates took their meals in a private dining room at tables reserved just for them. He likely had little reason or occasion to know many of the poorer students.

Roosevelt was going to fare much better in the social realm of Harvard than when he arrived at Groton, but he got another hard lesson in being second-rate when he was rejected by the Porcellian Club, which had accepted Theodore Roosevelt and had given Franklin's father, James, an honorary membership. One classmate called it the biggest disappointment of Roosevelt's life. But he rebounded, joining the Fly Club, which was considered almost as good as the Porcellian. He spent a lot of his energy having a good time. He liked to party, to boat, to dance. He joined a lot of campus organizations. He did some charity work, teaching classes and officiating at games at Boston's St. Andrew's Boys Club, which was supported by the Groton Missionary Society. A member of the Harvard Social Services Society, he headed a committee to provide relief for South African Boers who landed in a concentration camp after losing to the British. His efforts raised $336, which would be about $9,000 today, by some estimates.[8]

He joined the Republican Club, supporting William McKinley for president and Theodore Roosevelt for vice president. He and his father both derided Democratic candidate William Jennings Bryan as "a simple-minded prairie populist willing to destroy the national currency for the alleged benefit of downtrodden farmers."[9] He was still a long way from the man he would someday be.

In terms of his spiritual development, no decision in his life was more important than the one he took to marry Eleanor after graduation in 1905. It was a strange choice to many. Even the Roosevelts' children sometimes wondered why someone as full of fun as Franklin had married Eleanor. She was shy, often uncomfortable in social situations. Photos from that time show a willowy young woman with big eyes and beautiful hair drawn up into a pompadour. She was lovely then, but not the beauty a man as handsome as Franklin might have been expected to marry. Almost every photo of her from the following years shows her with her chin tucked in and her eyes downcast. Their friend and ally Frances Perkins, whose first opinion of the young Franklin was fairly low, believed he picked Eleanor because he didn't want a wife pretty or charming enough to take any attention away from him.

Eleanor had inherited money of her own, and she was Teddy Roosevelt's favorite niece. Some have said that she may have been a better catch than Franklin was. She certainly didn't think so. He was so handsome, she told a friend, that she didn't know how she would be able to hang on to him. Certainly she seems to have been the more sensitive, caring one. It would be nice to think he loved her for those qualities, as well as for the depth of her soul and her great intelligence. He did love her, there is little doubt of that.

After James's death during Franklin's first year at Harvard, Sara had moved herself to Boston so that she could be close to Franklin while he was in school. Always attentive to his mother, he managed to keep some of his life private without her being aware that he had secrets. One of them was Eleanor. Sara didn't know they were seeing each other until Franklin told her that he had proposed. Sara tried to discourage the union, but he would not yield. Finally she gave her blessing—only if he would go away with her for a Caribbean cruise. If he and Eleanor still wanted to marry after he returned, they would be free to do so.

Eleanor's childhood, mostly spent in New York City, was far more bruising than FDR's. For several years she wore braces to correct curvature of the spine. Her beautiful mother, Anna, gave her little affection, referring to the solemn child mockingly as "granny." Eleanor's handsome father, Elliott, adored the child, but he was an undependable alcoholic. When she was eight, Eleanor's mother died, and she was sent to stay in the gloomy house of her grandmother. She lived in the hope that someday her father would come and take her away. She saw him only rarely. He often promised to visit and didn't show up. When she was ten, he died.[10]

Her personality was in many ways more rigid than FDR's. She never quite got the hang of having fun. She found it difficult to forgive slights or betrayals. She was a public figure of great warmth, but with her own children, she was often distant and rarely physically demonstrative. At the same time, she had a great heart for people who suffered, and she was courageous in defending them. She wasn't merely a progressive; she was someone who suffered with the suffering.

As a young person she saw a man try to snatch a woman's purse. While others might have focused on the woman, the victim of an attempted crime, Eleanor couldn't stop seeing the misery in the face of the thief. When Eleanor's father took her to serve Thanksgiving dinner to the ragged newsboys who lived on the street, she encountered children who were poorer, hungrier, and more foulmouthed than any she had ever seen. Other girls of her class might have been repelled or frightened by the furious, clamorous energy of these street urchins, but Eleanor, so often the timid one, was not. She wanted to know all about them.[11]

It was Eleanor who gave Franklin a first glimpse of how bad life could be for the other half. During their courtship she was working at a settlement house in the slums of New York City. Although still a student at Harvard, Franklin often visited New York. When in the city, he would sometimes pick her up at the settlement house, and one day she asked him to help her take home a girl who had fallen ill. He was shocked to enter long, dark hallways smelling of grease and old food, ringing with the noise of families crowded into poorly ventilated rooms with thin walls. "My God," he said. "I didn't know anyone lived like that."[12]

After their marriage, Roosevelt went to law school at Columbia and became a law clerk. Eleanor bore six children,[13] dealt with her mother-in-law Sara's often unkind tyrannies, and supported FDR's political aspirations. In 1910, Roosevelt won a seat in the New York State Senate as a Democrat. In 1913, he followed in his distant cousin Theodore Roosevelt's footsteps by serving as assistant secretary of the navy. In 1918, FDR went on a tour of London, Paris, and the battle lines at Verdun in his role as secretary of the navy and returned home suffering from the flu and double pneumonia. He was so ill he had to be carried into the house on a stretcher. Unpacking his bags, Eleanor discovered love letters from her former social secretary, a young woman named Lucy Mercer.

Eleanor confronted her husband and demanded a divorce. When Sara was drawn into the quarrel, she reminded her son that a divorce would ruin his political career, and she told him that she would cut him off from all family money. Lucy was a Catholic who would be unlikely to be able to marry a divorced man. He quickly realized that the affair must end, promised Eleanor that he would never see Lucy again, and agreed to her stipulation that all marital relations between them would end.

He apparently kept the latter promise, but he broke the former. He invited Lucy to his first inauguration and to the White House on various occasions when Eleanor was absent, even engaging their daughter

Anna to serve as hostess. Eleanor discovered the extent of his perfidy in the most brutal way. The widowed Lucy Mercer, who had remarried and become Lucy Rutherfurd, was visiting Roosevelt's Warm Springs, Georgia, cottage on the April day in 1945 when FDR suffered a stroke and died. It was impossible then to keep the First Lady from knowing that her husband had spent his last conscious moments near the woman he had pledged to forswear.

Eleanor could not forgive him for his affair with Lucy. But the great pain he caused her eventually had some payoff. Before discovering the letters, Eleanor had been a shy, doting wife whose time was largely taken up by bearing and tending to one child after another. Discovery of the affair changed her. She no longer worshipped her husband. She no longer made pleasing him her goal. The pregnancies stopped, and the new Eleanor began to build her own life. She made friends outside the marriage; she worked in causes that interested her. Eventually she became a political force in her own right.

By the summer of 1921 FDR was out of political office, making his living in law and insurance, but his years of steadily accumulating political experience and power were reaping rewards. His prospects for achieving great office, the presidency even, seemed good. He was following closely in the footsteps of his idol Theodore. His political career had started in the New York State legislature, as TR's had. He had been appointed assistant secretary of the navy, as TR had been. He tried for the vice presidency in 1920, the office that TR held when William McKinley died and TR became president. Franklin lost this bid, but the effort allowed him to politick the country, making friends, gathering names of people who might be of support later. At the age of thirty-nine, he was full of the fabled Roosevelt energy, so good-looking, graceful, and lithe, seeming never to tire. He had lost an early habit of seeming to look down his nose at people and dropped the English way of talking that irritated the Grotties. His charm and looks made him the center of attention in most every setting. His health was basically good, although he often seemed to catch whatever virus was going around and might be sick enough to stay down for a week or so. That sweltering July, he was well.

Eleanor and the children had gone for their usual vacation at the family's Campobello summer home in Canada. He was eager to join them but had one last engagement to fulfill before he left New York City. He was a strong supporter of the Boy Scouts, as TR had been, and never turned down a sail if he could help it. The Scouts were camping at Bear Mountain, some forty miles north of New York. He and a party of friends were to sail up the Hudson River to the campground. They would have dinner with a few hundred Scouts and then sail back to the city.

Some have speculated that he encountered the polio virus at Bear Mountain from contaminated water.[14] No Scouts came down with the illness, and reports of outbreaks never turned up in the areas where the boys lived. If the virus was present there, however, it might have infected Roosevelt without harming anyone else. Fewer than 1 percent of those who encounter the polio virus suffer any ill effects. But he was tired, stressed from a Congressional investigation of the Wilson administration that he had successfully dealt with in the last weeks. Maybe his resistance was low.[15]

A few days after the Bear Mountain visit, on Friday, August 5, Roosevelt sailed with his friend and his employer in the insurance business, Van Leer Black, on Black's oceangoing yacht, *Sabalo*. He had invited Black with his family and friends to spend some time with him at Campobello. In the two days on the Atlantic between New York and New Brunswick, Roosevelt would later recall that he had "never laughed as much as we all did on the cruise up the Coast of Maine in 1921."[16]

When Roosevelt arrived at Campobello Island, his five children were waiting for their favorite playmate. They had "a wild, whooping, romping, running, sailing, picnicking time," son James remembered. His first days on the island, Roosevelt felt "logy and tired," he told Eleanor. Nevertheless he was determined to take Black and his friends on a fishing expedition before they left. Roosevelt had the job of baiting hooks for the party fishing from the *Sabalo*'s tender, which took the yacht's passengers to and from land. The small boat had two cockpits with a hot engine in between and only a narrow plank connecting them.

Roosevelt, an excellent sailor since boyhood, had superior coordination, but on this day he slipped and fell in the ocean. He was only in the water for a moment, then back on board and joking about how silly it was for an "old salt" like himself to lose his footing. The water averaged fifty-one degrees, which was too cold for a lot of people but nothing new to FDR. Only on this day, it seemed like the coldest water he had ever felt, "so cold it felt paralyzing," he said later. Eleven days had passed since the picnic at Bear Mountain. When the poliomyelitis virus infects, symptoms are likely to appear in seven to fourteen days. They sometimes include extreme sensitivity to hot and cold.

On Wednesday, August 10, he still didn't feel like himself, but he went for a day of sailing with Eleanor and the children on the twenty-foot, single-masted *Vireo*. Being on the sea always revived him. Not long after noon, they saw smoke coming from one of the islands near Campobello. He anchored the boat so that he and the children could join in fighting the fire. Breathing smoky air, they beat flames and stamped out sparks for hours. Then they sailed for home, sooty and tired. As they climbed toward the house, they decided a swim would cool them off. So they raced a mile and a half toward Lake Glensevern, a pond that wasn't as cold as the ocean. After swimming a hundred yards across the pond, Roosevelt leapt out, jogged over a rise, and took a swim in the ocean. They swam back across the pond and then trotted home.

Usually Roosevelt felt a glow after exercise, but not this time. While the children went to change out of their wet clothes, he sat down to open the mail and scan newspapers. He was too worn out to even put on dry clothes. As the family gathered for dinner, he rose, quietly saying his back ached. He headed upstairs to bed, telling everyone he only wanted to "get thoroughly warm." But he couldn't seem to warm up, and he felt achy all over.

The next morning, he was able to stand and walk to the bathroom in order to shave, but he was not all right. He felt "stabbing pains" in the back of his legs. Something felt strange about his right knee. There was no telephone in the house at Campobello. So Eleanor sent the older children off on the camping trip they had planned, telling them to stop in the village and ask Dr. Eben Homer Bennet, a general practitioner and old family friend, to come over.

The doctor found his patient achy, with a temperature of 102. It looked like a bad cold. But by the afternoon, his right knee wouldn't support his weight. By evening, his left knee was weakening. The next morning, when he tried to move his legs, they felt floppy and weak. Pain that has been compared to having nails driven into one's flesh began to spread through his muscles. Soon he could no longer tighten the muscles of his stomach or buttocks. That evening, he couldn't hold a pencil. He wasn't able to stand.

Louis Howe had rushed to Roosevelt's bedside as soon as he heard about the illness, and he stayed there day and night, reading to him, talking, massaging his legs. FDR repeatedly moaned to his friend, "I don't know what is the matter with me, Louis. I just don't know."

Howe had been offered a good job with an oil company, the first one in many years—FDR did not pay the people who served him generous salaries. This opportunity was a rare chance for Howe to make enough to money to support his family. He was going to take the job, but when he saw how ill Franklin was, Howe turned it down to devote himself to Roosevelt.

During the next weeks, Roosevelt would be misdiagnosed again. His second doctor would prescribe massages, which Eleanor and Louis would administer. They were excruciatingly painful and probably did further damage to his fragile nerves and muscles. As the paralysis and pain grew, Roosevelt's despair deepened, and he began to believe that God had deserted him.

If a child has been reared in a religious environment, as Franklin was, he won't remember a time when spiritual values weren't part of his consciousness. What he does with those values, how personal they become to him, how he applies them, and how widely he applies them will depend on whether or not his faith grows from its early stages.

Roosevelt had been loved and treated as an important person most of his life. While he and Eleanor both cared for the same causes, he could walk away from suffering without it seeming to haunt him. He did what he could for others, but he didn't seem to immerse himself in their pain. He had been taught to avoid the unpleasant and to avoid dwelling on it. He liked having people around, but some suspected that he liked them mainly as an audience to admire him. If he had the deep compassion Eleanor had, he kept it well controlled.

Polio changed everything. Disability and pain made him a more patient man, a better listener. He could no longer walk off and leave people who bored him. He now knew what it was to truly suffer—physically and emotionally. He had been among the world's most fortunate. That life was over.

The question of whether Roosevelt's nature changed during this crisis or whether the crisis brought out qualities that were already there has been often debated. That question is akin to asking whether he had a religious conversion that altered his basic self or merely developed a deeper sense of himself than before. It's impossible to know, but probably both occurred. When someone's body is altered so greatly, the basic self is also changed simply because the body, the mind, and the spirit are incontrovertibly linked. So, yes, he was already a man guided by religious faith and his sense of responsibility to others, and yes, he was also changed fundamentally.

He certainly had sympathy for the less fortunate before polio and may have truly wanted to help them, but sympathy is not experience. Being brought so low took him into realms of loss and helplessness that can't be understood unless they are experienced. He might have talked about the interdependence of humanity before polio; after polio he experienced it every moment of every day.

His friend Frances Perkins saw a great change in him. He was warmer. She had never been particularly close to either of the Roosevelts. Now she found herself feeling more fond of him: "I would like to think he would have done the things he did even without his paralysis, but knowing the streak of vanity and insincerity that there was in him, I don't think he would have unless somebody had dealt him a blow between the eyes," she later said.[7] When Eleanor was asked whether FDR would have been president if he hadn't been crippled, she said, "He would have been president, but he would have been a different kind of president."

One thing was clear from the beginning, when the pain was so terrible, and he couldn't move even his arms, and no one knew what would happen: Franklin would not be asking for sympathy. He would not whine or become demanding. He would not complain. He would not sulk or sink into self-pity.

Sara was visiting Europe when he fell ill. They hadn't wanted to ruin her trip by telling her. So they waited until she landed in New York and then gave her the news as gently as possible. She went right to his bedside, of course. The scene that greeted her was so cheerful as to be almost frightening. Even that tough old Victorian, she who had taught Franklin to hide sorrow and pain, was taken aback by his happy attitude. Franklin was freshly shaved, sitting up in bed and as chipper as she had ever seen him. Eleanor was the same. Both of them were upbeat, joking, and laughing, carrying on as though what had happened was no more than an inconvenience.

But Sara was no fool. She could see that her son's legs, those lovely legs that she had been so proud of, weren't working. She knew enough to suspect that they never would. As he first began to recover his ability to sit up and use his arms, Roosevelt's doctor worried that if he knew he would never be able to walk, it would crush his spirit. Eleanor agreed.

She decided that they would treat him as a normal human being who was temporarily unable to walk. That left politics open as a career. "She had never fooled herself about him getting back the full use of his legs, which he did believe in, and probably that belief helped him an awful lot," said Perkins. "She thought that he would die spiritually, die intellectually, and die in his personality if he didn't have political hope." Eleanor, whose work in the Democratic Party had made her a woman of considerable influence, believed that Roosevelt's name must be kept before the people. If he was consulted from time to time, he and they would know that he was still in the political scheme.[18]

Louis Howe believed Eleanor was right. Sara did not agree. She wanted Roosevelt to come back to Hyde Park and settle down as a gentleman farmer. That plan was far more likely to work out than what Eleanor and Howe wanted for him.

Sara was not fond of politics. Politicians were loud, ill bred, pushy. It really wasn't a proper career for a gentleman. Retiring to the country was an entirely suitable solution. The people of Hyde Park loved Franklin and would continue loving him just as much as always. And if they didn't, they certainly wouldn't dare show any disrespect. The larger world was unlikely to behave so well. Those with disabilities were treated quite badly. People shunned and insulted them. No one wanted to see them. They were put away in horrible institutions or locked in back rooms. With her sweet boy at Springwood, the family estate, she could protect him.

Franklin loved Springwood better than any other place in the world. He had plenty of hobbies, enjoyed collecting things. He would study, manage the estate. He could write. Theodore Roosevelt had written books, and Sara knew that Franklin had so many wonderful thoughts to share with the world. His books would certainly be successful. The family would have time to travel. They had plenty of money among them. The children loved Springwood. Why would he subject himself to a life of strain that might cause his health to suffer even more?

Eleanor and Louis were simply setting him up for humiliation, in her opinion. She went to Louis. He was devoted to Franklin, and a politically intelligent man. It was difficult to believe that he hadn't opposed Eleanor's ridiculous ideas.

Lela Stiles, an employee and friend of Howe's from 1928 until his death, tells the story she heard from him:[19]

> *"You have good common sense, Louis," Sara said. "Can't you see that a political future is now out of the question for my son?"*
>
> *Louis Howe looked at her long and steadily. "I expect him to be President," he said quietly. "Anyway he is going to have his chance."*
>
> *Then Louis flung his challenge to FDR: "Either you can retire and become a country squire, or gather up your courage and plunge forward as though nothing had happened. You are a man of destiny," he said firmly, "and I will go along with you every inch of the hard way, if that is the way you choose. Besides," he said, partly in earnest and partly to bring a smile to the tired face, "this makes it certain that you'll be President. My reason? You'll get the sympathy of the public and you will be spared the hand-shaking, the platform stumping, the bazaar openings, in short all the political nonsense that ruins so many men."*
>
> *"As far as I was concerned though," Louis Howe said later, "I was betting on a sure thing. I knew my man would win because I knew my man. He accepted the challenge too, and his courage through those black years was so magnificent I decided that the greatest adventure of which a man could dream would be to put him in the White House."*
>
> *Roosevelt listened intently.*
>
> *When Louis had finished, the future president flashed him a smile. "Well," he said cheerfully, "when do we begin?"*
>
> *"I knew then," said Louis Howe, "that you could never lick Franklin!"*[20]

Author James Tobin cast doubt on the idea that Howe or anyone else ever made up Roosevelt's mind. "Before and after he became ill, it was FDR, not Louis, who made the decisions about his career," wrote Tobin, "and he did not need Howe to define this critical choice. In fact, no surviving evidence suggests that Roosevelt ever allowed himself to think seriously of quitting politics."[21]

Rexford Tugwell, a Columbia University economist who was one of the president's close advisers, concurred. Roosevelt had a "ferocious drive" toward destiny that was like "a fierce flame burning" at his core.

"The head of steam it generated allowed its containing vessel no rest even in invalidism, much less in seeming defeat; it drove his turbines with merciless impatience," he wrote.[22]

FDR had transformed his sense of being abandoned by God into the belief that polio was a test of his faith and his resolve. He believed he would walk again, and when he did, he would resume his place in life. Howe and Eleanor may have doubted that he would ever walk again, but both knew him to be a man of tremendous will. With such a person, permanent failure is never a certainty.

For the next seven years, Roosevelt worked tremendously hard to walk again. He strapped on braces and dragged himself along step by step using parallel bars at waist height. When that didn't work, he tried raising the bars above his head so that he could hang from them. He learned just about everything that could be known about leg muscles. He corresponded with polio patients and experts all over the country. He investigated every kind of cure. He was willing to try anything that might help: ultraviolet light, massage, electric currents.

His mother bought him an electric tricycle he could ride. He had himself hoisted onto horses. He tried osteopathy. He worked his muscles against gravity and with gravity. He tried exercising with resistance and without it, in warm water and in cold water. He even consulted French psychologist Dr. Emile Coué, who discovered the placebo effect and believed that people could cure themselves by a regimen of repeating, "Day by day, in every way, I'm getting better and better" to change unconscious thoughts that were keeping them back.[23]

His legs could not support his weight at all unless they were strapped into heavy iron braces. But with the braces, he was able to use crutches to get about. His doctors did not discourage him. So day after day, he worked at building strength in every part of his body that still had working muscles—arms, shoulders, and back—believing that eventually he would regain the use of his legs.

His daughter Anna told of watching him try to walk from the house to the road at Hyde Park when she was fifteen. Hour after hour would pass as he slowly inched his way forward, gripping his crutches, dragging his braces, gritting his teeth. Every few steps he would be so tired he had to rest. As she watched, she remembered how he once had been such a wonderful playmate, jumping and running faster than anyone. "Suddenly you look up and you see him walking on crutches—trying, struggling in heavy steel braces. And you see the sweat pouring down his face, and hear him saying, 'I must get down the driveway today—all the way down the driveway.'"[24] He never did make it to the mailbox.

He began to spend his winters on the *Lorooco*, a small houseboat in Florida. He generally had friends with him. They did not see him angry or out of sorts or depressed. Missy LeHand, his personal secretary and probably the person who knew him best, was the only one aware of the black moods that wouldn't allow him to leave his cabin at all until after noon.

Meanwhile, Eleanor and Louis were doing their part in keeping FDR's name in circulation by staying active in political causes and committees. Roosevelt also kept in touch with people of influence by writing letters. So while nobody saw him, he was being heard from. Eleanor and Louis began working behind the scenes to convince Al Smith, governor of New York, that he ought to have Roosevelt make the nominating speech for Smith as the 1924 Democratic presidential candidate.[25]

Roosevelt agreed to do it. It would be his first public appearance since he contracted polio. He took his seat at the convention hall early so that no one would see him arrive. When the time came for him to speak, he struggled out of his chair, put a crutch under each arm, and with his son beside him started up the long aisle. A hush fell over the room, people saddened by the sight of him, almost holding their breath. Many delegates remembered him as a young man so energetic, strong, and agile that he could leap over chairs just to get to the front of the room faster. Now he was pale and thin, almost delicate looking. Roosevelt kept thumping forward for what seemed like forever.

Finally he reached the lectern and began to speak. The hand he held his speech with was trembling, but most people did not know that. All they saw was his great smile flashing over the crowd and his voice coming forth as strong and inspiring as they remembered it. He hadn't written the speech himself and had little influence on its content. He hadn't wanted to use the phrase "Happy Warrior" to describe Smith, but he did. He delivered that sobriquet so perfectly that it is still remembered today by people who have no idea that it was applied to Al Smith, by people who don't even know Al Smith existed. Roosevelt's speech was a tremendous success.[26]

At the convention, a wealthy friend named George Peabody told him the story of a boy disabled by polio who was able to walk after exercising in a spring-fed thermal pool in Bullochville, Georgia, a town soon to be renamed Warm Springs. He suggested that Roosevelt visit the Meriwether Inn, a resort of which he was half owner near the springs. And thus began the next phase of Roosevelt's spiritual development. In a backwoods southern town ten miles away from paved roads, he would learn how to be truly great.

Franklin D. Roosevelt in Warm Springs, Georgia, in 1931.

4

LEAD MY SHEEP

In October of 1924, when Roosevelt's train pulled into the little town with the hot springs, the Peach State was in worse shape than he was. He couldn't walk; Georgia could hardly crawl. While the rest of the country was reveling in the Roaring Twenties, Georgia was turning into a wasteland of dry gullies and dusty fields tended by farmers as rundown as the land. Cotton had sucked everything out of the soil. The state's forests had been hacked down, letting the wind blow all the way from Texas without a break. Bad plowing had loosed and tossed the topsoil until it dissolved into dust. The price of cotton fell. And then came the boll weevils.

Two-thirds of the state's land was farmed by sharecroppers, most of them white families whose dawn-to-dusk labor earned a worker about $200 per year. Times were even worse for African Americans. They had to take whatever land the white folks didn't want, and what they didn't want wasn't worth having. Most farm families lived in shacks with outdoor privies with no water and no electricity. They ate fatback, molasses, and corn bread. They tried to plant gardens, but who would keep them? Even children had to work the fields. And who could afford the seed? Raising a cash crop out took everything they had. If they couldn't make money, they would be tossed off the land and have nothing.

And then times got worse. In 1925, a three-year drought began that withered whatever cotton the boll weevils didn't get. In 1930, another drought started, the worst one ever seen. In the midst of all this was the village of Bullochville, a ramshackle dip in a dirt road with fewer than 400 residents. But it was where FDR looked to find a cure.

Word had spread of the famous Yankees who were coming to visit, and a crowd of about a hundred turned up at the train depot to welcome them. Some had never seen a Yankee, certainly not rich and famous ones. The train's worn coaches clanked slowly past. The conductor standing on the high steps of one coach pointed to the back: "Mr. Roosevelt's in the last car."

Soon Roosevelt's big head and shoulders emerged from the train door. Happy to see a crowd, he lit up at the sight of the welcoming committee. They watched silently, moving back to give him room as his valet and a man drafted from the crowd helped carry him down the train steps. Once his crutches were under his arms, he tossed his head back in a friendly way and said, "How nice of you all to welcome us." For him, and them, it was love at first sight. Most likely it wouldn't have been the same if he had come there able-bodied. He might have so intimidated them that they would have been shy and stayed away. But for all its faults and pretensions, the South has a great fondness for the peculiar. Having its own New York aristocrat suited that little farming town just fine.

The resort George Peabody touted to the Roosevelts turned out to be a rundown 200-room monstrosity called the Meriwether Inn. Eleanor was with her husband on that first trip to this place where verandas were called porches, lawns were yards, and a mess of possum stew was reason to have a party. Eleanor observed that the hotel looked like something a southern belle would emerge from. (She was being kind—or she didn't know many southern belles.) The hotel was missing windows and leaned a bit. Trash was dumped indiscriminately along the road. It was shabby, dirty, and to the eyes of these world travelers, quite tasteless.

Luckily they had their own cottage. Declared "delightful and very comfortable" by Roosevelt, it had gaps between the wallboards large enough to see light through. At night they could hear animals' claws scratching over the roof. Squirrels (they hoped). The cottage owner had kindly sent over a cook and a gardener to look after them. When the cook announced a chicken dinner was on the menu, Eleanor expected the chicken to arrive ready to be eaten, as it always had. Instead the cook grabbed one of the chickens pecking around the house, wrung its neck, and started plucking. Eleanor, near enough to hear the flurry and the squawking, found herself somewhat less eager to eat than she had been.

Franklin didn't mind any of it. All he could think of was the pool. But for Eleanor, it wasn't just the discomfort or even the poverty that she really couldn't stomach, it was the casual, constant racism. What Arthur Schlesinger called Roosevelt's "genial obliviousness" let him pass over behavior that Eleanor could not ignore. She did not enjoy Georgia and rarely visited afterward.

Over the next days, gifts arrived. Hardly anybody in Meriwether County had money to spare; nevertheless, they brought eggs and loads of wood, hot dishes of food, and sometimes flowers arranged in vases of silver or china, clearly heirlooms that Eleanor worried over until they could be emptied, cleaned, and returned safely.

The day after their arrival, FDR visited the spring-fed pool he hoped would help him build his muscles enough to walk again. The eighty-eight-degree pool was like an Epsom salt bath, so dense with minerals that people couldn't sink if they tried. He was able to splash around for hours. His skin felt soothed, and his limbs glided through the water. To his surprise and delight, he found that he was able to stand in four-foot water. Perhaps he was only able to float with his feet touching the pool bottom, but it felt like standing to him. He took a couple of steps, and he was thrilled. Here was the place he had been looking for, the exercise environment where he might regain what he had lost. He began to write his friends and family about the springs. He intensified his research on what kinds of exercises he might do and what kinds of muscles he could strengthen. He already knew more about the effects of polio than most doctors.

Louis Joseph, the boy whose story had attracted Roosevelt to Warm Springs, came to introduce himself. Paralysis had weakened his lower back and abdominal muscles. He had arrived at the springs wearing braces, unable to walk. And now he could. He used two canes, and he lurched a bit, but he walked. Putting his weight heavily on his canes, balancing carefully, he even walked up the steps. No braces. He and his family had come to the resort three summers. During the third one, Joseph found himself able to support his own weight. He had no explanation, but he was walking proof that it happened.

Word that Roosevelt, a former vice presidential candidate, was at Warm Springs spread to Atlanta, and the paper sent a reporter to get his story. The story did not claim that the springs restored Roosevelt's walking ability, but it was clear that he had high hopes, and that he was having a good time. The news spread all over the country. Before FDR returned the next April, six hundred people had written to him or the Meriwether Inn for more information. Some didn't bother to write; they just showed up—the "uninvited, unheralded, the hopeful, and the all but hopeless."[1]

One of the first of them was a Roosevelt favorite, Fred Botts. The twenty-five-year-old had been stricken in the polio epidemic of 1916. He had spent most of nine years in a bedroom on his family's Elizabeth, Pennsylvania, farm. Once a singer with hopes of an operatic career as a baritone, Botts had wasted since his illness into a pale, skinny kid. One day, he saw a headline in the Sunday paper, "Healing of Paralysis." It was a long way to Georgia, but Botts was determined to go. Because he couldn't stand, his younger brother built him a wooden cage that he could use to travel in the baggage car. He and his brother made their way to Warm Springs together.

The day after he arrived, Botts was paddling around in the pool marveling at the warmth and lightness when Roosevelt arrived and bade him good morning. Roosevelt, wearing swimming trunks and seeming not the least bit self-conscious, looked as pale-skinned as Botts did, and his lower body looked almost as wasted as Botts's. Roosevelt had been swimming for hours every day, and he was entirely confident.

He had also begun instructing guests paralyzed by polio on how to exercise. As each polio survivor came to town, he helped find them lodging, and then took them to the pool. There he sized them up, making notes of how each of their muscles functioned, its strength, and its range of motion. Mrs. Steiger had arrived from Missouri, "a very bad case from the waist down." A boy named Hersheimer came in but his attitude was bad, and Roosevelt feared he wouldn't stick to the routine. A teen from Arkansas named Philpot had the opposite problem. He was so eager that he wanted to do more than was healthy. Retan, a young woman from Boston, had just one leg that was quite damaged. Treatment was so poor and doctors knew so little that sometimes limbs were amputated when physicians judged them useless enough that they would only cause more problems.[2]

Roosevelt exercised with the guests each day, showing them what he knew, helping them learn how to push their progress forward without injuring themselves. He loved to tell the story of two rather well-rounded women whom he was trying to encourage to place their feet on the bottom of the pool. They couldn't seem to make their limbs do what he wanted. When one of the ladies' dimpled knees popped up, Roosevelt pushed it down. No sooner had it left his hand than the other knee popped up. Soon he was swatting at this knee and that knee like a crazy game of whack-a-mole.

One of Botts's first questions for Roosevelt was, "What about nurses and doctors?"

We'll be our own nurses and doctors, Roosevelt said. Soon people began calling him Doctor Roosevelt and referring to themselves as "the companions." The trickle of companions began to grow, from thirty-one the first year to fifty the next, to seventy the year after. By then Roosevelt had spent $200,000, two-thirds of his net worth, to buy the springs, the hotel, and the land around it. His plan was to turn it into a fashionable resort, as it had once been; he envisioned a shooting preserve, a fish-stocked lake, a golf course, and riding trails. His family and friends thought it was not a good idea. And it quickly became clear that paying guests didn't want to swim with people paralyzed by polio. Nobody knew how the virus spread, and they were afraid. A separate pool was constructed, but that didn't solve the problem for long. The vacationing guests didn't want to even see the "polios," sometimes also called the "infantiles," presumably because infantile paralysis was a synonym for polio. So Roosevelt gave up the idea of combining the two groups and began focusing just on the companions.

He had liked the idea of making the hotel a vacation destination as a way of generating funds to help his work with the companions. Helping them had always been his first priority; the resort was merely a way to support his work with them. So when he realized that he couldn't make money that way, he transferred ownership of the resort to a foundation he set up that would allow him to raise money from charitable donors. Edsel Ford, son of the carmaker, gave one of the largest gifts, $25,000, to build a glass building over the pool.

The Georgia Warm Springs Foundation policy was to charge those who could afford to pay just enough to cover expenses. For those who couldn't pay, there was no charge. Nobody ever knew who paid and who didn't. Roosevelt followed his old headmaster Endicott Peabody's example in treating the foundation like a family, not an institution. But he was a far different father. He was Doc, the playmate, the confidant, the laughing, joking, game-playing example of how good life could be.

He organized community-wide picnics and variety shows. He loved jokes and gossip, and wasn't above sharing a bit of moonshine in those Prohibition days. Things that had once seemed so dreadfully sad became normal and a source of new fun. When a quartet of "Powder Puff" girls in wheelchairs sang "I Won't Dance, Don't Ask Me," a newsman was so overcome he was seen wiping tears from his eyes; Roosevelt roared with laughter, and the girls did, too. Roosevelt hired young men called "push boys" to wheel chairs from place to place. They were at the ready to take the patients for coffee, to get mail, or just on an outing. He hired young women from a nearby college to act as assistant therapists. When several of the push boys lowered themselves into the fountain on the lawn as though they were paralyzed and then sprang from the water shouting, "I'm healed," Roosevelt thought it hilarious. Romances sprung up between town kids and the companions. Eventually some of the youngsters fell in love. There were even some marriages.

In the pool, he was generally the one showing someone how to do something that would help them. He talked a doctor into signing on. He hired Helen Mahoney, a crackerjack physical therapist. They put together a chart of muscles that helped the patients see which muscles they were trying to work. A board was installed under the water so patients could lie on it while doing their exercises. Exercise rings were installed over the water so patients could pull themselves up. Bars were installed so they could practice walking. People were getting stronger, and some of them even walked.

Tom Bradshaw, the local blacksmith, suggested he could modify a car so that Roosevelt could operate it with just his hands. Then the blacksmith took a look at Roosevelt's leg braces and modified them so that they were lighter and easier to manage. When he was able to drive himself where he wanted to go, Roosevelt cruised the lanes of the town, calling out to people as he passed, "Hiya, neighbor." He would often pull into a farmer's driveway just to chat. The kids would run out to perch on his running board. He and their dad would talk crops and weather. He started trying to convince the farmers to move away from planting cotton. It exhausted the soil, and with the prices going up and down, it wasn't reliable. Sometimes they listened.

He liked to pull up to the ice cream shop on Broad Street and honk his horn. Everyone else had to go inside to order their treat, but for Roosevelt, the shop provided curb service. He also liked meeting the school bus and treating all the children to ice cream. He returned to Warm Springs every Thanksgiving to carve the turkey for dinner with the foundation patients.

Roosevelt had come to Warm Springs for himself. His sole focus had been to help himself. His friends and family had advised him to remember that focus. Don't get in too deep, they said. Don't risk too much. This could overwhelm you. You might fail, they said.

Polio had humbled him, but he was a man of great confidence. He punched back. And that little patch of Georgia gave him something he had found nowhere else. At the Warm Springs pool his spirit came into the greatness that the Groton headmaster, Endicott Peabody, had promised it could attain. They came to him, weakened, their spirits crushed, their limbs crippled. He had no cure. No quick solution. Just some water and his own faith. That's what he gave them. He gave them the water and himself, the great exuberance of himself, so that they could have his hope and confidence, so that they could heal. And it worked out just as he hoped it would. While he was helping them, he was also getting stronger, closer to his dream of walking.

It was four years since FDR had nominated New York governor Al Smith for a presidential run. The Democrats hadn't given Smith the nomination then, despite FDR's stellar performance, but in 1928 Smith put his hat in the ring again. An important part of his presidential strategy was to have FDR run for governor of New York. With such a strong Democratic candidate for governor, Smith believed he could carry the state in the race for president. The New York State governorship was a great launching pad for the presidency. Smith was determined to win Roosevelt over.

But Roosevelt wasn't ready to make his move. With the help of Howe and Eleanor, he was building a solid political base mostly by voluminous letter-writing. He needed eight more years in the background, they believed. And even more importantly to FDR, with seven more years of exercise and therapy, he believed he would be walking again.

He didn't attend the 1928 New York State Democratic Convention. Smith, who was there, kept calling. Roosevelt avoided the phones as the convention was meeting.

Finally Smith called Eleanor, who was not at Hyde Park, asking her to phone her husband and convince him to talk with Smith. On her third call, Roosevelt answered. She persuaded him to take Smith's call. Smith pleaded with Roosevelt, but could get no assent. Then Smith asked, "What if they nominate you? Would you refuse it?" Roosevelt hesitated and then said he didn't know what he would do. That was enough. Smith hung up the phone and nominated FDR to be the party's choice for governor of New York.[3]

Roosevelt would never walk unaided again, but he would become governor of New York. In 1929 the stock market crashed. President Herbert Hoover, who had won against Al Smith, handled the crisis and ensuing depression so poorly that a progressive Democrat would have a good shot at unseating him in 1932.

Roosevelt knew that if he wanted to be president, his time had come. He got the Democratic nomination and campaigned hard against Hoover, who sought a second term. FDR trounced the sitting president with a 17.7 percent margin.

Finally Roosevelt attained the goal he had pursued his entire adult life. He knew exactly what he needed to do. The Squire of Hyde Park would remember pulling into the hard-packed dirt yards of the farmers in Warm Springs to talk about the crops that weren't coming up. He would remember watching their wives haul water and their skinny children go barefoot. From them he learned lessons that he would use to help millions of people like them. At the same time, his agenda would polarize the country, inspiring such hatred among people of his own class that many would refuse to even utter his name. They would call him simply "that man," and everyone knew exactly whom they meant.

Franklin D. Roosevelt giving a speech from the rear platform of the "Roosevelt Special."

5

"THEY WILL FORGET I'M A CRIPPLE"

On the eve of his first inauguration, Roosevelt was traveling on his private train, the Roosevelt Special. From New York, he rode through the mist and cold rain of New Jersey, Pennsylvania, Delaware, and Maryland into Washington, D.C. His destination was the Mayflower Hotel, named after the ship on which some of his ancestors had come to America. But Roosevelt had little chance to enjoy the image of peace outside his window.[1]

Two days earlier, gold deposits at the Federal Reserve Bank of New York had fallen below the legal limit, which was 40 percent of the paper currency a Federal Reserve bank issued. The bank's head, George L. Harrison, declared to Hoover officials that he would no longer "take responsibility" for running the New York bank "with deficient reserves."[2] Closing the most important Federal Reserve bank in the country would halt business transactions all over the United States and stall them in much of the world. When Roosevelt reached Washington, the table in his hotel would be covered with slips of paper informing him that as he had been traveling, the situation had worsened. One state after another was closing its banks. The economy was in full collapse.

Roosevelt knew about total collapse. He had once been a man who could spend an entire day running, swimming, and sailing, fight a brush fire, jog home, then dress for dinner and be charming company. In the space of one night, he became a man racked by pain, filled with fear, a man who couldn't do anything. He knew what it took to come back from complete collapse. Faith. Will. And a plan. If the first plan didn't work, you needed more faith, more will, and another plan.

He could fix the banks. He had some of the smartest people in America working on that. The bigger problem was how to pull Americans out of despair. That problem was his alone.

The Depression had soured the American dream like a milk bottle left too long in the sun. A country that symbolized hope now had none. He'd had the same problem as he lay in his bed after contracting polio, unable to move, trying for hours just to wiggle a toe—and failing. "He knew that the soul needed healing first. . . . People have to have the courage to keep seeking a cure, no matter what the cure is. America had lost its will to recover, and Roosevelt was certain that regaining it was the first order of business," observed Garry Wills years later.[3]

During his campaign people had thronged to hear him. They'd filled the streets, climbed on rooftops, and shinnied up into trees just to see him pass. The little bit of faith they had left, they put in him. His faith, his solutions, his spirit would rescue them only if he could ignite *their* faith, their solutions, and their spirits. To rouse people's darkest selves was no great challenge. Any demagogue could shovel enough manure to make fear and hatred grow. Empowering people's better angels was not so easy. Washington had done it. Lincoln had done it. Did Roosevelt think he was a Washington or a Lincoln? All presidents want to be. But he was a fifty-one-year-old man. Life had tempered the confidence of youth. Polio had made him dependent on others in a way able-bodied people couldn't imagine. It had taught him that he could do almost anything—if he had the will and the help. The American people needed strength. It made sense to him that they would get it from the same divine source he had.

He was sitting alone in the living room of his private car when his campaign manager, James A. Farley, sat down beside him. Roosevelt wasn't the kind of guy who dropped God's name in every conversation, but he was in a musing mood. Maybe it was Farley's reputation as a devout Catholic that caused the president-elect to open up. When Farley related Roosevelt's next words in his memoir, the campaign manager didn't put them in direct quotes, but he remembered the gist of it.

A thought to God is the right way to start off my administration, Roosevelt said. A proper attitude toward religion and belief in God will in the end be the salvation of all peoples, he told Farley; it will be the means of bringing us out of the depths of despair into which so many have fallen. Then Roosevelt went further. On Inauguration Day, before the actual ceremony, he said he was going to have all members of the cabinet and their families accompany him to St. John's Episcopal Church, sometimes known as the Church of the Presidents.[4]

No president had ever called future cabinet members to prayer and worship before the inauguration. It wasn't expected. So why do it? That this particular president would begin on such a religious note was counter to most of what the public believed about him—then and now. Claiming that only religion and belief in God would bring Americans out of despair sounded more like preacher talk than the words of a rich politician with an amber cigarette holder clenched between his teeth.

Nevertheless, late on the evening of March 3, members of FDR's future cabinet received telephone messages asking them to gather the next morning in the chapel of St. John's Episcopal Church for a private service of worship and intercession. They were told that FDR wanted to pray, and he wanted everyone to pray for him.

Prayer requests were a part of life they might as well get used to. He liked praying, and he liked other people to pray, too. He had asked his son James to pray for him on election night. "I'm afraid I won't be able to do this job," Roosevelt said as he lay in bed ready to sleep after that long day. "I'm going to pray, and I want you to pray with me." In the coming years, he would ask his cabinet to pray for him before making other big decisions. Each year, Roosevelt would commemorate his first inauguration as president with a prayer service.

At ten o'clock on March 4, 1933, the seventy-five-year-old Reverend Endicott Peabody led the service. Peabody had married Eleanor and Franklin and corresponded with Franklin over the years since Groton.[5] Peabody's blond hair had receded, but his straight, patrician nose was still imposing, his posture as erect as ever, as he stood at the front of St. John's before a group of about one hundred Roosevelt supporters and advisors sitting with their families beside them. As the service was about to begin, Roosevelt slipped in a side door.

Quite a different scene was taking place outside the sacred hush of the Lafayette Square church. Shortly after two o'clock in the morning a wave of anxiety had spread from hotel to hotel as people realized money was disappearing. All twelve Federal Reserve banks planned to keep their doors locked on March 4, and banks in thirty-seven states were either closed completely or operated under state-imposed restrictions on withdrawals.[6]

Overnight, the cash people had in their wallets became the only money that counted. Checks were worthless. No business wanted to extend credit knowing it might never be paid.

As Roosevelt and his associates sang, "Faith of our fathers! living still in spite of dungeon, fire, and sword," women still in evening wear from the night before were jostling with assembly-line workers, doctors, and teachers, going from bank to bank, finding the doors locked. Then they tried retail establishments, restaurants, shoe shops, anyplace that might have cash. But they were too late. Anybody with cash was holding on to it.

Visitors couldn't pay their hotel bills, couldn't eat in restaurants. They couldn't buy train tickets to return home. They couldn't wire to ask relatives for money because they couldn't pay for the telegram. They couldn't even catch a bus; to take a taxi or ride a bus, you had to have correct change, and coins were scarcer than bills. One story went around about a man who wanted to buy shaving supplies but didn't have correct change. When he gave the clerk a fifty-dollar bill, the clerk took his supplies back and returned the bill. If he had change, he wasn't giving it up. When the customer protested, the clerk suggested he grow a beard.

People in other places were having similar experiences. In New York City, when word went out that ticket clerks at Pennsylvania Station had coins, crowds began showing up with dollar bills, $100, $500, and $1,000 notes, trying to buy tickets to Newark that they didn't need and wouldn't use. A traveling salesman sold his shoe samples in a hotel lobby to get money to return home. Doctors around the country couldn't make house calls because they didn't have cash for gas. Even the rate of divorces went down that week, as people who wanted them couldn't come up with change for the bus fare to get to court. In Elgin, Ohio, the story spread that a sixteen-year-old boy had saved 11,357 pennies for his college education; local shop owners surrounded his home, begging for the copper coins. Hotel owners planned to send bellhops to church the next day, Sunday, telling them to put bills in the collection plates and scoop up the change.

Inside St. John's, Peabody was reading psalms chosen by Roosevelt. Then he prayed, "O Lord, our Heavenly Father, the high and mighty ruler of the Universe, Who dost from Thy throne behold all the dwellers upon earth; most heartily we beseech Thee, with Thy favor to behold and bless Thy servant, Franklin, chosen to be the President of the United States."

After Peabody's amen, the president-elect remained with his head in his hands. Minutes passed as his closest friends and advisors, Catholics, Protestants, and Jews, waited, ready to rise but keeping their heads bowed, checking now and then to see what FDR was doing. Church was a good place for Roosevelt to find inspiration. He'd recently been in his childhood Hyde Park church, St. James' Episcopal, when a Bible story he would use in his upcoming speech had come to him—the story of Jesus chasing the money changers from the temple.[7]

Finally, Roosevelt's big head came up. Pulling himself to his feet, he squared his shoulders, turned, and "smiled at all of us in a sort of friendly, fatherly way," Frances Perkins remembered.[8] As he walked out of St. John's, "a brief streak of sunlight shot down upon him through grey wintry clouds," *Time* magazine reported.[9] FDR had first turned to God, as would be his practice in the presidency. Now he would move forward, perfectly at ease, secure in the formidable confidence that seemed always with him. He was ready to lead.

As Hoover and Roosevelt rode in an open car from the White House to the Capitol, Democrats, who hadn't elected a president for sixteen years, lined Pennsylvania Avenue, hanging from windows, perched in trees, standing on soapboxes, children sitting on fathers' shoulders. The parade afterward would stretch three miles, making it the longest inaugural parade ever marched to date. It would include African American men pushing lawnmowers, a rebuke to Hoover's claim that grass would grow in the streets of American cities if Roosevelt's trade policy was followed.

Roosevelt waved and tipped his hat to the smattering of cheers as they rode, but Hoover stared straight ahead, unsmiling, brooding as though he were alone in the car. The outgoing president had good reason to be glum. By the last months of his administration Hoover was so psychologically depressed that Secretary of State Henry L. Stimson reported cabinet meetings were like taking a bath in black ink.[10] It would be said of Hoover that if he so much as held a rose, it wilted. Instead of being remembered as a great leader, he would be remembered as the man who sent tanks and troops to fire on a protest by the Bonus Army's war veterans and their families. They had come to Washington, D.C., hoping to get the bonuses promised to them earlier than scheduled. By FDR's inaugural day, a man who had never failed at anything seemed to have become a president who failed at everything.

Before he became president, he had earned a fortune as a mining engineer. He organized relief work in China before he was forty, and later on a more massive scale for Europe after World War I. The food he helped deliver to starving people is credited with saving more than ten million French and Belgian lives. He was so revered in Finland for the many lives he saved that his name became a verb meaning "to help." He accomplished relief efforts with such efficiency and excellence that he was acclaimed as the "Great Humanitarian." A 1928 presidential campaign film was titled *Herbert Hoover: Master of Emergencies.*[11] His reputation propelled him into the presidency.

Once there, he put complete faith in capitalism's ability to right itself. As he waited for the free enterprise system to work its magic, he failed to give Americans the succor and hope they so desperately needed. In his penultimate 1928 campaign speech about American ideals and traditions, Hoover had declared that the American system was based on rugged individualism and self-reliance. He said his countrymen must choose whether to continue the tradition of unfettered capitalism that had brought so much prosperity or to go the way of Europe, which was paternalism and socialism. He chose unfettered capitalism.

The stock market crash and ensuing depression didn't change his mind. He believed that private charity should take care of most need during the depression and that the free enterprise system would return prosperity to the country in a short time. Hoover's remedies were so inadequate that he admitted to a dubious historical honor: "I am the only person of distinction who has ever had a depression named for him." Makeshift encampments where people lived in cardboard boxes, tin shelters, or simply slept on the ground were known as Hoovervilles. Newspapers used to keep out the cold were called a Hoover blanket. Hoover wagons were cars that had been stripped down and modified to be pulled by horses because people couldn't afford gas. Turned-out pockets with nothing in them were called Hoover flags.[12]

Raised a Quaker, Hoover had worked tirelessly to feed people of other countries, but he simply did not believe his own people, digging through garbage cans for food, were starving. He did initiate relief programs, but he feared direct payments to the unemployed would destroy the country's moral fiber. When his administration provided money to help farmers, they were directed to use it only for animal feed and equipment. "The Great Humanitarian who had fed the starving Belgians in 1914, The Great Engineer so hopefully elevated to the presidency in 1928, now appeared to be the Great Scrooge, a corrupted ideologue who could swallow government relief for the banks but priggishly scrupled over government provisions for the unemployed," wrote Stanford University historian David M. Kennedy.[13]

Hoover's vision may have been clouded by one of the most revered tenets of what sociologist Robert Bellah called civil religion: shared beliefs about a country's essence and values that are outside formal religion. Hoover's desire to help the suffering ran up against the idea that free enterprise was sacred, that anyone can make it in the United States if he or she works hard. Self-reliance, individualism, and respect for free enterprise were values that this self-made man and many others considered integral to America's survival.[14]

The crowd facing the inaugural platform at the east front of the Capitol was one hundred thousand strong, packed tightly enough to blacken forty acres of park and pavement, and so somber that they might have been taken for sullen. Radio announcers read from prepared copy that "a mighty cheer had risen from the throats of one hundred thousand

Americans." But it hadn't. The crowd was "as silent as a group of mourners around a grave." The air was so still that the clop-clop of police horses' hooves echoed as they fell on pavement.[15]

As the hour for the changeover approached, a bugle sounded, and through the great bronze doors cast with the story of Columbus on their surface, the president-elect came from the Capitol into the cold day wearing a morning coat and striped trousers. He was without his hat or overcoat, holding onto his son James's arm.

Now the crowd really did burst into cheers. Political dignitaries were bunched together on a raised platform decorated with flags, garlands, wreaths, and the Great Seal of the United States. Underneath the rostrum where Roosevelt would speak was the image of a huge eagle, wings spread. At the sight of Roosevelt, John W. Davis, the Democratic Party's presidential candidate in 1924, pounded on the wooden flooring with his walking stick. Former secretary of the navy Josephus Daniels, the portly North Carolinian editor who had been Roosevelt's boss when the president-elect was assistant secretary of the navy, scrambled nimbly across the pine benches to his seat. Bernard Baruch, financier and advisor to both presidents Woodrow Wilson and Theodore Roosevelt, stood on a bench like a boy and doffed his high silk hat.[16]

As father and son moved slowly across the lawn to a specially constructed ramp carpeted in maroon, the crowd cheered and the Marine Band played "Hail to the Chief." From the massive doors to the lectern was thirty-seven steps. The laborious process he used to walk required such strength and concentration that Roosevelt's face often beaded with perspiration.[17] The cold air on that day was a blessing. Balancing his massive upper body on heavy, locked braces with shoes built into them, he walked by swinging one leg from hip out and forward, and then shifting his weight to the other side, swinging the other leg out and forward. Like a man walking on the heaving deck of a ship, he listed from side to side.

James had to hold his 195-pound father erect using only one arm and at the same time watch Roosevelt's feet, ready to place one of his own in front of FDR's shoe if his father's stiffened leg seemed in danger of slipping as he shifted to the other side. James and his brother Elliott had lifted weights to make sure their arms were strong enough. Sometimes their father's grip was so fierce that their arms bruised. Each step was a gamble. The slightest mistake would send the big man crashing like a felled tree. It was an easy walk from the vantage point of the audience; for the two Roosevelts, it was a slippery path they had to traverse safely with complete self-assurance and not the slightest hesitation. It had taken years of building strength, practicing balance, and perfecting technique for this thirty-seven-step presidential walk to look normal enough that it accomplished a goal FDR had set years earlier.

Although he never seems to have admitted to anyone that he knew he would not walk again, his Warm Springs, Georgia, physical therapist Helen Mahoney wasn't a woman who skirted the truth. After watching him labor hour after hour on legs that weren't doing much better, she asked him what he was working for. He didn't try to sell her any impossible dream, but he did aim high. He said, "I'll walk without crutches. I'll walk into a room without scaring everybody half to death. I'll stand easily enough in front of people that they will forget I'm a cripple."[18] He was willing to walk with a cane. Lots of people used canes. But crutches, no.

Finally Roosevelt and James arrived safely at their place on the platform. He released James's arm. Then Roosevelt stood with perfect posture, his head up, his expression solemn. Everyone had seen how slowly he moved forward. Clearly he could not walk normally. Nobody could miss that. Now he was about to make them forget it.

His first message to America came from the scripture he chose for his oath of office: one of the loveliest and most reassuring in the Bible. Standing at the east entrance to the Capitol, he placed his hand on his family's 247-year-old Dutch Bible. It was so fragile and so precious to him that Roosevelt had hand-carried it from New York to Washington. That Bible would also be used in his three subsequent presidential inaugurations. It was opened to First Corinthians 13, as it had been when he was sworn in as governor of New York.

Roosevelt was notorious for his aversion to the number thirteen. No dinner party he gave could have thirteen guests.[19] No sailing party he embarked with could have thirteen sailors. That he would choose text from chapter thirteen must have required a great love for the passage. Two verses have been singled out as important to him. The first verse was said to be his favorite: "If I speak in the tongues of men or of angels, but do not have love, I am only a resounding gong or a clanging cymbal." The thirteenth verse was also one he loved. It reads in modern translation: "And now these three remain: faith, hope, and love. But the greatest of these is love."

Other presidents had either paid little attention to the selection of a verse or chose much sterner readings. Law and commandments were popular. In their first inaugurations, Washington and Lincoln swore on Bibles opened hastily and at random. For his second inauguration, Lincoln chose three verses, among them Matthew 7:1, apt for the ending of the Civil War: "Do not judge, lest you be judged." Hoover selected Proverbs 29:18: "Where there is no vision, the people perish: but he that keepeth the law, happy is he." In light of his administration's end, that seems a fitting foreshadowing and a reproof of the social unrest his leadership inspired.[20]

FDR is the only president to have ever chosen a verse with such inspiring promises. On that day, as his words began infusing faith and hope into the American people, they would give him admiration, allegiance, and even love. The relationship between leader and led would become one of the most amazing love fests in history.

Roosevelt wasn't the only American who thought faith in God would deliver the people from despair. A lot of Americans were already pairing God and FDR in their minds. Clouds were heavy on that cold, gray day, but a Mississippi onlooker later wrote to Roosevelt that "when you came and put your hand on [the Bible] . . . the sun broke through the clouds and gave a ray of light through upon you. I said then, and I still say, that the Supreme Power above blessed your administration."[21] *Time* magazine had noted a shaft of light as he left St. John's. Now someone had seen a shaft of light when he took the oath of office. As Roosevelt finished his speech, a diarist would record yet another ray of light breaking through to shine as if God were sending a blessing. There would be more notice of light coming from the heavens to rest on him. Even after his death, people would talk of the sun breaking through to shine on his coffin being carried forward.

As Chief Justice Charles Evans Hughes recited the oath of office, the crowd quieted quickly. Unlike other presidents, Roosevelt waited until the chief justice finished the entire oath. Then he repeated each word "like a bride groom repeating his marriage vows," wrote the *New York Times*.

At eight minutes after one o'clock, Roosevelt attained the office he sought all his adult life. The last words of his oath, "So help me God," had hardly faded before the new president swung sharply around to face the crowd. The genial smile that has so defined him was gone, his head was back, his large chin was thrust defiantly forward as though he was about to start a fight. In the crowd, cheers died and smiles evaporated, leaving worried, frightened, and angry faces. Some seemed "terror-stricken," said Perkins.[22]

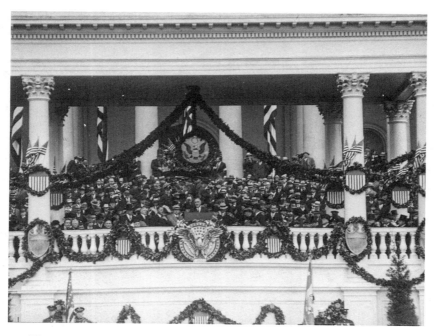
Franklin D. Roosevelt giving his inaugural speech in 1933.
IMAGE COURTESY OF THE FRANKLIN DELANO ROOSEVELT PRESIDENTIAL LIBRARY

"A Day of Consecration"

The land of the free was so desperate on Inauguration Day 1933 that civil war seemed at hand. Machine guns trained on the throng were armed and ready. Secret Service agents kept hands close to their guns. No one in the crowd knew what to expect from Roosevelt. Many didn't expect much.

"No one knows his heart and few have seen behind the masking smile that wreathes his face," grumped editor William Allen White from Emporia, Kansas. "We have had to be satisfied with urbanity when we needed wisdom, with mastery when we should have a complete understanding. We are putting our hands in a grab-bag. Heaven only knows what we shall pull out."[1] Journalist Walter Lippmann could see no real strength in the new president, calling him "a kind of amiable Boy Scout."[2]

Those who questioned his resolve to go in a new direction would have done well to consult his friend John Kingsbury. In 1930, Roosevelt told him, "There is no question in my mind that it is time for the country to become fairly radical for a generation. History shows that where this occurs occasionally, nations are saved from revolution."

Roosevelt was at heart a conservative man. But he loved democracy more than he loved stasis. "Democracy is not a static thing," he said. "It is an everlasting march."[3]

⊷⇌◉⇋⊷

Most presidents follow the oath of office with a speech of bland assurances and easy promises, lackluster addresses that no one remembers. Not this time. One of the most amazing twenty minutes in American history began when the new president opened his mouth. He spoke fewer than two thousand words, and despairing Americans began to feel like the can-do winners they once were.

His clear, patrician tenor ringing through the chill air, Roosevelt started, *"This is a day of national consecration."*

This line was not in the official copy given to the journalists. He penciled it in above the typed copy of his speech while waiting for the ceremony to begin. No sentence he uttered that day so completely captured what he intended. Consecration is how a priest is raised up to become God's bishop, how wine and bread are transmuted into the blood and body of Christ, how land becomes holy. These words are a vow. He is pledging to be bound by God and to consider the tasks before him sacred. The words are also a request. He is asking Americans to consecrate themselves in service of a new vision. He is about to call upon this nation to be more like the kingdom of God. He plans to make the law of the land hew closer to God's mercy than it ever has been before. He is bold. They must be, too.

He delivered his most famous line early. *"So, first of all, let me assert my firm belief that the only thing we have to fear is fear itself—nameless, unreasoning, unjustified terror which paralyzes needed efforts to convert retreat into advance."*

Newspapers didn't put much emphasis on that part of the speech the next day. Some could scoff that there was plenty to be afraid of. Laid-off miners and their families were living in shut-down coke ovens near Pittsburgh. The Detroit zoo was so broke that it gave away its animals to other zoos and slaughtered the buffalo and deer to feed the hungry. Families scavenged in trash heaps for food and slept huddled over street grates. Upstanding, hardworking citizens who had always paid their own way were destitute, scorned, blamed, and shunned as if they, the victims of it all, were at fault.

But fear is not the way to heal a country. It's a way to go to war. It's a way to divide, not to show people that they are one. Believe and be not afraid was one of Jesus's central teachings.

Their troubles are real, the president tells them next, but "[t]hey concern, thank God, only material things."

This was Roosevelt's first expression of faith in them, these defeated and destitute (or about to be) people. They didn't have to wait long for this bucking up. And they would get more. Nobody has had much good to say about them. With this short, simple sentence, he told them so much that they needed to hear: as long as you're solid—and you are—everything else can be fixed. After recognizing the economic situation with some vivid description, he raised them and their suffering into the realm of God's grace merely by his choice of words.

He recognized that "a host of unemployed citizens face the grim problem of existence, and an equally great number toil with little return." Only in the Bible is a crowd a host. Most of the time the host is a heavenly host; sometimes members of the host are not identified, but usually the host is thought to be composed of angels. Sometimes they are God's army. Once they came to welcome God's son to earth. Is he saying that this crowd of dispirited listeners are all God's angels? His avengers? No, of course not. They are poor, grimy losers, or afraid of being such. He isn't saying they are God's own angels, not overtly, but for these people steeped in the Bible all their lives the word host pulls with it a big load of stories, a lot of feelings. It elevates everyone hearing it.

He also used the word toil. Humans work in the actual world, but in the King James Version of the Bible, which is what Christians had in those days, they toil. Toil is sweat and calluses and weariness that makes your bones ache and your flesh sag. Toil is never-ending. Toil is sorrowful and poorly rewarded unless it is in the vineyards of the Lord. Americans are feeling far cast out of the vineyards and far from the Lord's blessings. Roosevelt is about to bring them back. Carefully. Sweetly. With ancient words.

"Yet our distress comes from no failure of substance. We are stricken by no plague of locusts." The word substance instantly had two meanings for these good Americans. They didn't need time to ponder it. He aimed straight for their souls. Substance is that which sustains: food, water, the living word of God. Substance is also the character of the people. It could be money. Lord knows they would have loved to have some of that. But it's more than money. It's character, it's being upstanding citizens, it's working for your family, being a human being worthy of respect. It's all that so many of them have lost.

And then he said that there had been no plague of locusts. The plague of locusts was one of the punishments inflicted on Egypt because the pharaoh wouldn't let the Israelites go free. You are the chosen ones, he was telling them. You are not the pharaohs, not the puffed-up sinners. You are not being punished for your sins.

His words spoke to the truth beyond truth, to the great stories that spoke to their hearts. He told them they were innocent, beloved. If he said it straight out, they would not be able to tolerate such goodness. So he didn't. He told it through a language of spiritual import.

"*Nature still offers her bounty and human efforts have multiplied it. Plenty is at our doorstep, but a generous use of it languishes in the very sight of the supply.*" This is one of the deepest truths he knows. Nature, God's handmaiden, has provided bounty. More than enough for everyone. And they have done their part. Their work has multiplied it. *Plenty is at our doorstep.* Jesus said the kingdom of God is at hand. Roosevelt said that plenty is at our doorstep. Is there a difference?

But "*generous use of it languishes in the very sight of the supply.*" Like Moses, they can see the promised land, but they can't cross over. Is that because they've sinned? Been greedy? Forsaken God? People in trouble this deep can't stop asking why. Are they fools? Are they sinners?

No, Roosevelt told them, this poverty came upon the people "*because rulers of the exchange of mankind's goods have failed through their own stubbornness and their own incompetence.*" Stubbornness? Oh, yes, they knew without any reflection at all that the pharaoh was stubborn. God's prophets always rail against the stiff-necked and stubborn.

Then he reassured the people again, don't be afraid. The false leaders "*have admitted their failure, and have abdicated. Practices of the unscrupulous money changers stand indicted in the court of public opinion, rejected by the hearts and minds of men.*"

Money changers. Those were such bad men that Jesus, meek and mild, lost his temper and cast them out of the temple.

> *True they have tried, but their efforts have been cast in the pattern of an outworn tradition. Faced by failure of credit they*

have proposed only the lending of more money. Stripped of the lure of profit by which to induce our people to follow their false leadership, they have resorted to exhortations, pleading tearfully for restored confidence. They know only the rules of a generation of self-seekers. They have no vision, and when there is no vision the people perish.

The lure of profit. Oh, yes, the people followed these false leaders, but the mighty are defeated and crying now.

The money changers have fled from their high seats in the temple of our civilization. We may now restore that temple to the ancient truths. The measure of the restoration lies in the extent to which we apply social values more noble than mere monetary profit.

The new president vanquished the bad men. Then he turned his attention to the people. What must they do? They must realize what really matters.

Happiness lies not in the mere possession of money; it lies in the joy of achievement, in the thrill of creative effort. The joy and moral stimulation of work no longer must be forgotten in the mad chase of evanescent profits. These dark days will be worth all they cost us if they teach us that our true destiny is not to be ministered unto but to minister to ourselves and to our fellow men.

Roosevelt claimed consecration. He put fear aside. Now he called these people, good people of substance, to return to their high values. They must serve each other.

Recognition of the falsity of material wealth as the standard of success goes hand in hand with the abandonment of the false belief that public office and high political position are to be valued only by the standards of pride of place and personal profit; and there must be an end to a conduct in banking and in business which too often has given to a sacred trust the likeness of callous and selfish wrongdoing. Small wonder that confidence languishes, for it thrives only on honesty, on honor, on the sacredness of obligations, on faithful protection, on unselfish performance;

without them it cannot live. Restoration calls, however, not
for changes in ethics alone. This Nation asks for action, and
action now.

It was a sounding of the trumpet, which in politics and churches usually leads to nothing. But not this time. This time, a president intended to make the highest, most stringent of spiritual values into governmental policy. He found the enemy, and it was them, the money men. And he would go after them like a prophet of old. He also had a long list of actions he would take. They promised quick help and changes that went to the crux of the problem.

Hoover and his wife sat in the first row. The former president kept his eyes on his knees during the address, but dark little knots of disagreement passed over his forehead more than once as Roosevelt continued. His time in the limelight, however, had ended. When the address was over, he and his wife would slip quietly away to board a train for home.

Roosevelt delivered a few more punches at those whose *"callous and selfish wrongdoing,"* whose lack of honesty and honor, whose failure to respect *"the sacredness of obligations"* and failure to give *"faithful protection"* or *"unselfish performance"* betrayed a sacred trust.

Those doubting that a constitutionally empowered democracy would be strong enough to pull the country out of depression could rest easy, he told them. He had no doubts. The Constitution is simple and flexible enough to meet modern needs. The government is solid. But if the normal balance of executive and legislative authority wasn't sufficient to meet the crisis, he said he would ask Congress for *"broad Executive power to wage a war against the emergency, as great as the power that would be given to me if we were in fact invaded by a foreign foe."* At this pledge, the closest he came to saying that he would seize power, the crowd roared its approval with such ferocity that Eleanor was afraid of what they might be willing to do. They were ready for a man of strength. If he could take power and do it in a democracy, fine, but whatever it took, they wanted him to do it.

When he began at 1:08 p.m., they had no faith in anybody or anything. By 1:30, they were his followers, aroused and ready.

As the inaugural speech moved toward its close, Roosevelt made another pledge: *"For the trust reposed in me I will return the courage and the devotion that befit the time. I can do no less."* He gave assurance:

> *We face the arduous days that lie before us in the warm courage of national unity; with the clear consciousness of seeking old and precious moral values; with the clean satisfaction that comes from the stern performance of duty by old and young alike. We aim at the assurance of a rounded and permanent national life.*
>
> *We do not distrust the future of essential democracy. The people of the United States have not failed. In their need they have registered a mandate that they want direct, vigorous action. They have asked for discipline and direction under leadership. They have made me the present instrument of their wishes. In the spirit of the gift I take it.*

And then, for the first time, he addressed God. *"In this dedication of a Nation we humbly ask the blessing of God. May He protect each and every one of us. May He guide me in the days to come."*

"It was very, very solemn and a little terrifying," Eleanor said later. "The crowds were so tremendous and you felt that they would do anything—if only someone would tell them what to do."

Roosevelt remained solemn as he left the platform and was seated in his car. His face was still "so grim as to seem unfamiliar to those who have long known him," wrote Arthur Krock.[4] The president departed in the same open limo he had arrived in, but now Eleanor was beside him. As the crowd cheered, he smiled and raised his clasped hands like a boxer announcing his win. Traveling in his car through streets crowded with admirers, he tipped his top hat one way and another, so enthusiastically that his wife finally felt compelled to tell him it would be better to keep his hat on. She worried about his health.[5]

Reflecting on the day many years later, Frances Perkins said, "People cried. Tears streamed down the faces of strong men in the audience as they listened to it. It was a revival of faith. He said, 'Come on now, do you believe?' They said, 'Yes, we do.'"

The day felt like a religious revival to her. In fact, it was the beginning of a revival, a revival of hope and spirit, a revival of brotherhood, an application of Christian precepts to American public life, the likes of which would not be seen again. It was the beginning of a twelve-year period when biblical truths would be cited repeatedly as the proper basis for the conduct of government by a president who could put those ideals into law.

FRANKLIN DELANO ROOSEVELT'S

FIRST INAUGURAL ADDRESS

President Hoover, Mr. Chief Justice, my friends:

This is a day of national consecration. And I am certain that on this day my fellow Americans expect that on my induction into the Presidency I will address them with a candor and a decision which the present situation of our people impels. This is preeminently the time to speak the truth, the whole truth, frankly and boldly. Nor need we shrink from honestly facing conditions in our country today. This great Nation will endure as it has endured, will revive and will prosper. So, first of all, let me assert my firm belief that the only thing we have to fear is fear itself—nameless, unreasoning, unjustified terror which paralyzes needed efforts to convert retreat into advance. In every dark hour of our national life a leadership of frankness and vigor has met with that understanding and support of the people themselves which is essential to victory. I am convinced that you will again give that support to leadership in these critical days.

In such a spirit on my part and on yours we face our common difficulties. They concern, thank God, only material things. Values have shrunken to fantastic levels; taxes have risen; our ability to pay has fallen; government of all kinds is faced by serious curtailment of income; the means of exchange are frozen in the currents of trade; the withered leaves of industrial enterprise lie on every side; farmers find no markets for their produce; the savings of many years in thousands of families are gone.

More important, a host of unemployed citizens face the grim problem of existence,
and an equally great number toil with little return.
Only a foolish optimist can deny the dark realities of the moment.

Yet our distress comes from no failure of substance. We are stricken by no plague
of locusts. Compared with the perils which our forefathers conquered because they
believed and were not afraid, we have still much to be thankful for. Nature still offers
her bounty and human efforts have multiplied it. Plenty is at our doorstep, but a
generous use of it languishes in the very sight of the supply. Primarily this is because
rulers of the exchange of mankind's goods have failed through their own stubbornness
and their own incompetence, have admitted their failure, and have abdicated.
Practices of the unscrupulous money changers stand indicted in the court of public
opinion, rejected by the hearts and minds of men.

True they have tried, but their efforts have been cast in the pattern of an outworn
tradition. Faced by failure of credit they have proposed only the lending of more
money. Stripped of the lure of profit by which to induce our people to follow their false
leadership, they have resorted to exhortations, pleading tearfully for
restored confidence. They know only the rules of a generation of self-seekers.
They have no vision, and when there is no vision the people perish.

The money changers have fled from their high seats in the temple of our civilization.
We may now restore that temple to the ancient truths. The measure
of the restoration lies in the extent to which we apply
social values more noble than mere monetary profit.

Happiness lies not in the mere possession of money; it lies in the joy of achievement,
in the thrill of creative effort. The joy and moral stimulation of work no
longer must be forgotten in the mad chase of evanescent profits. These dark
days will be worth all they cost us if they teach us that our true destiny is not
to be ministered unto but to minister to ourselves and to our fellow men.

Recognition of the falsity of material wealth as the standard of success goes hand in
hand with the abandonment of the false belief that public office and high political
position are to be valued only by the standards of pride of place and personal profit;
and there must be an end to a conduct in banking and in business which too often has
given to a sacred trust the likeness of callous and selfish wrongdoing.
Small wonder that confidence languishes, for it thrives only on honesty,

on honor, on the sacredness of obligations, on faithful protection, on unselfish performance; without them it cannot live. Restoration calls, however, not for changes in ethics alone. This Nation asks for action, and action now.

Our greatest primary task is to put people to work. This is no unsolvable problem if we face it wisely and courageously. It can be accomplished in part by direct recruiting by the Government itself, treating the task as we would treat the emergency of a war, but at the same time, through this employment, accomplishing greatly needed projects to stimulate and reorganize the use of our natural resources.

Hand in hand with this we must frankly recognize the overbalance of population in our industrial centers and, by engaging on a national scale in a redistribution, endeavor to provide a better use of the land for those best fitted for the land. The task can be helped by definite efforts to raise the values of agricultural products and with this the power to purchase the output of our cities. It can be helped by preventing realistically the tragedy of the growing loss through foreclosure of our small homes and our farms. It can be helped by insistence that the Federal, State, and local governments act forthwith on the demand that their cost be drastically reduced. It can be helped by the unifying of relief activities which today are often scattered, uneconomical, and unequal. It can be helped by national planning for and supervision of all forms of transportation and of communications and other utilities which have a definitely public character. There are many ways in which it can be helped, but it can never be helped merely by talking about it. We must act and act quickly.

Finally, in our progress toward a resumption of work we require two safeguards against a return of the evils of the old order: there must be a strict supervision of all banking and credits and investments, so that there will be an end to speculation with other people's money; and there must be provision for an adequate but sound currency.

These are the lines of attack. I shall presently urge upon a new Congress, in special session, detailed measures for their fulfillment, and I shall seek the immediate assistance of the several States.

Through this program of action we address ourselves to putting our own national house in order and making income balance outgo. Our international trade relations, though

vastly important, are in point of time and necessity secondary to the establishment
of a sound national economy. I favor as a practical policy the putting of first
things first. I shall spare no effort to restore world trade by international economic
readjustment, but the emergency at home cannot wait on that accomplishment.

The basic thought that guides these specific means of national recovery is not narrowly
nationalistic. It is the insistence, as a first consideration, upon the interdependence
of the various elements in and parts of the United States—a recognition of the old and
permanently important manifestation of the American spirit of the pioneer.
It is the way to recovery. It is the immediate way. It is the strongest
assurance that the recovery will endure.

In the field of world policy I would dedicate this Nation to the policy of the good
neighbor—the neighbor who resolutely respects himself and, because he does so,
respects the rights of others—the neighbor who respects his obligations and respects
the sanctity of his agreements in and with a world of neighbors.

If I read the temper of our people correctly, we now realize as we have never realized
before our interdependence on each other; that we cannot merely take but we must give
as well; that if we are to go forward, we must move as a trained and loyal army willing
to sacrifice for the good of a common discipline, because without such discipline no
progress is made, no leadership becomes effective. We are, I know, ready and willing to
submit our lives and property to such discipline, because it makes possible a leadership
which aims at a larger good. This I propose to offer, pledging that the
larger purposes will bind upon us all as a sacred obligation with
a unity of duty hitherto evoked only in time of armed strife.

With this pledge taken, I assume unhesitatingly the leadership of this great army
of our people dedicated to a disciplined attack upon our common problems.

Action in this image and to this end is feasible under the form of government which
we have inherited from our ancestors. Our Constitution is so simple and practical
that it is possible always to meet extraordinary needs by changes in emphasis and
arrangement without loss of essential form. That is why our constitutional system
has proved itself the most superbly enduring political mechanism the
modern world has produced. It has met every stress of vast expansion of territory,
of foreign wars, of bitter internal strife, of world relations.

It is to be hoped that the normal balance of Executive and legislative authority may be wholly adequate to meet the unprecedented task before us. But it may be that an unprecedented demand and need for undelayed action may call for temporary departure from that normal balance of public procedure.

I am prepared under my constitutional duty to recommend the measures that a stricken Nation in the midst of a stricken world may require. These measures, or such other measures as the Congress may build out of its experience and wisdom, I shall seek, within my constitutional authority, to bring to speedy adoption.

But in the event that the Congress shall fail to take one of these two courses, and in the event that the national emergency is still critical, I shall not evade the clear course of duty that will then confront me. I shall ask the Congress for the one remaining instrument to meet the crisis—broad Executive power to wage a war against the emergency, as great as the power that would be given to me if we were in fact invaded by a foreign foe.

For the trust reposed in me I will return the courage and the devotion that befit the time. I can do no less.

We face the arduous days that lie before us in the warm courage of national unity; with the clear consciousness of seeking old and precious moral values; with the clean satisfaction that comes from the stern performance of duty by old and young alike. We aim at the assurance of a rounded and permanent national life.

We do not distrust the future of essential democracy. The people of the United States have not failed. In their need they have registered a mandate that they want direct, vigorous action. They have asked for discipline and direction under leadership. They have made me the present instrument of their wishes. In the spirit of the gift I take it.

In this dedication of a Nation we humbly ask the blessing of God. May He protect each and every one of us. May He guide me in the days to come.[6]

A pro-Roosevelt crowd in 1932.

IMAGE COURTESY OF THE FRANKLIN DELANO ROOSEVELT PRESIDENTIAL LIBRARY

"The Boss, the Dynamo, the Works"

Before Inauguration Day was over, telegrams began pouring into the White House, most of them saying, in one way or another, "Go for it. We are with you." Blacks and whites, blue-collar workers, doctors, lawyers, farmers, immigrants, widows, government officials in small towns and big cities wrote. Schoolchildren used lined paper torn from their notebooks to say thank-you and tell him how happy they felt after hearing him. Businessmen dictated letters to their secretaries using company stationery to give their counsel the proper stature. Housewives sent greeting cards. Half a million of them wrote that week. And already the people were responding to his expert evocation of divinity by projecting some of that godliness on him: "It was the finest thing this side of heaven"; "Yours is the first opportunity to carve a name in the halls of the immortals beside Jesus"; "People are looking to you almost as they look to God."[1]

That was the beginning, and the letters didn't stop. Over the next years, they kept coming by the millions. Hoover had averaged five thousand letters a week; FDR got fifty thousand.[2] In the letters, citizens greeted him with salutations ranging from "Dear humanitarian friend of the people" to "My Pal" and "Dear Buddy."[3]

The press, the pundits, the political wise men hadn't cared for him when he was running and wouldn't care for him later, but that first week they were giddy with love for him. The man was superb, said even the staunchest Republican papers. The *Atlanta Constitution*'s editorial writers were fulsome: "The address takes its place among the greatest of historic State papers of the nation, ranking with Lincoln's address at Gettysburg and the most striking of the war utterances of Woodrow Wilson. No more vital utterance was ever made by a President of the United States."[4] In Mississippi the editor of the *Clarion-Ledger* compared the address to the Sermon on the Mount.[5]

Overnight, one eyewitness later remembered, Washington, D.C., seemed like Cambridge on the morning of the Harvard-Yale game: "All the shops were on display, everyone was joyous, crowds moved excitedly. There was something in the air that had not been there before."[6]

But this was no ordinary holiday when everyone thinks only of his own pleasure. It was something else, something rarer. "For a deceptive moment in 1933," Arthur Schlesinger wrote, "clouds of inertia and self-ishness seemed to lift."

Hitler was on the cover of the *Time* magazine issue that reported on FDR's inauguration; early Nazi actions were already alarming. Many in Germany were also feeling a surge of excitement and holiness around their new leader. Others were fearful and filled with dread.[7]

But Hitler's first address as chancellor placed his objectives in terms as lofty as those employed by FDR. He announced, "The Almighty has withdrawn his blessing from our *Volk*." He promised that the state would protect Christianity "as the basis of our entire morality." He named an enemy, the communists. He ended by saying, "May Almighty God look mercifully upon our work, lead our will on the right path, bless our wisdom, and reward us with the confidence of our *volk*. We are not fighting for ourselves, but for Germany!" Both Roosevelt and Hitler were masters of rhetoric. Both invoked God for their purposes. Both inspired their followers to great loyalty.

The new president was calling on the American people's highest values, laying the groundwork for the spiritual and political demands he would make in the next months and years. Together we will not fail, he said. He was building an army in his speeches, more figuratively than Hitler was, but both were intent on shaping their people's goals. Hitler was calling upon his people to realize their own superiority; Roosevelt was calling on his to recognize that they were all brothers, equal in the sight of God. Hitler's inspiration was his own fear, bitterness, and need for vengeance. Roosevelt's inspiration was, from start to finish, the Sermon on the Mount.

The Sermon on the Mount raises up the humble, the afflicted, the weak, says that God values them, and promises that God will reward them. Then Jesus demands what few humans can accomplish. Love your enemies. Don't harbor anger. Don't have lust even in your heart. Don't worry about anything. Don't judge anyone.

Roosevelt didn't meet all Jesus's standards, not by a long shot. But judging by what he said and did, he believed in them. Most of all he believed in the sermon's underlying message, which was that God had different standards for success than people do, and he believed that God was leading him to help make those standards into the laws of the land.

The day after the inauguration was a Sunday, and Roosevelt went to church again. That afternoon he decided to call Congress into special session on Thursday and to declare a four-day bank holiday—a cheerful name which meant that none of the banks would open on Monday and neither would the Federal Reserve. General counsel of the Federal Reserve Board Walter Wyatt convinced the president that, having started his administration on such a religious note, he ought to delay issuing the proclamation until after midnight. That way it would be dated on Monday instead of Sunday.

One reason for the nationwide bank closing was that Roosevelt had to stop the gold drain. During the month-long run on the banks in February, patrons thronged to the teller windows demanding gold for the dollars they had on deposit. Once they had their gold, many hoarded it at home or sent it to another country. By the week before the inauguration, Treasury gold reserves were down by $226 million. If the nation's gold were lost for good, keeping currency on the gold standard would be impossible.[8]

It might seem that suspending all banking operations would have terrified a public that was already frightened. But banks had been closing in state after state in a haphazard and unannounced way. Americans who had resisted federal control from the beginning of the nation's founding were now ready for some centralized rigor. Only the federal government had the resources and power to right what was going wrong. The president's swift action seemed to reassure Americans that he had control and wasn't going to sit in his high seat watching as the slide continued.

The holiday put the country in an almost springtime mood. "Anything was better than nagging uncertainty. Now everyone knew where he stood," wrote Schlesinger. The president's speech followed by his quick action gave people a sense of a common plight.[9]

Police, who had seen mobs threaten to tear the banks apart, feared there would be trouble. In Boston, three times the usual number of officers were on duty from midnight on. Officials feared that radicals would stage some kind of insurrection, or mobs would storm stores to seize the large amounts of cash they were stockpiling.[10]

But none of that happened. The anger of the Election Day crowd had been replaced with good humor. Police officers standing outside banks turned away a few who wanted to withdraw cash, and in an entirely unforeseen turn of events, they turned away many who wanted to make deposits. The depositors seemed to think it was a great joke that the banks' doors were shut against those who wanted to give them money.[11]

Paychecks couldn't be cashed, but businesses and customers pulled together so people could get what they needed. Stores extended credit more liberally. Railroads also broadened credit and assured travelers they would "not be left stranded because of banking difficulties."[12] An ad for Pebeco Tooth Paste declared, "The 'I Will' spirit of the nation is on the move. Things are happening. And better times are not far away. To back our faith in the current emergency program, we stand ready to keep millions of America's families supplied with tooth paste . . . on three months credit. Get three tubes. Take three months to pay."[13]

Even some of America's shadier enterprises got into the spirit. "Confident in the success of business and future prosperity, I am extending credit to our patrons who may be embarrassed by lack of cash. During the bank moratoria your signature will be accepted and credit extended as long as you want to dine without money inconvenience." The wire, signed by Percival Marshall's bootlegger, was quoted in a letter that author and engineer Marshall sent to the *New York Times*. Marshall's cheery addendum: "Here is the patriotic and human touch."[14]

Milwaukee ministers agreed not to pass collection plates until the bank holiday was over, and the First Baptist Church in El Paso arranged to accept IOUs.[15] "Scores of church leaders were solicited . . . by businessmen, particularly chain restaurant and store managers who had run short of coins and $1 and $2 bills, and in virtually every instance the clergy responded by turning over the cash and taking checks in return," wrote the *Boston Herald*. In Milwaukee, the West Allis Presbyterian Church provided free gasoline and oil to all worshippers, and placed the collection baskets in an obscure spot to avoid embarrassment to the changeless.[16]

Even the justice system responded to the crisis. In Boston twenty-three federal jurors, some of whom had been forced to break their children's banks to get their carfares to court, were paid off by United States Deputy Marshall Ralph Gray after Judge James A. Lowell had discharged them from further attendance in the United States District Court, according to the *Boston Post*.[17] The governor of California gave a reprieve to condemned murderer Peter Farrington because of the "doubtful legality of hanging on a holiday."[18] There was, however, no reprieve for those who owed federal income tax. The IRS was perfectly willing to accept checks, according to the *New York Times*.[19]

Gold hoarders were denounced in newspapers and from pulpits. Shamed and afraid, people began pulling gold from wherever they had hidden it, in safes, under beds, in holes they'd dug in their yards. *New York Times* reader David A. Lunden-Moore wrote the paper urging people to bring their jewelry to the Treasury and convert it into gold coin. "Old rings, antiquated mountings, bracelets, chains, pins and other articles of gold are of no value to the average person. Yes, there is sentiment but why not convert sentiment to patriotism?"[20]

Even the very rich were moved. Irénée du Pont turned in gold pieces he had been given for attending board of directors meetings for I. E. du Pont de Nemours & Co. over twenty years. His wife had retained them for sentimental reasons, her husband wrote the Wilmington Trust Company, but now she "feels it her duty to get them into the government's gold reserves."[21]

Meanwhile, the new administration was trying to rescue the entire economy. To do that Roosevelt needed an even bigger change in public faith. The country's big bankers, whom he had so reviled as money changers on Inauguration Day, were now being summoned to give advice. Culpable they might be, but saving the country meant saving them first. The bankers must have gagged at the thought of helping this name-calling new administration, and some of the administration's reformers must have choked at helping the bankers. But they were desperate.

Stoked on coffee and cigarettes, officials labored by day and by night. "When some of the calmest men about him were worrying themselves threadbare, the President kept his shirt on," wrote Arthur Krock. He is "the boss, the dynamo, the works."

Roosevelt nixed a federal guarantee of deposits, reasoning that the government shouldn't prop up bad banks along with good ones.[22] Instead new money would be printed, which the Federal Reserve would begin sending to the banks as each was examined, declared sound, and scheduled to open. The Federal Reserve was encouraged to send each bank as much as was needed. So no matter how big the run on a bank might be, the federal government was making sure it had the money to meet all demands.

The thorniest question was what to back all this new money with. Gold reserves weren't nearly enough to support it. The honeymoon glow left after Roosevelt's first inaugural address was inspiring people to bring back their treasure. In case their faith faltered, new law would give the secretary of the treasury power to demand that citizens hand over all their gold coin, gold bullion, or gold certificates and allow hoarders to be charged with a federal crime.

Until the gold reserves recovered fully, the good faith of the United States would stand behind the money, they decided. Nothing more, just that. It's all they had. No one knew if the people would trust money with no solid assets behind it. If they didn't, all the good feelings created on Inauguration Day would dissolve. The banknotes would be worthless. People would be more cynical and angry than ever. The country would plummet into a whole new kind of hell.

The Senate received the Emergency Banking Act of 1933 on Thursday, March 9, at 1:40 p.m. The House began consideration at 2:55 p.m. At about

8:00 p.m., shortly after eating a liver and onions dinner, the president was handed the banking bill. It had passed without amendment. Some members of Congress voted for it without even reading the bill. "The house is burning down, and the President of the United States says this is the way to put out the fire," said House Minority Leader Bertrand H. Snell. "And to me at this time there is only one answer to this question, and that is to give the President what he demands and says is necessary to meet the situation."[23]

Cameramen were at the White House to record the moment. As they were setting up, Eleanor entered the room and cried out, "Franklin, fix your hair!" When Roosevelt just grinned, Eleanor turned to Secretary of the Treasury William Woodlin. "Mr. Secretary, please help Franklin brush his hair down." The secretary patted the president's head. Then the Roosevelts' longtime friend, Nancy Cook, handed him a $1.50 fountain pen—a cheap pen even in those days—and at 8:36, seven hours after its introduction, Roosevelt signed his first bill into federal law.[24]

Also on Thursday, the president extended the bank holiday for three more days. Once again the public, already spooked, might have been expected to panic. But they didn't. Their new president was doing exactly what he'd promised. In four days, he had been able to get a banking act through Congress that the Hoover administration had been unable to pass in three years. He had told them that he knew they would stand with him if he took vigorous action. And he was right.[25]

Letters continued to flood into the White House. No president before had ever received so much mail. He told his staff to answer every letter. Forty-six percent of those who wrote the president that March were laborers, 17 percent were businessmen, and 14 percent were clerical workers.[26]

With the banks set to open on Monday, Roosevelt gave his first fireside chat on Sunday night. Other presidents had used radio, but none had ever spoken to the American people as he was about to do. "The president wants to come into your home and sit beside your fireside for a little fireside chat," the announcer said. An estimated sixty million people gathered around their radios to hear a president speak to them as if they were his neighbors. "I tried to picture a mason at work on a new building, a girl behind a counter, a farmer in his field," Roosevelt would explain later.

He wasn't in front of a fire, he was in an upstairs study at the White House sitting at a table with microphones in front of him. A small audience was watching. A pitcher of water and a glass were next to him. He stubbed out his cigarette. Then he began to talk. It wasn't long before he began nodding and gesturing as if the radio audience could see him. He was so completely engrossed in his words that it was as if none of those other people, holding their breath and bodies so still, were even in the room.

He explained why perfectly solid banks couldn't give all their depositors all of their money at once. He told them how the government was going examine and reopen the banks. He enlisted the people's help. Then FDR ended with his favorite sentiment: higher calling. "After all, there is an element in the readjustment of our financial system more important than currency, more important than gold, and that is the confidence of the people themselves. Confidence and courage are the essentials of success in carrying out our plan. You people must have faith; you must not be stampeded by rumors or guesses. Let us unite in banishing fear. We have provided the machinery to restore our financial system, and it is up to you to support and make it work.

"It is your problem, my friends, your problem no less than it is mine.

"Together we cannot fail."

The novelty of this event was captured by the description, the day after the talk, in the *Christian Science Monitor*:

> *He speaks to the nation over the radio in what is quite possibly the most remarkable address ever made by any President. In man-to-man fashion, in words of only one syllable, he uses the tones of a friend on the inside to assure a people . . . that the bank situation is sound. He recites the problems [and] explains the remedy: "when people find they can get their money when they want it the phantom of fear will soon be laid [to rest]. . . . It was the government's job to straighten out this situation and the job is being performed."* [27]

In New York, a justice of the state supreme court and his wife had invited neighbors over; some were Democrats, some were Republicans. They all had opinions on whether the president could or would do all he promised. "When your radio talk began everyone seems to become hypnotized, because there isn't a word spoken by anyone," he wrote the president. When the president finished, as if in one voice, the Democrats and the Republicans spoke in unison: "We are saved." "The frantic individuals of a few moments before declared that they would leave their money in the banks, and they were not afraid of the future," the judge wrote in his letter to the White House.[28]

When the fireside chat began, Ruth Lieberman in Brooklyn was listening to her father, a determined pessimist, airing his views on the banking situation. Certain that the banks would never reopen, he declared glumly that he would never regain his savings. After the president signed off, Lieberman's dad sat silent for fifteen minutes, his brow wrinkled in thought. Ruth wrote Roosevelt, "Then . . . he grinned sheepishly and said, 'Oh well, I wasn't really afraid of losing my money anyhow.'"[29]

In Birmingham, Alabama, a widow, Mrs. J. R. Adams, was having a sort of religious experience. She waited a week, and the feeling didn't lift. It just got stronger. So she sat down to share her thoughts. "Dear Presedent—Our Presedent after listening to your wonderful talk Sunday a week ago—we all felt the magnetism, of the tone of your Voice—that you were sent for our delivery," she wrote in her letter to FDR. "When in times of deep distress God took pity on His people. He sent Moses to deliver the oppressed. Then He sent Jesus Christ—to show his people how to live—to redeem them—Then you a Comforter to put confidence in this so great a people. And you will do it—for God is at the helm."[30]

Roosevelt's brilliant speechwriter, Rexford Tugwell, an intellectual accustomed to weighing and analyzing, watched from the sidelines of the White House broadcasting room. "Never can there have been a closer, a more intense union of leader and led. . . . His mastery of radio was something never before known," he wrote years later. "His stature increased. He glowed and gave out light. The people responded."[31]

Secretary of Labor Frances Perkins leaving a 1938 meeting after giving President
Roosevelt a progress report on the Wage-Hour law.

8

"Be Ye Steadfast"

Along with the New Deal came the New Dealers. The Great Depression had left idealistic, well-educated men of all ages without work: lawyers, managers, accountants, economists, and social workers. Washington was hiring, and they were ready. "They brought with them an alertness, an excitement, an appetite for power, an instinct for crisis and a dedication to public service which became during the thirties the essence of government," wrote Arthur Schlesinger.[1]

Roosevelt's deputies were Democrats and Republicans. Progressives and conservatives. He certainly did not vet his appointees to make sure they had the same religious convictions he did. Louis Howe, a scruffy little chain smoker, renowned for his gnome-like ugliness and sharp tongue, had allegiance to no god but Roosevelt, which perhaps did not entirely displease the president. One of FDR's closest advisors, Harry Hopkins, had been raised by a devout mother but left his faith behind, keeping just enough of it to quote a Bible verse or two when needed.

One the most famous of those occasions was in 1941, when Hopkins was sent to assess Britain's situation. Before Hopkins returned, Churchill hosted a small dinner during which Hopkins rose to propose a toast. "I suppose you wish to know what I am going to say to President Roosevelt on my return? Well I am going to quote to you one verse from the Book of Books . . . 'Whither thou goest, I will go and where thou lodgest I will lodge, thy people shall be my people, and thy God my God.'" He then added, "Even to the end." One of the other guests looked at Churchill and saw tears streaming down his face.[2]

One powerful member of FDR's cabinet was seriously Christian, and a bit more. Republican Henry Wallace, FDR's secretary of agriculture in his first administration and vice president during the third, was a scientist and a deeply religious man whose bold ideas and hard work made a great and lasting change in the lives of American farmers. "You cannot expect to be a really big man," his grandfather told him, "unless you live a sincere, earnest, and religious life. . . . We are in a really big world, the servants of a God who is infinitely bigger than we can possibly comprehend." Wallace's ideas about serving God seemed quite a bit more rigorous and certainly more esoteric than FDR's. He spoke of "that blissful unmanifested reality which we call God" and quoted the prophets as though they were "elder liberal statesman with whom he lunched the day before," wrote Schlesinger in *The Coming of the New Deal*.[3] Wallace's search for God had already led him to explore a range of occult ideas before he joined FDR's administration. It was he who convinced the secretary of the treasury to put the Eye of Providence, the reverse of the Great Seal of the United States, on the new dollar bill in 1935. It's a mark of Roosevelt's openness toward religious belief that although he could make no sense of Wallace's unorthodox notions, he dismissed questions about his secretary of agriculture's religious peculiarities by describing him amiably as "a kind of mystic." But when the talk was crops, land, water, and the American farmer, nobody suited FDR more.

Most of the recruits were men, of course. But also among those serving the new administration were two strong, stubborn women. They would dedicate their entire selves to making sure that Roosevelt never rested in his well-doing. The most officially powerful woman in FDR's administration was Frances Perkins, his secretary of labor and the first female in a presidential cabinet; the most famous was Eleanor Roosevelt.

Perkins's name is unknown to many Americans today, but Eleanor Roosevelt's is still revered worldwide. Her influence on FDR was incalculable. Roosevelt aide Stanley High believed her spiritual and practical influence on the New Deal was vital long before FDR became president: "She gave substance to his inclinations. She spurred a faith that might have flagged," he wrote. "In the end, the plight of the dispossessed became a crusade with him as it was with her. When, therefore, the times turned ripe for that kind of gospel, he had the gospel ready for the times. . . . Her sympathy, passion and energy was such that she became a symbol of mercy and access to power for millions."[4]

"She is the president's Number One Advisor on sociological problems," *U.S. News* asserted. During the war, she retained her influence, traveling constantly, investigating, speaking out. She harried him so constantly for causes and people she believed needed help that he had to have a basket placed near his bed for her barrage of notes. The joke in Washington during the war was that Roosevelt went to bed each night praying, "Dear God, please make Eleanor a little tired."[5]

Eleanor had shed quiet tears on the night of FDR's first presidential election. She had struggled for years to build a life of her own, and it had finally begun to take shape. She believed she would have to give up her own priorities in order to serve the ceremonial duties of a First Lady. Instead, she was about to enter a period of great public influence that would last until the end of her life. Realizing that he couldn't be all the places he needed to be, Roosevelt tutored her on the kind of information he wanted, and sent her out in his stead. She brought reams of impressions and details back. Her sensitivity and intelligence gave him a feeling for the people that nothing else would have.

Eleanor's value as a presidential emissary became apparent almost as soon as Roosevelt took office. After President Hoover had infamously allowed army tanks, mounted troops, and infantry armed with rifles and fixed bayonets to roust the Bonus Army, an encampment of military veterans and their families in Washington, D.C., that group went home. But a second group arrived when FDR became president. Roosevelt gave them a place to camp, a big tent for their meetings, and made sure they had three meals a day with unlimited coffee. However, intent on fulfilling a campaign promise to balance the federal budget, the president didn't give in to their demands, refusing to speed up the disbursal of their bonuses.

Louis Howe, stymied in his attempts to solve the impasse, took Eleanor to their encampment. While he lounged in the car, she trudged through ankle-deep mud, unaccompanied. She drank tea, listened to a performance of songs, talked to the protestors about her memories of World War I. All she had to promise them was that she would tell FDR about their feelings and that they would have a chance at jobs in FDR's new Civilian Conservation Corps. For the men, some of whom had been unemployed for years, jobs were a welcome offer. They were so charmed by her that one man remarked: "Hoover sent the army. Roosevelt sent his wife."

Those who loved her, loved her fiercely, and sometimes saw her in a holy light of her own. One woman wrote to her, "Centuries back Catholics prayed to the Virgin Mary because they thought she might intercede with a deity who could not take time to hear every petition. In that spirit, we turn to you."

She paid a steep price for the causes she championed. She was investigated by the FBI because of the people she talked to and helped. She was savagely reviled by those who disagreed with her. She was so hated during the 1930s by her own social set that telling crude, humiliating, and often lewd jokes about her became common at parties.[6] The vulgarity came entirely from those who relayed the jokes, because nobody ever saw Eleanor do anything crude, humiliating, or lewd. Her only fault was that she gave her opinions freely, and she had power through her influence on Roosevelt. Perhaps part of the ill will came from the fact that her husband simply would not control her. His attitude seemed to be that she should advocate as she liked, and if he could, he would follow her.[7] His answer to complaints about her was to say that he could control many things but not "the missus."

Francis Perkins knew Roosevelt well from his early days in Albany as a state senator. Like so many people who met him, then and later, Perkins hadn't been impressed. His great crusade that year was a fight over the election by the legislature of William Sheehan to fill the vacant seat of

United States senator from New York. Roosevelt saw Sheehan's selection as dirty politics and took on the Tammany Hall crowd to defeat it. He won, but he didn't make many friends doing it.

"Awful arrogant fellow, that Roosevelt," said "Big Tim" Sullivan after a bout with the young politician.[8] "You know those Roosevelts. This fellow is still young. Wouldn't it be a good idea to drown him before he grows up?"[9]

Roosevelt had "a youthful lack of humility, a streak of self-righteousness, and a deafness to the hopes, fears, and aspirations which are the common lot," Perkins later wrote. As whole, "he really didn't like people much." He also had a habit of tossing his head back as he looked through his pince-nez, as though he was looking down on people.

"I can still see 'that Roosevelt,' now," she said, "standing back of the brass rail with two or three Democratic senators arguing with him to be 'reasonable,' as they called it, about something; his small mouth pursed up and slightly open, his nostrils distended, his head in the air, and his cool, remote voice saying, 'No, no, I won't hear of it!'"[10] When he had shown up for a committee meeting before his election wearing riding breeches, Perkins told him to go home and put on some pants.

In those days, Perkins was a labor activist working hard on a bill to establish a fifty-five-hour workweek for women. She approached Roosevelt to come out for it. But he wouldn't. It failed. Twenty years later a similar measure to restrict the workweek would bring Roosevelt, then governor of New York, and Perkins, his industrial commissioner, national attention.

Perkins had not expected the new president to give her a cabinet position and had hesitated to accept the post of secretary of labor. No cabinet office was more central to the legislative changes FDR would make in the next years. No cabinet position had a constituency that would be more outraged over the appointment of a woman. "The attitude of both labor and employers [toward her] is a good deal like that of *habitues* of a waterfront saloon toward a visiting lady slummer—grim, polite, and unimpressed," as New York city planner Robert Moses put it later.

Their scorn was understandable. Women had been able to vote in national elections for only thirteen years. The impression that women were emotionally unstable and intellectually unfit for responsibility was widely embraced. Females weren't considered capable enough to have credit in their own names, and they wouldn't be for another forty years. The idea that women ought to be paid as much as men for equal work would have been considered absurd in 1933. A woman simply was not worth as much as a man. Catholics, Jews, and African Americans were not worth much either in a lot of white Protestant voters' minds.

But apparently FDR didn't agree. More Catholics would serve in his administration than that of any president before him, along with the larger number of Jews that he appointed. During a time when American Jews were denied membership in social clubs, discriminated against in university admissions, and routinely kept from positions of power by the white Anglo-Saxon Protestant establishment, Roosevelt hired more Jews than any other administration ever had, so many that the New Deal was nicknamed the "Jew Deal" by his enemies.[11] He would form an advisory cabinet of influential African Americans and appoint more blacks to federal positions than any president since Reconstruction.[12]

He had started his political career in a state where the most powerful people came from New York City, the country's most urban, most diverse metropolis. To get his legislation passed he had to negotiate with Jews, Catholics, and other immigrants, as well as powerful women. But the rest of the country wasn't New York City. Putting a woman in charge of Labor would seem like madness to many in the labor movement. An insult, really. As for blacks, Jews, and Catholics, in the South and the Midwest, many voters considered them foreign and dangerous. Roosevelt could lose a lot of votes taking on such a crew, but that doesn't seem to have bothered him.[13]

When Perkins heard that Roosevelt might offer her a place in his cabinet, she talked with people close to her about the offer: the activists she had worked with, fellow Christians who gave her spiritual advice. They said take it. It will be a great day for women. It will be a great opportunity for serving God.

Serving God was important to her. Her favorite scripture came from First Corinthians: "Be ye steadfast, immovable, always abounding in the work of the Lord, forasmuch as ye know that your labour is not in vain in the Lord." Frances Perkins would become FDR's steadiest counsel of Christian conscience in the cabinet.

When asked why she did what she did, Perkins didn't hesitate to say she did it for Jesus. She liked the story of two charitable men who were debating about why a poor man ought to be given shoes. The first man said because his feet are cold. The second man said, "for Jesus's sake." The first man's humanitarian impulse wouldn't last, Perkins believed. "The poor aren't grateful in the long run and quarrels come up," she said. Humanitarians get discouraged, and sometimes bitter. But those who serve Jesus by extending compassion and seeking justice don't look toward humans for their reward.[14]

But Perkins and Roosevelt had more in common than their faith. They were also fiercely dedicated to reaching their goals. For both that involved cultivating a certain restraint in their daily interactions. Almost everyone who knew FDR as president remarked on his extraordinary patience and good humor. Economist and longtime aide Rexford Tugwell credited Roosevelt's unshakeable faith in a benign, protective God as the source of his consistent aplomb: "The secret of his unassailable serenity and his easy gaiety lay in this sense of oneness with the ongoing processes of the universe and his feeling of being, as Emerson said, in tune with the infinite."

What seemed so effortless for Roosevelt, Perkins clearly worked at. At least once a month while in Washington, Perkins visited a community of Episcopal nuns for silent retreats. "It preserves me from the temptation of the idle word, the fresh remark, the wisecrack, the angry challenge, the hot-tempered reaction, the argument about nothing, the foolish question, the unnecessary noise of the human clacking," she wrote a friend.[15]

Perkins and FDR also were alike in believing that God expected them—them specifically—to help people with less power than themselves. "I had to do something about unnecessary hazards to life, unnecessary poverty. It was sort of up to me," she said. Roosevelt felt the same, she believed. His religion was more than a moral code, she said. His faith "was a real relationship of man to God, and he felt as certain of it as of the reality of his life," she wrote. It was a motivating force. "He saw the betterment of life and people as part of God's work, and he felt that man's devotion to God expressed itself by serving his fellow man."

Perkins had graduated from Mount Holyoke, a women's college founded by activist and educator Mary Lyon. "Go where no one else will go, do what no one else will do," Lyon advised Mount Holyoke students.[16] Being a social worker, one of the high-minded, well-educated women and men who were gradually moving the work of helping the downtrodden beyond being primarily a job for church volunteers, had been Perkins's first goal. Instead she had become involved in making political change with the New York Consumers League.

The focus of her life work was irrevocably set the afternoon of March 25, 1911, the same year FDR took his seat as a New York state senator. She and friends were having tea in Washington Square when they heard fire engines. Running outside to see what was happening, they joined a large crowd of New Yorkers watching the Triangle Shirtwaist Factory go up in flames.

March 25 was a warm Saturday when the air was beginning to smell like spring. A small fire had started in the building, perhaps from a discarded cigarette or match. A manager tried to put it out himself, but stacks of material sitting on the floor soon caught fire. The fire escape door on the floor leading to the outside had been locked by management. Workers could get to a fire escape on other floors, but only a few of them were able to climb down before it broke away from the building, twisting from the heat.

A United Press reporter named William Shepherd reported from the scene, phoning in details as screaming women began to crowd the windows, flames from the floors below licking up toward their faces. Soon he heard a sound that he called too horrible to describe. "Thud-dead, thud-dead, thud-dead, thud-dead," he wrote. He counted the sound sixty-two times. "It was the sound of a speeding, living body hitting a stone sidewalk," falling from eighty feet up. Every person, balancing against the wind current as they fell, trying to stay upright, became "a silent, unmoving pile of clothing and twisted, broken limbs" when they hit the sidewalk.

In one room where young women were screaming as an inferno of smoke and flames approached, a young man assisted three women. With what Shepherd called "a terrible chivalry," the young man extended his hand to help them up to the window ledge as though he were inviting them to dance; then gently holding them away from the building, he let go. A fourth girl embraced and kissed him before he eased her toward death. The young man then jumped with great energy himself, as if to beat his love to the ground, wrote Shepherd. As he fell, his coat fluttered up and his pant legs filled with air, showing that he wore tan shoes and hose. His hat stayed on his head.

One hundred and forty-six people died that day. Donations flowed in to help the injured and bury the dead. Memorials were held. Leading citizens called a public meeting a week later at the Metropolitan Opera House. Frances was among them when the fiery strike leader Rose Schneiderman stood to speak. Instead of praising the audience for its concern, she chided them.

> *This is not the first time girls have been burned alive in this city. Every week I must learn of the untimely death of one of my sister workers. Every year thousands of us are maimed. The life of men and women is so cheap, and property is so sacred! There are so many of us for one job, it matters little if 140-odd are burned to death. . . . We have tried you citizens! We are trying you now.*

Then, with fury, she indicted their response: "You have a couple of dollars for the sorrow of mothers and brothers and sisters by way of a charity gift. But if the workers come out in the only way they know to protest against conditions which are unbearable, the strong hand of the law is allowed to press down heavily upon us."

That night, Perkins felt the guilt of having not done more. She heard the call to greater commitment. The tragedy might be used to save thousands more lives—or the moment might pass and be forgotten. When a Citizens Committee on Safety was formed, Perkins was hired as the executive secretary on the recommendation of Theodore Roosevelt, who knew her from work on other reforms. Years later, she would say the day of the Triangle factory fire was "the day the New Deal was born."[17]

Perkins decided she would take the job of secretary of labor only if Roosevelt agreed to a list of demands. FDR, a son of crafty Dutch traders, was about to contend with a woman of flinty Maine stock who would not be moved. She had watched him put people off by seeming to agree when he was merely encouraging them to talk and didn't plan to do what they asked at all. She would not fall for that. She would also resist his charm, even though the weight of it was considerable.

After the president-elect made his offer, Perkins told him it was a bad idea. Men didn't like taking orders from a woman. Labor leaders would also oppose her because she hadn't been a labor organizer. She would be an easy target for his critics. His administration didn't need the controversy. He was not persuaded. They had done great things for labor in New York. He wanted to extend those things to the nation. But did he really? She didn't quite trust him, a sentiment many people would echo as the years went on.

She took out her list. The things she wanted to get done weren't radical in her opinion. They'd been tried in states but not on a national scale. He might think her reforms were too ambitious. If he wouldn't go along, she would rather serve outside his administration than inside it. So she started to read: a forty-hour workweek, a ban on child labor, a minimum wage, unemployment compensation, worker's compensation. Old-age insurance. A federal employment system.

This was not only an absurdly optimistic wish list in 1933, in the middle of a national employment meltdown, it was a politically danger-ous one for Roosevelt. The eight-hour workday was a favorite cause of the Socialist Party, a crowd much more radical than FDR and not one he wanted to be associated with. There had never been a federal mini-mum wage. Business would howl that such thinking was un-American, and plenty would agree. Unemployment compensation was nothing more than the idea of paying people who didn't work, which was not the American way. Her ideas would kill FDR's chances of balancing the budget as he'd promised he'd do in his campaign. One-fourth of Ameri-cans were out of work, but three-fourths were still working, and they wouldn't like supporting freeloaders.

She continued reading: Social Security, health insurance, direct fed-eral aid for unemployment relief. The list would be a utopian dream for some, to others a nightmare.

She finished. She waited. Roosevelt argued. She countered. He pro-tested. She parried. Finally he agreed.[18]

He was not only true to his word, he was swift about it. In the first one hundred days of his presidency, FDR passed so much New Deal legislation that every president since has been judged during his own first hundred days and found wanting. No one has ever matched him. Roosevelt's administration passed fifteen major bills, a "presidential barrage of ideas and programs," historian Schlesinger observed, "unlike anything known to American history."[19] By June, when the Congress finally adjourned, the so-called welfare state had been created. A small central government with a hands-off attitude had been transformed into a much more activist government with its hands in almost everything.

Farmers were rescued from overproduction and disastrously low prices with the Agricultural Adjustment Act, which paid them not to plant crops. Homeowners about to lose their homes could secure mortgage refinancing through the Home Owners' Loan Act. Relief checks went to hungry families through the Federal Emergency Relief Administration. Millions were employed in the Civilian Conservation Corps and a $3.3 billion employment plan that later became the Works Progress Administration. A massive partnership between government and business, the National Industrial Recovery Act, was set in motion, with participating partners identified through their display of unforgettable blue eagle posters.[20] And more.

Those hundred days began the most enormous and fundamental change in American government before or since—a shift motivated by religious faith, led by a man rarely lauded for his faith. As Roosevelt said years later in a speech on Social Security, "We are going to make a country in which no one is left out."

Franklin D. Roosevelt with the family Bible on which he swore the presidential oath of office at each of his four inaugurations.

"A Christian and a Democrat"

One day a reporter tried to pin the president down by presenting some of the labels others applied to him.

"Mr. President," he asked, "are you a communist?"

"No," Roosevelt replied.

"Are you a capitalist?" the reporter asked.

"No," the president said.

"Are you a socialist?" the reporter asked.

For the third time the president said no. The reporter had run through the Big Three and was out of guesses.

"Well, what is your philosophy then?" he asked.

"Philosophy?" Roosevelt replied. "I am a Christian and a Democrat—that is all."[1] Apparently he repeated this description on other occasions. Sometimes he added slyly, "a little left of center."[2]

This story is a famous one particularly because his answer was so unexpected. If Woodrow Wilson had said such a thing, it would have been noteworthy but not surprising. Although Roosevelt's faith was apparent in many ways—he consulted religious organizations and clergy, he used religious language and gave religious motivations for what he did—his answer to the reporter has rarely been examined closely, perhaps partly because some have read it as flippant and even insincere. But this little story bears looking at because it points toward understanding how his Christianity intersected with his economic policies.

We don't know if he intended the D in *democrat* to be capitalized or not. Either way is fine. He was a Democrat and a democrat. For Roosevelt democracy and religion were intertwined. He believed that they supported each other, and both were holy. If freedom of religion was lost, democracy was imperiled. And vice versa.

It's somewhat surprising that Roosevelt didn't admit to being a capitalist. He certainly was one—so much so that his more leftist supporters criticized him for failing to nationalize important industries while he had the power. He could have created a much more equal society with a greatly expanded governmental role than he did.

The day after scourging the "money changers" in his inaugural address, he called those very rascals to the White House for help in fixing the economy so that they could continue making money. "I think back to events of March 4, 1933, with a sick heart," Senator Bronson Cutting of New Mexico later wrote. "For then . . . the nationalization of banks by President Roosevelt could have been accomplished without a word of protest. It was President Roosevelt's great mistake." But Roosevelt was a fairly conservative man by inclination. Two other senators directly asked him to nationalize the banks before he presented the Emergency Banking Act to Congress. He didn't want to.[3]

He was often called a communist and a socialist. He clearly was not a communist; they didn't even believe in God.

As for being a socialist, there is no doubt that he helped move the United States toward being a country that guaranteed its people some standard of security, what has been referred to as a welfare state. His biggest social welfare program, Social Security, however, wasn't a federal giveaway but rather a program that Americans paid into and then could take their money out of if they were disabled or retired. By protecting savings, setting a minimum wage, regulating Wall Street, and giving employees rights, he softened the hardest edges of the free market. The gross abuses that socialists could hold up as examples of capitalism's failure were blunted, and the dissatisfaction with free market policies that had been building within the general public began to abate. Perhaps the cleverest and most succinct answer to the socialist charge came from Presbyterian minister and socialist Norman Thomas, who noted that when Roosevelt finished with socialism, it had to be carried out on a stretcher.

The truly surprising part of the president's answer to the question about his philosophy, of course, was that FDR would describe it—not his religion, but his economic and political philosophy—as Christian. Christianity is a religion, of course, and one that many people leave at the church door. Some of the biggest churchmen in the country at that time were also industrialists and slumlords who treated the poor quite harshly. They and sometimes their ministers simply did not believe there was a contradiction between Christian beliefs and such actions; quite the opposite in fact. A New York City judge told striking seamstresses before the 1911 Triangle Shirtwaist Factory fire, "You are striking against God."

The idea that God favors rich capitalists is backed up by a certain kind of theology that was furthered specifically to counter FDR's policies and will be examined in more detail a later chapter. The first plank of such theology is that Christianity and capitalism are both systems in which individuals rise and fall according to their own merits and choices. As Princeton historian Kevin M. Kruse illustrates, "So in Christianity, if you're good you go to heaven, if you're bad you go to hell. In capitalism if you're good you make a profit and if you're bad you fail." Roosevelt's economic ideas were built around quite different religious convictions. He saw how changes in the economy were hurting working people, and he believed God expected him to do what he could with the presidential power he had to help them.

But FDR's Christian economics weren't merely religious dreaming devoid of reference to real life. He realized long before he gained the presidency that the industrial age called for radically new thinking about the rights of human beings. He saw, as many others did, that American democracy itself could be endangered if workers became disillusioned enough to band together. Russia's revolutionary shift from monarchy to communism put governments all over the world on alert. Russian communists were spreading their new atheistic gospel as widely as possible, and it was gaining a following even in America.

With assembly lines replacing skilled work with jobs that almost anybody could be quickly trained to do, workers who had earned job security with experience and skill found themselves with no advantage. As labor activist Rose Schneiderman had put it after the 1911 Triangle Shirtwaist Factory fire, workers were so plentiful and so desperate that they could be easily replaced. At the same time, workers operating the new machines were being treated as if they themselves were machines that could be pushed to work faster and faster. Injuries resulted, and sometimes deaths. It wasn't only workers who were being affected. These factors put responsible factory owners in a tough spot, too. If competition remained unfettered by universal regulations, business owners who resisted exploiting workers could quickly be out of business. Their costs would be higher, their output lower, and they wouldn't be able to compete.

Other factors were also in play. Technology and corporate control were concentrating great power in fewer and fewer hands. Craftsmen, small-business owners, and farmers who had been able to control their own work and to a large extent set their own wages were now being controlled by market forces and faraway business owners intent on amassing great wealth by keeping labor cheap and shifting production to ever-higher levels. As corporations grew in number and size, and as the stock market grew in importance, businesses were less and less accountable to workers or individual communities.

Part of the reason Roosevelt saw these forces so clearly was that he was a rural man at heart. He had formed his ideals within a community held together by personal bonds. Like Thomas Jefferson, he believed that the best society was one based on small farmers and small businesses. But he knew that such a world was rapidly disappearing. As it did, the bonds that held society together were fraying. Religion was an important one of those bonds, which may be one of the reasons that FDR talked about freedom of religion more often than he mentioned any of the other rights set out in the first ten amendments to the US Constitution.

FDR supported free enterprise and the right of property, but he was also a Christian who believed in what the founding fathers called God-given rights, and he believed that the United States had arrived at a time when such God-given rights needed to be expanded. FDR wasn't alone in having such ideas; scholars, economists, and religious thinkers also saw what was happening. Catholics had been supporting ways to counter the massive changes created by the Industrial Revolution since the turn of the century. In 1891 Pope Leo XIII published *Rerum novarum*, which translates as "revolutionary change," an encyclical addressing the misery of workers in the new industrial age. The encyclical promoted the right of labor unions to organize and the right of workers to receive a wage that provided at least frugal comfort. It became a foundational document for Catholic social teaching.

Monsignor John A. Ryan, America's leading Catholic moral theologian at the time, expounded on the pope's ideas by noting that economic theory had been separated from any moral dimension—a mistake that was allowing technologies (such as the assembly line, machines, faster transportation, long-distance communication) to damage communities and workers instead of serving them.[4] In such situations, there needed to be countervailing legal and governmental influences. The concept of a just wage, rooted in the idea that freedom of contract is a value of less importance than the transcendent dignity of every human being, is an example of such economic morality.[5] Roosevelt agreed so completely that in 1938 he signed into law the Fair Labor Standards Act, a hard-fought legislative victory that set the nation's first enduring federal minimum wage at twenty-five cents an hour. Ryan became such a strong proponent of the New Deal that he was tagged with the derisive nickname "the Right Reverend New Dealer" by right-wing radio priest Charles Coughlin.

So what was FDR's economic policy? How did his faith affect it? Some have written that he didn't have any policies built on coherent theory. He just tried whatever might work, and if it didn't work, he tried something else. He encouraged that impression by saying as much. But there *was* thinking behind what he did—a goal at least. One particular quote that's featured prominently at the Franklin Delano Roosevelt Library gives a pretty good answer. It's not socialist, it's not communist, and it certainly isn't capitalist. But it does sound Christian. It's not as poetic as the Sermon on the Mount or as demanding. But it might fit there fairly well. "The test of our progress," he said, "is not whether we add more to the abundance of those who have much; it is whether we provide enough for those who have too little."

A tendency to gloss over the importance of FDR's Christianity in influencing his policies may be one reason that people then and now have found him so mystifying. In trying to put together the puzzle of his personality, they are missing a big piece. Those who were able to observe FDR closely while he was alive and scholars who focused on his faith later verify that his religion went deep and wide. Biographer Kenneth Davis wrote that FDR's faith was "the most potent of clues to the innermost workings of his psyche."[6] Frances Perkins went even further. His Christian belief was "the deepest, most real part of him," she said. When Winston Churchill praised Roosevelt to FDR Jr., saying, "Your father is a great man," the young man replied, "My father is a very religious man and has risen to great heights by his strength of character and determination."[7]

Four-time Pulitzer Prize–winning playwright, author, and FDR speechwriter Robert Sherwood watched Roosevelt with a writer's eye for detail and a playwright's ear for meanings beneath conversation, which should have given him an edge on figuring the man out. But even Sherwood got nothing more than rare glimpses beneath the president's closely woven emotional cloak. He saw only that Roosevelt's interior world was "heavily forested." The words speak to mystery, depth, darkness, and not at all to the open, sunny, vacant place so many imagined his interior world to be.

"He could appear utterly cynical, worldly, illusionless," Sherwood wrote, "and yet his religious faith was the strongest and most mysterious force."[8]

His religious faith was a mysterious force, as Sherwood wrote, because FDR did not talk about faith or any other personal, deeply felt emotion. That reticence was reinforced by the type of faith he had. His Christianity was quiet, doesn't appear to have been outwardly emotional, and wasn't heavy on repentance. It was pretty much what might be expected from an East Coast Episcopalian of the upper class. Another reason his faith may not have been noticeable is that he seems to have been among what psychologist William James called the healthy-minded and once-born. The once-born don't fret over their sins. They don't have anguished moments of doubt. They feel confident of themselves, of God, and of God's agency in the world. In the Gifford Lectures that became his famous book *The Varieties of Religious Experience*, James said, "In the religion of the once-born the world is a sort of rectilinear or one-storied affair whose accounts are kept in one denomination, whose parts have just the values which naturally they appear to have, and of which a simple algebraic sum of pluses and minuses will give the total worth. Happiness and religious peace consist in living on the plus side of the account." That was Roosevelt to a T. That was how he saw America. That was how he wanted government to position itself. It was all quite simple and do-able, in his mind.

James goes on to describe the once-born with a paragraph that could have Roosevelt's name on it. "Some persons are born with an inner con-stitution which is harmonious and well balanced from the outset. Their impulses are consistent with one another, their will follows without trouble the guidance of their intellect, their passions are not excessive, and their lives are little haunted by regrets."

What of the spiritual battles of the once-born? There often appear to be few. Their spiritual lives are so stable that, while James tells many tales of the twice-born, he doesn't present any stories about the once-born. There just isn't much to say. Roosevelt's faith was so completely embedded in his life that few who have studied his life give faith much credit for molding his politics. Longtime speechwriter and judge Samuel Rosenman, who knew him better than most people, puzzled for years over why Roosevelt had such a strong sense of social justice. Rosenman rejected the usual explanations—his family, his polio, his times. Finally he concluded that FDR's concern for the underdog was simply an innate quality. But, as looking at his early life shows, his concern did develop and deepen over time.

Another reason FDR's faith may not be readily apparent to some is that Roosevelt saw his faith as a private matter, not for public consump-tion. Far from using his faith for political capital, he seemed to go out of his way to avoid supplying the bona fides that would have convinced conservatives of his religious sincerity. As an example, one of his first actions as president was to initiate the repeal of Prohibition, which he and many others believed was contributing to a breakdown of law and order. His justification was that government had overreached into an area that was best controlled by American families.[9] As policy, it was the right move, but it didn't burnish his reputation as a stalwart of the faith. Many of the "dries," as those who favored Prohibition were called, especially those in churches, never forgave him. Some of them approved of his social policies, but they just couldn't believe any man of God would loose the demon of drink upon the people.

He might have regained some ground if he had responded by showing up at church every Sunday, but he didn't. As president, with all eyes on him, he so rarely attended Sunday services that a good many of his critics were able to paint him as a man with little religion. The reason he gave for staying home was to avoid exactly the public attention that his critics believed he wanted. Getting into the church caused such a commotion that by the time he was settled, all impulse toward prayer was gone, he said. "I can do almost anything in the 'Goldfish Bowl' of the president's life, but I'll be hanged if I can say my prayers in it."

The privacy of his faith was so important to him that he wouldn't even publicize moments of special religious observance that could have made him seem quite pious. As an early example, the precedent-setting church service he, his family, and his cabinet attended before his first inauguration remained so secret that the public and press didn't hear about it until the ceremonies were over. No other president had ever attended church before an inauguration. It could have been quite the event. If he had let the cameras in, given a few front-steps interviews to the press, maybe preached a little sermonette of his own before he got in the car, he could have scored big points with the church people. But he didn't. The services held before his three subsequent inaugurations were also low-key. So were the special services held each year to commemorate his first inauguration—except for the first of them, and that wasn't by intention.

When Bishop James E. Freeman invited FDR and his cabinet to celebrate the anniversary of his first inauguration at the Washington National Cathedral, Roosevelt accepted. Perhaps Roosevelt expected the rector to keep his attendance under wraps. But word had gotten out on that cold, rainy Sunday in March of 1934, and the sanctuary was filled with tourists who stood to look at him, talking and pointing through the service. The president bore it all with good humor, smiling and nodding to the congregation as he laboriously moved forward, leaning to one side and then the other side, balancing and rebalancing himself in his stiff braces, the uniformed arm of Navy captain Walter Vernon keeping him stable.

After the service, Bishop Freeman waited expectantly. Having the president in the cathedral that Freeman had devoted his life to building was a great opportunity. The bishop meant for the National Cathedral to become an American Westminster Abbey, where presidents worshipped and luminaries were buried. President Wilson and Admiral George Dewey were already among those in the crypt of the Chapel of St. Joseph of Arimathea. This anniversary was Freeman's chance to ensure that FDR's final resting place would also be in the cathedral.

After they shook hands at the door, Freeman brought up the idea, reminding the president that he would be joining an illustrious company. Roosevelt kept smiling, as he so famously did even when he was not happy. When no answer was forthcoming, the bishop pressed on. Perhaps the president would dictate a memorandum stating that he wished to be buried at the cathedral, the bishop suggested. It would be a shame if some misunderstanding caused him to be placed elsewhere. Roosevelt kept smiling. He was helped into his automobile and began waving at the crowd as the car drew away. The bishop was left standing in the rain without his answer.

If Roosevelt had wished to burnish his reputation as a Christian, what better place to be buried than in a cathedral, near one of the country's greatest Christian presidents, Woodrow Wilson? But Roosevelt did not wish to glorify himself in that way. He so did not wish it that, instead of being honored by the suggestion, he was infuriated. As the limousine moved away, he was muttering, "The old body snatcher. The old body snatcher." FDR intended to be buried at Hyde Park in his mother's rose garden with Eleanor beside him. A simple ceremony could be held in the East Room of the White House, as it had been for other presidents, but the cathedral would not be involved, he told his staff.[10]

Many of FDR's personal habits were those that spiritual people have aspired to. He might well have publicized such habits as virtues that marked him as holier than others. Germans certainly made much of Hitler's spartan ways to paint him as a simple man of the people and help create what became known as the Hitler myth. The president could easily have spun his habits as those of a man so righteous that, rich as he was, he eschewed materialism. That he didn't is another example of his failure to make political points off religion and could be seen as a point in favor of the idea that he was sincerely religious. Jesus was pretty hard on those who used religion to make themselves seem holy.

He didn't care much for comfort or what many consider the finer things of life, which could have been touted as asceticism. He slept most of his life in a narrow bed much like the one he had had as a boy. That bed could have been presented as evidence of monkish austerity. In his houses the furniture was plain, and the rooms were cluttered with collections. As a matter of fact, the Roosevelts' rooms were all ugly, Arthur Schlesinger wrote. Roosevelt prided himself on wearing clothes that he had owned for years or had been passed down from his father. Food in his White House was notoriously awful. It was sometimes said to be cheap and poorly prepared, not because the Roosevelts lacked money or even because they were cheap, although sometimes they were, but because neither Eleanor nor Franklin cared much about food. When asked what he might like to eat, he usually looked bewildered and if pressed generally came up with: "Let's just have some scrambled eggs."[11]

In an era where drinking alcohol was considered ungodly by many, the man who repealed Prohibition might have stayed away from alcohol in order to win some credit from religious teetotalers. But he liked to drink with friends before dinner. Although his mother disapproved, he didn't give it up and he didn't keep the practice secret.

There was a lot about Roosevelt that didn't reflect well on his faith, and he doesn't seem to have tried to hide those traits and behaviors either. He liked power, and he didn't try to disguise his love of it by calling it sacrificial service to humanity. He liked to have a good time. He liked to travel. He liked to brag on himself. He liked women, and he liked to flirt with them. He had such close relationships with various women that many suspect he did more than talk with them. If so, he kept those affairs quiet, but he never hid that he was spending time with them or that they enchanted him. He did hide his continuing relationship with Lucy Mercer from Eleanor, which was reprehensible, and he didn't try hard enough to hide it from others, which was doubly bad. It didn't bother him a bit to be thought of as a bit of a rogue. In fact, he liked it.

That isn't to say that he deserves praise for these desires and behaviors. It's likely that he was unabashed about them merely because he was so completely satisfied with himself, another less-than-holy trait. It simply means that this extremely adroit politician, often guilty of duplicity, does not seem to have cloaked his ambitions or his flaws to appear a better Christian than he was. He used his religion to form his values, and he used scripture to convince his friends and enemies that he was right. He prayed a lot, asking people to pray with and for him when big decisions were being made, but as the next chapter will make clear, he was a bit playful about the ways God might be responding. In short, he did not put his religiosity on display in many ways he might have, and that was part of the reason he had the reputation of a man who wasn't very religious.

FDR's own faith may have also been easily underestimated because he was so open to people of different faiths. Today that might be counted among Christian virtues, but it hasn't always been. Christianity has traditionally maintained that only those in the Christian church will go to heaven. Especially in the 1930s, many Christians saw intolerance of other faiths as a mark of a true believer. Protestants didn't generally like Catholics. Catholics didn't care much for Protestants. Even Methodists and Baptists had trouble getting along. Giving Jews a hard time or discriminating against them wasn't considered a sin by many Christians. Roosevelt didn't go in for any of that.

He wanted everyone to believe in God, but having others believe in God the way he did wasn't important to him. He believed religion was important to people's lives, and that it was a central, moral, governing force. He wanted to be sure there were no roadblocks for people to worship as they saw fit. Or not to worship at all. His ideas about freedom of religion put emphasis on freedom, just as the founding fathers had.

His attitude toward Jews and Catholics wasn't merely tolerance, it was appreciation, and sometimes friendship. Religious prejudice appears not to have been in his nature. Neither was racial prejudice, according to many accounts. That virtue discomfited many of his constituents, especially in the South, a Democratic stronghold he could not afford to lose. During the 1930s membership in the Ku Klux Klan rose and spread throughout the country. Anti-Semitism soared. It was not uncommon for blacks and young Jewish men to be attacked in the cities.

When Al Smith, a Catholic, was running for president and Roosevelt was running for New York governor in 1928, fierce opposition to Smith's Catholicism was common even in New York State, where Smith had been governor.[12] The prejudice so enraged FDR and he spent so much time speaking against it that his campaign manager sent a message reminding him that *he* was running for office and needed to spend more time talking about himself.

In the first year of his presidential administration, when foreign governments were sending emissaries to meet him, Hitler's minister of finance, Hjalmar Schacht, who would be put on trial at Nuremberg as a war criminal in 1946, came to see Roosevelt. The president arranged a small luncheon for the Nazi. One of the men he invited was Samuel Rosenman. Afterward Rosenman remarked, "I don't think Schacht liked me being there very much."

"I'm sure he took notice," Roosevelt said, "and the exposure is good for him. If it were not for this protocol business, I would have seated you right next to him."[13]

In 1936, when the president was about to start his main campaign trip for a second term, he invited Rosenman and his wife, Dorothy, to go with him. "Mr. President, you know that your train is going principally through the Bible Belt. You know how bigoted a great many people are who live there. While, of course, I would be delighted to go, I don't think two Jews should be on that train with you."

Roosevelt seldom lost his temper, but he did then. "That's sheer nonsense! The only way to meet that sort of thing is head-on—and not duck it. Make arrangements for you and Dorothy to come; and let's not discuss it any further."

FDR's openness toward women's abilities and opportunities also aroused the ire of some fundamentalist Christians. During the war years, he urged women to fill jobs left by men who were fighting overseas. The country needed them if the United States was going to win the war. America's role as the arsenal of democracy, that great outpouring of weapons, planes, tanks, and ships, is often credited with actually winning the war. Women in large numbers accepted the president's challenge and were able to excel at jobs previously given only to men.

Before the war only 1 percent of jobs in the aircraft industry were filled by women. By 1943, women held 65 percent of those jobs. Earning about 50 percent of what men made for the same jobs, one out of every four women was in the workforce in 1945. When soldiers returned from war, most of the women returned home. But the fundamentalists were right to fear FDR's urgings. Women's experience of being in the workplace, doing jobs no one had believed they could do, was not forgotten. The star of the administration's push for women workers in the munitions industry, Rosie the Riveter flexing her muscles, is still a symbol of female power championed by feminists.

Roosevelt fit easily within the ranks of liberal Christians, which were then and now heavily influenced by social gospel ideas. But putting him in that company may also have contributed to his faith having been minimized. Social gospel ideas have been so roundly negated as ineffectual and so successfully challenged by Christian conservatives as a weak and unbiblical that it's almost as though those who followed them aren't considered Christians in good standing. None of that is an accurate rendition of a movement that affected America tremendously, but even if it were, FDR's kind of faith did not comply with many of the stereotypes. For instance, social gospel proponents are often accused of putting little emphasis on Christian conversion. On that one, he was not guilty. He was, in fact, something of a revivalist about the importance of people seeking God.

"No greater thing could come to our land today than a revival of the spirit of religion—a revival that would sweep through the homes of the Nation and stir the hearts of men and women of all faiths to a reassertion of their belief in God and their dedication to His will for themselves and for their world," he said during a 1936 radio address honoring Brotherhood Day, February 23, a day set aside by the National Conference of Christians and Jews for people to dwell on what united them rather than what divided them.[14]

When the occasion called for it, he also supported conversion. His old friend and senior advisor, Army major general Edwin "Pa" Watson, fell ill as he was returning with Roosevelt from the 1945 Yalta Conference where Stalin, Churchill, and Roosevelt met to decide the fate of postwar Europe. Knowing that Watson had never been confirmed as a Catholic, and that his wife very much wanted him to accept the Catholic faith, FDR arranged for a priest to accept Watson's confession and give him last rites before he died at sea.

Roosevelt came from the kind of background where speaking about religion too personally was considered bad form. But if a little evangelizing seemed called for, he would do it and tell the story proudly ever afterward. An example was his 1933 exchange with Russian diplomat Maxim Litvinoff when they were negotiating US recognition of the USSR. During the lead-up to World War II and after the war began, the president kept freedom of religion front and center in the discussions. Roosevelt insisted he must have Stalin's assurance that freedom of religion was allowed in Russia. That request was a good political move, to help get support for aid to the USSR, but the issue also had personal meaning for Roosevelt, as the diplomat realized when he replied that Russia had all the freedom of religion it needed. Nobody was punished for going to church; they were merely discouraged, he said.

"Well now, Max, you know what I mean by religion," Roosevelt said.

> You know what religion gives a man. You know the difference between the religious and the irreligious person. Why, you must know, Max. You were brought up by pious parents. Look here, some time you're going to die, and when you come to die, Max, you are going to remember your old father and mother—good, pious Jewish people who believed in God and taught you to pray to God. You had a religious bringing up, and when you come to die, Max, that's what is going to come before you, that is what you are going to think about, that's what you are going to grasp for. You know it's important.

Roosevelt was convinced that his words had impressed Litvinoff. "You know, Max got red and fumbled and seemed embarrassed and just didn't know what to say," he liked to tell his audiences. Frances Perkins, who related the story years later, was not so convinced. She suspected the diplomat was taken aback by the improperly personal nature of Roosevelt's appeal and couldn't think of how to move on without offending the president.[15] When Churchill heard the story, he was so amused that he jokingly suggested he might appoint FDR archbishop of Canterbury when the position next came open.

Followers of social gospel tenets have also been accused of having low regard for the Bible. Once again FDR is not guilty. After Pearl Harbor, he was described by *Time* magazine as working on a speech with the Bible before him, open to the book of Isaiah. He wove frequent references to the Bible into his off-the-cuff comments as well as his prepared speeches. In his many efforts to preserve the environment, he loved quoting part of Deuteronomy 20:19: "When you besiege a city a long time to make war against it in order to capture it, you shall not destroy its trees by swinging an axe against them." In a speech often referred to as the "Green Pastures" speech, he compared the Psalms picture of what God wanted for humans to the sad state of the real world. When he talked of justice, he defined it as doing to others as you want them to do unto you.

In World War II millions of servicemen were given copies of a book containing the New Testament, Psalms, and a prologue by the president, which said in part that the Bible "is a fountain of strength and now, as always, an aid in attaining the highest aspirations of the human soul." In his 1944 Thanksgiving Day proclamation he declared,

> To the end that we may bear more earnest witness to our gratitude to Almighty God, I suggest a nationwide reading of the Holy Scriptures during the period from Thanksgiving Day to Christmas. Let every man of every creed go to his own version of the Scriptures for a renewed and strengthening contact with those eternal truths and majestic principles which have inspired such measure of true greatness as this nation has achieved.

One of the gifts spiritual faith sometimes gives people is the imagination to see the world as God would like it to be and the will to work toward making that vision real. Christians sometimes call it "bringing in the Kingdom." FDR's reliance on faith opened his mind to religious teachings that might seem ridiculously idealistic and positively un-American to more secular people and to many religious people as well.

In his New Deal, fair dealing was not enough. He set a biblical, a New Testament standard. The Federal Trade Commission must insure that businesses follow the Golden Rule, he said.[16] Three months later, he told the National Foreign Trade Commission that US trade agreements would likewise be based on the Golden Rule. In the New World, "we live for each other and in the service of a Christian faith," he told the Pan American Scientific Congress. "Physical strength can never permanently withstand the impact of spiritual force," he said on another occasion in a tribute to Woodrow Wilson.

If everyone would only follow God, most of the country's problems, domestic and international, would disappear, he said. "I doubt if there is any problem—social, political or economic—that would not melt away before the fire of such a spiritual awakening," he said during the 1936 radio address honoring Brotherhood Day.[17]

Roosevelt's great optimism caused him to see evidence of fundamental moral shifts. "With every passing year I become more confident that humanity is moving forward to the practical application of the teachings of Christianity as they affect the individual lives of men and women everywhere," he told the National Conference of Catholic Charities in October of 1933. He also believed that God was in the middle of it all, citing "my deep belief that God is marching on."

In his second term he exulted during an Oklahoma City speech that

> during these past six years the people of this Nation have definitely said "yes" with no "but" about it to the old biblical question, "Am I my brother's keeper?" In those six years I sense a growing devotion to the teachings of the Scriptures, to the quickenings of religion, to a greater willingness on the part of the individual to help his neighbor and to live less unto and for himself alone.[18]

The president leaving St. John's Episcopal Church after the traditional prayer service before his inauguration in 1941.

☙10❧

LISTENING TO THE

ALMIGHTY

Roosevelt asked others to pray for him and prayed a lot himself, as has already been noted. But he didn't pray to a silent universe; he seems to have believed God sent signs in response, and maybe more than that. FDR wasn't the only one who believed something out of the ordinary was happening with him. People who watched him make decisions often had the sense that he was able to draw upon resources they didn't have access to. They said he relied on his hunches. Or his intuition. They said he had a sixth sense for what ought to be done.

The president got messages directly from God even when he wasn't aware of them, according to Frances Perkins. "He had an intuitive knack for doing something decisive," she said. "I call it the ability to receive divine guidance without knowing whether you're getting it or something else." The secretary of labor, who believed she was aided in judging people by an ability to perceive auras, thought that FDR had a kind of clairvoyance.[1]

Eleanor once wrote that she believed her husband actually did think God answered him. But her statement was clearly conjecture. What she did know was more down to earth. "He felt that human beings were given tasks to perform and with those tasks the ability and strength to put them through. He could pray for help and guidance and have faith in his own judgment as a result," she said. Without his faith, making so many difficult decisions would have been "well-nigh impossible."[2]

Roosevelt believed he was an agent of divine beneficence, and an instrument of God, but nothing more than an instrument, wrote Kenneth Davis. He never lost awareness of his humble place in God's plan. "The notion of attempting a mystical union with God, becoming one with him, had it ever occurred to FDR, would have been rejected as an absurd, outrageous presumption," he wrote.[3] Any idea that God was speaking directly to him would have seemed in much the same vein.

Heartfelt, grandiose declarations about his own relationship with divinity were simply not his style. Roosevelt's style was to make jokes. When he made jokes about his luck or his lack of luck, he liked to link them with the idea that God was communicating his approval or disapproval of what his servant was doing or about to do.

Roosevelt was uncommonly lucky, so lucky that even journalists noticed and began to give certain kinds of good fortune his name: the Roosevelt luck, they called it. He was so lucky in weather that when he had a speech planned, it seemed always to fall on a day with the kind of delightful weather that made people want to come out and hear him. If it was raining or storming, he would roll into town and the skies would simply dry up. The reporters called that Roosevelt Weather. And Sometimes Roosevelt's weather luck worked the other way. That kind of luck won him a nickname: "Roosevelt the Rainmaker." That's what happened in the middle of the Dust Bowl on the day the president came to Amarillo.

By July 11, 1938, Franklin D. Roosevelt had governed the United States for five years. Things weren't looking so good. The Great Plains drought wasn't over, and neither was the Great Depression. Roosevelt had cut back federal spending in 1937, causing a downturn often called the Roosevelt Recession. The Supreme Court was overturning so much of his legislation that he had tried to change the rules for the justices' appointment so that he could pack the court with his own supporters. His failure was particularly humiliating. Now he was on a tour to defeat his political opponents and secure the Democratic Party for progressives. He would fail at that, too.

But the American people were still with him. More than a hundred thousand of them gathered in Amarillo for the president's visit. Some traveled two days on dirt roads that were little more than ruts, riding buckboards drawn by mules, crowded into the back of pickup trucks, steering jalopies, and if they had no other way, walking. Dressed in overalls and flour-sack dresses, they were coming to see an Eastern toff who used a cigarette holder for his store-bought smokes and clipped his words like Hollywood's version of a millionaire. They brought their own food because Amarillo couldn't feed them. And they brought their own bedrolls because Amarillo couldn't house them even if they could afford hotels, and they couldn't.

For a week, the president's impending visit had been front-page news. Texans like to do things big, and Amarillo more than proved it. Every musician in five states who could get a cowboy shirt and play "The Eyes of Texas" in the key of B flat in 4/4 time was invited to march in "the world's largest band." Twenty-five hundred instruments would play for the president. Amarillo seamstresses sewed the world's largest American flag. It was so tall that five six-foot men would have had to stand on one another's shoulders just to hold it up. It was so long that eight six-foot men could stretch out on the ground head to foot and still not reach the end.[4]

Amarillo was the epicenter of suffering in a nation driven to its knees. Texas and the states around it had been in such a desperate drought for such a long time that many in this religion-soaked region believed the end of the world was coming. FDR was their primary reason to hope it might not be. No wonder they crowded together to see him.

Lack of rain was just the beginning of the woes visited upon those long-suffering folk. In the spring of 1934, a two-mile-high dust storm called the "black blizzard" came across the Great Plains. Traveling two thousand miles until it hit the East Coast, it stalled for five hours, shrouding the Statue of Liberty and the US Capitol. Ironically, legislators were that day debating a soil conservation bill. The black blizzard was the worst of the dust storms, but the lesser ones regularly turned daylight into dark and thickened the air so that old people and children died just from breathing it. So much static electricity built up between the dust overhead and the ground beneath that a man might reach out to shake his neighbor's hand, and they'd both be knocked to the ground by the electrical spark that flashed between them. Barbed wire fences glowed blue with flame. Cars were so likely to short out during the storms that people took to dragging chains behind their cars to ground the electricity.

At the same time, warm weather in the early 1930s caused litters of black-tailed jackrabbits to contain more offspring that usual. The jackrabbits, which may produce litters of two only when weather is cold, began to produce as many as eight offspring every thirty-two days. Drought, brush fires, and loss of habitat caused by farming were also killing off the birds and larger mammals that keep the rabbit population down. In 1935 these two-foot-long jackrabbits, weighing as much as six pounds, began to migrate looking for food. Hundreds of thousands of them, so many you couldn't see the end of them, overran the land, racing across the fields, leaping ten feet at a time, moving at forty miles an hour, right into the towns, down the streets, onto the porches, into the houses if they weren't locked up tight. Nobody could catch or shoot that many jackrabbits because they just kept coming. They ate anything green, and so much of it that the farmers began calling them "Hoover hogs," after the president they blamed for the Great Depression. Finally the townsmen built corrals so they could pen them in and smash their brains out with clubs and baseball bats. It wasn't easy work.

Next came thick clouds of grasshoppers, twenty-three thousand insects per acre, some estimates made it. They came flying in so thick that the only way to know the difference between them and a dust storm was to look for the glinting of the sun on their wings. Even the sound of them, that high-pitched buzzing turned so loud that nothing else could be heard, could drive a person nearly crazy. Farmers plowing on tractors would be hit in the face by so many that they "would knock you cuckoo," said one farmer. They'd eat anything—the shirt off your back, the handle of the hoe you were using to squash them.

People told stories of cars running over so many insects that the roads were slick. Trains couldn't get up their tracks because the hoppers' bodies were so thick they'd "greased" the tracks.[5] The National Guard was called out to crush them with tractors. When that didn't work, soldiers burned the fields, which must have meant they lit the cloud of insects itself because the fields had nothing left in them to burn. In Colorado the National Guard shot flamethrowers from slow-moving trains and set off bombs to kill the insects, but the bugs just kept coming. The Civilian Conservation Corps pitched in by bringing a poison of arsenic, molasses, and bran that was mixed with sawdust and spread in the fields. That killed them, but the stench of a billion insects sickened even the strong-stomached farmers.[6]

The idea that the end of the world was near didn't seem far-fetched at all.[7] That kind of talk was coming from the preachers, and the old folks, but not from Roosevelt. We'll get out of this, he kept telling them, stick together, have faith, don't give up. He was with them all the way. And God? He acted as if God was, too, though it sure didn't look like it, which made that grinning president and his stuck-out chin all the more important to the people of the plains.

Two years earlier, the president had visited nine drought-stricken states to see conditions for himself and to make sure the federal government was doing the job he intended for it to do. After his trip, he sat down with the country for one of his periodic fireside chats. All over the country people who had radios in their homes gathered close around them, fiddling with the dial to keep the staticky sound coming. People who didn't have radios stood outside buildings where radios were playing. If a cab pulled over with the driver listening to FDR, people would cluster around the vehicle, just standing there to hear him.

The disasters were not permanent, he told the nation. "No cracked earth, no blistering sun, no burning wind, no grasshoppers are a permanent match for the indomitable American farmers and stockmen, and their wives and children who have carried on through desperate days and inspire us with their self-reliance, their tenacity and their courage," he said. "It was their fathers' task to make homes; it is their task to keep those homes; it is our task to help them with their fight."

Lots of experts wanted to write off the Great Plains, let it go to desert and then to hell for all they cared. But Roosevelt loved the land of

America almost as much as he loved its people. He could no more back off and let the land die than he could know children were going hungry and not devise a plan to feed them.

He said, "I talked with families who had lost their wheat crop, lost their corn crop, lost their livestock, lost the water in their well, lost their garden and come through the summer without one dollar of cash resources, facing a winter without feed or food—facing a planting season without seed to put in the ground."[8]

If those who need help get it, everyone will benefit, he told those listening to his fireside chat. "The very existence of the men and women working in the clothing factories of New York, making clothes worn by farmers and their families; of the workers in the steel mills in Pittsburgh, in the automobile factories of Detroit, and in the harvester factories of Illinois, depend upon the farmers' ability to purchase the commodities they produce," he told his listeners. "In the same way it is the purchasing power of the workers in these factories in the cities that enables them and their wives and children to eat more beef, more pork, more wheat, more corn, more fruit and more dairy products, and to buy more clothing made from cotton, wool and leather. In a physical and a property sense, as well as in a spiritual sense, we are members one of another."

FDR had a simple faith grounded on unquestioning belief, as Eleanor once said. But his simple faith led him to an idea so deeply religious that only the greatest spiritual masters embrace it. Few others believe it, and almost no one attempts to bring it into the material world. But he did. "We are members one of another," he told the country. The spiritual was political for Roosevelt.

FDR had done quite a bit to help the drought-withered states in the years before his 1938 visit. He had sent a determined expert named Hugh Bennett to hire an army of Civilian Conservation Corps workers and put them to work planting nearly forty million trees in Texas, Oklahoma, and Kansas. The spindly plants were little more than sticks in the ground and many of them wouldn't survive, but they looked like hope to the residents of the Dust Bowl. Bennett taught famers to plow their fields in ways that didn't cause the soil to blow away with every gust. He put nearly a million acres under contract in his plan to restore the great, grassy prairie to health. He paid the farmers to plant the grass. He planned to plant grass on six million more acres, which meant men who had been idle and despairing could earn wages enough to feed their families.

That spring it had looked as if the government plan might be working. Rain gentle enough to soak the fields turned them a color almost forgotten in West Texas—pale, tender, just-coming-out-of-the-ground green, one of the prettiest colors on earth. The people of the plains gave God the credit first. And then they threw some thanks Roosevelt's way.

When the summer came, hot, dry, and windy, the plants shriveled and turned brown as they had in past years. But Roosevelt's own ebullient determination had given the people hope, a commodity once as rare as rain. The president arrived in Amarillo at 6:45 p.m. As he stepped out the door of his private train, he checked the sky. Just like a dirt farmer, the *Amarillo Daily News* reported approvingly. The day had been clear, but as the open Cadillac that Amarillo had borrowed for the event began moving into the streets, clouds gathered and rain began to fall in sheets.

The parade route from the train to the park where he was to speak was three miles long. "The president rode . . . between seas of yelling humanity and a flood of rain everywhere," the *Amarillo Globe-News* reported. "He didn't flinch. He made no attempt to keep off the rain. He lifted his hat and flashed his smile."[9]

The band's tubas filled with water. The borrowed convertible's interior was soaked. As rain pummeled the great flag, burly farm boys struggled to hold its weight aloft, while the field of blue and the stripes ran down the cloth, coloring the flooded gutters purple.

Along the parade route, dry dirt farmers stood next to cattlemen, everyone dressed in their best. Amarillo's most fashionable ladies were having unforeseen trouble of their own. The latest style that summer was to wear gauzy dresses made from a new material called rayon. Since these precious dresses were dry-cleaned and few of the women had been caught in the rain, no one knew that the material they wore would shrink as soon as it got wet. By the end of the event, the good women of Amarillo were wearing skirts that barely covered their bottoms.[10] If FDR, inveterate flirt that he was, noticed, he was too much the gentleman to stare. It was quite a day.

A "big time" was had by all, the paper reported. That the July 11 rains coincidentally came just as FDR arrived could hardly have seemed a matter of pure chance to many who looked toward the heavens every day for God's punishment and his blessings. FDR himself did not claim the rain as a sign from God, but he did not miss the opportunity to point out how unlikely such a downpour was.

"If I had asked the newspapermen on the train what the odds were, they would have given me 100 to 1 that it wouldn't be raining in Amarillo. But it is," he proclaimed jauntily to the crowd. The newspaper account doesn't record it, but the crowd must have laughed happily at that. It was so precisely the happy-go-lucky attitude they'd come for. And what impromptu brilliance to have used the newspapermen, those hard-nosed, cynical adherents of just the facts, as a foil. If it was indeed the Almighty who had sent the rain to show his favor toward Roosevelt, he sure had showered his blessing on a man who could make good use of it.

Roosevelt's own luck was at issue here because in their great lack of luck, he was their best hope. After that bit of happy bragging, FDR went on to the matters at hand. He followed a script that had worked so well for him in his first speech as president and all the years since. He praised them, damned those who might stand against them, and talked of what he had done. He assured them he would keep working for them and that he knew they would keep working with him.

Once his prepared remarks ended, he gave them a little more of that old Doc New Deal charm and confidence. Then he ad-libbed, "I think this little shower we've had is a mighty good omen." He was far too good a politician to let rain in the middle of a drought go without noting that it had come just when he did.

Roosevelt wasn't shy about pointing out good omens and taking them as signs of God's favor. Everyone close to him was also aware that he might see misfortune as a sign that God wasn't with him. When word arrived on March 2, 1933, just before his first inaugural that attorney general–designate Thomas Walsh, Montana's beloved and respected senator, had died, campaign manager Jim Farley knew he needed to move fast before the idea of a bad omen took hold in FDR's mind. After hurried consultation, it was decided to give the post to Homer Cummings, and the threat of a presidential funk receded.

FDR would sometimes set a test by saying to himself that if the trivial event occurred within an immediate time span (the next minute, perhaps, or before he could count to ten), it meant that God approved what he was considering; if it did not occur, God disapproved. If he won at poker or a type of solitaire called Miss Milligan, if he caught a particularly big fish on one of his sailing trips, if his favorite food was served for dinner, he might exclaim in happy, boyish triumph that he now knew whatever decision he had just made was the right one. If he lost at cards or didn't catch any fish, he might reconsider his reasons for what he had been planning to do.

It's impossible to know just how seriously Roosevelt took the divine signs he pointed out to people—or whether the notice he took of signs was just another way to play. He was a man who loved to have fun. His time with his children was fun. Writing speeches with him was so much fun that his speechwriters marveled. His laugh was famously infectious. Often when he talked about what he wanted Americans to have, he included recreation. He also liked hearing messages from astrologers and palm readers, but it was all for relaxation, according to his secretary Grace Tully. "It amused me very much to have him even take time out to read the results of their work, because I knew he had great faith in God—not planets, nor numbers, nor turning up the best luck card in the deck at a given moment," she wrote.[11]

He was also a superstitious man who believed in lucky objects, especially hats. In 1910 his grip slipped as he tried to board a Lexington Avenue streetcar in New York City, and he fell backward. The battered brown felt hat he was wearing cushioned the blow to his skull and kept him from being injured. "Don't you make fun of that old hat of mine," he told a reporter who mentioned that FDR's health seemed good but wondered if the hat he was wearing wasn't a bit sickly. "I have a peculiar superstition about hats." The old brown one wouldn't be traded for a new hat until after he won the election he was in at the time for New York's governor.[12]

Journalist and author John Gunther noted with some dismay the reason FDR gave for raising the price of gold by twenty-one cents. "It makes one shudder to learn that when he decided in 1933 to raise the price of gold, he chose 21 cents as the amount, partly because 'that's a lucky number,—three times seven.'"[13]

The Roosevelt luck never seemed more like divine protection than on the evening of February 15, 1933, when a thirty-three-year-old Italian immigrant named Giuseppe Zangara tried to kill him. Roosevelt had spoken briefly with a crowd at Miami's Bayfront Park from his open convertible, and then he prepared to leave. A camera crew asked him to stay a bit longer and turn around so they could shoot some film. He was generally obliging with the press, but this time he was tired and said no.

Although the cameraman protested, FDR wouldn't relent. He slid down from the top of the seat and was leaning forward, ready to take a telegram from an approaching man, when a sharp retort was heard. The president-elect thought it was a firecracker. Speechwriter Raymond Moley, who was with him, thought it was a car backfiring. As four more retorts sounded, shouts were heard from the crowd, and then screaming. The man with the telegram was yanked away from Roosevelt. His driver started the car, shifted into gear, and stomped on the gas pedal so hard that the motor roared.

The mayor of Chicago, Anton J. Cermak, who had come to talk to Roosevelt about his city's economic situation, was standing nearby and was hit by a bullet in the chest. The car was gaining speed, but Roosevelt had seen Cermak's white face and bloody chest, and ordered the driver to back up. The mortally wounded mayor was loaded into the car. Roosevelt held him all the way to the hospital, assuring him that everything was going to be all right.

Zangara had stationed himself on the second row of a bandstand bleacher sixteen feet from where Roosevelt's car was stopped. As the president-elect began speaking, people rose to their feet in front of Zangara, who at only an inch over five feet tall couldn't see over them. When Roosevelt stopped talking and slid down in his seat, the people blocking Zangara's view sat down. So he sprang onto the bench behind him, but it wobbled, causing the gun he held toward Roosevelt to shake. Standing next to him was Lillian Cross, the wife of a local physician and surgeon. She was only a few inches taller than Zangara and had climbed on a bench herself to get a better look at the president-elect.

Zangara almost toppled her over when he jumped onto the bench behind her. She turned to protest, and she saw his pistol, aimed over her right shoulder. Immediately she knew he had come to kill Roosevelt. Instead of freezing or running, as most people would have, she switched her handbag to her left hand and caught Zangara's arm, forcing it upward just as he fired the trigger. The pistol, an inch or two from her right ear, smudged her cheek with gunpowder and temporarily deafened her, "but I held on," she told reporters later.

That evening as the president-elect's companions gathered around, shaky and ready to discuss the close call, Roosevelt behaved exactly as though nothing out of the ordinary had happened. "There was nothing—not so much as the twitching of a muscle, the mopping of a brow, or even the hint of a false gaiety—to indicate that it wasn't any other evening in any other place," Moley remembered years later. "I have never in my life seen anything more magnificent." Roosevelt retired at the usual time and fell asleep right away, as usual. The Secret Service agent in charge was so struck by his calm attitude that he checked on him during the night. He was sleeping soundly.[14]

Although many believers would have praised God for their deliverance, Roosevelt did not do so, at least not publicly. In the wake of Cermak's death, it would have been most impolitic, the kind of mistake FDR rarely made. Lots of others did praise the Lord, however. The next Sunday, plenty of clergy gave the Almighty thanks for delivering the president-elect. The assassination attempt further burnished FDR's image as the martyred savior. Having been stricken by polio and resurrected to deliver America while still a young man, he had once again been lifted out of peril by God. His bravery and compassion as he held the bleeding mayor, whispering reassurance, helped cement his image as the heroic comforter. "Just as God made You the President of the American people, as He preserved You at Miami, I feel sure that he has destined You to be the Saviour of Our Country," wrote Joseph Williams.[15] FDR's secretary Missy LeHand commented cryptically to Rex Tugwell, "There is a star."[16]

Roosevelt may have seen his luck as one way God communicated his favor, but it would be a mistake to believe that the president didn't help God out. He was an amazingly hard worker. He campaigned so tirelessly that younger, healthier men who didn't have to carry a load of steel strapped to their legs were exhausted long before he was. Sometimes what appeared to be luck wasn't luck at all. It was preparation, effort, and Roosevelt's fierce drive to win, no matter what he had to do. He made it look like luck—and if that required deception, well, he could do that, and he would.

One of the times he helped his luck along doesn't show him in a Christian light at all. Before he ran for his first three terms as president, Roosevelt's opponents tried to convince the public that he was not mentally or physically robust enough to govern. As he aged and the outrage over him continuing to hold on to power grew, they tried harder. But each time he outmaneuvered them. Sometimes he released physicians' reports that declared him well and robust. Other times he simply kept going as other men with less energy and will fell by the wayside.

During the whistle-stop campaigns he conducted for his first three terms, FDR traveled thousands of miles on the Roosevelt Special, greeting people at each little stop, often saying a few words, sometimes making speeches from the back of the train, always standing. To anyone watching from the outside, it looked effortless; to those on the inside, it was an amazing feat of endurance. Roosevelt, who hated wearing his leg braces, would retreat into his private car after each stop, sit down, and unstrap the heavy, confining metal. Before the next stop, he would put the braces back on, be pulled to his feet, and begin the slow swing of one leg and then other that would put him on the train platform.

When he was running for his fourth term, Roosevelt's opponents began a campaign to show that he was too frail to complete four years in office. He campaigned only five days during that wartime run for the presidency, but in October it became clear that the people needed to get a look at him before the election.

In the 1940 election, he had toured New York in his open limousine. He decided to silence his critics with a similar tour in 1944. In fact his health was declining so rapidly that during the dinner before a Teamsters' speech three weeks earlier his hand shook as he ate. On the day his cavalcade was to tour five boroughs of New York, Jersey City, and nearby towns, a distance of fifty miles, the famed Roosevelt luck with weather failed. The cold was biting as rain whipped an estimated three million bystanders who cheered themselves hoarse, craning to get a look their president. Everyone was asking the same question: "How does he look?"

At 9:46 a.m. Roosevelt began the parade from the Brooklyn Army Base of the New York Port of Embarkation. Not only was the weather against him, but the president had to start without a traditional gunfire salute because there were no guns. As the base commander, Major General

Homer N. Groningen, told reporters, "We have no guns: the only guns I have I move overseas." But FDR wasn't watching for ill omens on that day. He had it all covered.

Hatless and coatless in the open car, FDR waved gaily through the entire four hours of the parade, cheerful, conversing, throwing his head back with laughter. That night, he gave a speech. And true to his phenomenal luck, he didn't come down with so much as a sniffle. The verdict of throngs that stood, teeth chattering, to cheer him? He looked pretty good for a man dealing with the strain of war.

What the world didn't know was how he did it. At points along the parade route, the car slid into garages blocked off from other traffic. FDR was scooped out of the car and laid on a pallet. His clothes were taken off down to the skin. He was toweled down and massaged until he was dry and warm. Then he was dressed in dry clothes. He was reseated in the car and rejoined the parade.[7] Did he ever confess to the public and repent of his deceit? No, he did not.

Franklin D. and Eleanor Roosevelt in front of the White House after his 1941 inauguration.

11

"JUDGE ME BY MY ENEMIES"

When dealing with the common folk of America, Roosevelt had few equals. His easy ways and simple talk allowed them to feel that he was talking straight to them. He encouraged and united them when no one else could. The country trusted him. Many thought of him as their friend.

But among the powerful people of his own class, FDR was considered a traitor, a liar, an enemy of the state, a threat to all that was precious in America.

A less egotistical, less confident man, a milder Christian might have soothed the feelings of his enemies, but Franklin Roosevelt did not. In his addresses, when speaking of those who opposed him, he cast off his cloak of kind savior and became the avenging force of righteousness. Superhero he may have been, but oh my, he was a mean one.

Those who misunderstand Christianity may believe his name calling went against his faith. But brotherhood and peace making are only one side of Judaism and Christianity. Calling out wrong-doers is part of the religious task. For Christianity, which started as a Jewish counterculture movement, those in power were prime targets from the beginning. The new religion's greatest number of followers were among the poor, led by a man who had nothing. What Jesus had to say was so threatening to those in power that they killed him. He was preceded by and inspired by prophets whose words were harsh enough to blister the ears of those who listened. So it must be said that FDR was in good company even at his most insulting. Among those politicians who attempt to "comfort the afflicted and afflict the comfortable," few have spoken with the boldness of the president in the wheelchair.

✦⟶◉⟵✦

The fervor with which he took after the "money changers" in his first inaugural address was no surprise to American businessmen. He had been smearing their good name for months. The "many amongst us [who] have made obeisance to Mammon" were to blame for the Depression, he said in his nomination speech at the 1932 Democratic convention.

"Judge me by the enemies I have made. Judge me by the selfish purposes of these utility leaders who have talked of radicalism while they were selling watered stock to the people and using our schools to deceive the coming generation," he said in September of 1932. The "lone wolf, the unethical competitor, the reckless promoter" were blocking those who have a right to work, he said in a San Francisco speech that year. "It was a real shocker for those who simply assumed that free competition was no more to be questioned than home and mother," noted one biographer.[1]

In his first State of the Union speech he attacked so fiercely that even the left-leaning *Nation* seemed rattled, calling him a "complete master of the grammar of vituperation."[2] "Entrenched greed" was the motive of those who hated his administration, he told the nation. "They seek the restoration of their selfish power. . . . Give them their way and they will take the course of every autocracy of the past—power for themselves, enslavement for the public."

By that time, he had probably made his point, but he wasn't even nearly through. He continued to bait the established powers of finance and industry savagely. He was almost boastful about the fury he aroused: "Never before in all our history have these forces been so united against one candidate as they stand today. They are unanimous in their hate for me—and I welcome their hatred," he said three years later at Madison Square Garden.

He hadn't lightened up a bit by the time he was nominated for a second term. He attacked leaders who had given the country "nine mocking years with the golden calf and three long years of the scourge," in his 1936 nomination acceptance speech at the Democratic convention. He assured his listeners that "your government is still on the same side of the street with the Good Samaritan and not with those who pass by on the other side."

Name calling was just the beginning. Roosevelt's ideas undermined everything his own socioeconomic class held most sacred. "I believe that our industrial and economic system is made for individual men and women, not individual men and women for the benefit of the system," he said. "I believe in the sacredness of private property, which means I do not believe that it should be subjected to the ruthless manipulation of professional gamblers and the corporate system."[3]

Ruthless capitalism had its purpose during the settling of America's vast lands, he told Americans, but the country must move beyond such tactics. It was now time to think of those who had been left behind in the country's march toward progress. "I see one-third of a nation ill-housed, ill-clad, ill-nourished," he said, promising that such inequity would not continue because Americans would not allow it to. "We are determined to make every American citizen the subject of his country's interest and concern; and we will never regard any faithful law-abiding group within our borders as superfluous. The test of our progress is not whether we add more to the abundance of those who have much; it is whether we provide enough for those who have too little."

For all of American history, everyone had agreed that free enterprise meant freedom to run your business the way you wanted. If someone didn't like it, they could work for another employer or start their own business. Laws that FDR and his Democratic allies passed forbidding practices that many Americans considered merely good business were insane, immoral meddling, his enemies believed, and would ruin the country.

He was concentrating so much power in the federal government that many feared he might be a fascist. Propaganda posters, the NRA (National Recovery Administration) symbols in windows of businesses, and military-like work camps that housed millions of young men in uniforms all seemed a lot like what was going on in Germany and Italy. Even some of those who supported him became afraid after his second election, when he tried to change appointment rules for the Supreme Court so he could pack the court, and when he set out to purge Congress of Democrats who weren't progressive enough.

One result of all this hubbub and change was that the people Roosevelt had dined with, danced with, worshipped with, and taken innumerable cups of tea with all his life truly did hate him. Even FDR's former friends and classmates despised him. The Groton School alumni so disdained their fellow graduate that on the fiftieth anniversary of the school's founding, Endicott Peabody told graduates who could not give proper respect to the president that they should not attend. On another occasion he told a group of Grotties, "I believe Franklin Roosevelt to be a gallant and courageous gentleman. I am happy to count him as my friend." His audience would not have dared boo him. Instead they met his words with complete silence.[4]

Even Harvard did not like him. In his first election, a straw poll conducted by the *Harvard Crimson* showed a three-to-one preference for Hoover. Roosevelt was called "a traitor to his fine education" in a *Crimson* editorial four years later.[5] Harvard president A. Lawrence Lowell was rude when FDR was invited to speak at Harvard's Tercentennial. Lowell sent him a letter specifying that he should keep his remarks to ten minutes. Roosevelt replied that he would certainly keep his words to a time limit if he was being invited as an alumnus, but if he was being invited as the president of the United States, he would take whatever time was needed.

Thousands of men and women in the upper stratum of American society nurtured a "fanatical hatred" of him. "It is a passion, a fury, that is wholly unreasoning," wrote Marquis W. Childs in *Harper's* magazine. Consuming and personal, it was encountered over meals, in locker rooms, in clubs, and in card rooms, and it frequently took "a violent and unlawful form, the expression of desires and wishes that can be explained only, it would seem, in terms of abnormal psychology. . . . The larger the house, the more numerous the servants, the more resplendent the linen and silver, the more scathing is likely to be the indictment of the President."[6]

The upper 2 percent vied with each other to demonstrate the bile he inspired. They called him "that megalomaniac cripple in the White House." One well-off American traveling to tropical islands refused to hear any news, saying, "There is only one bit of news I want to hear and that is the death of Franklin D. Roosevelt. If he is not dead, you don't need to tell me anything else."[7] Radio manufacturer Atwater Kent retired rather than do business while FDR was running the country. J. P. Morgan's family supposedly hid newspapers with pictures of Roosevelt. In a health club in Connecticut, mention of his name was "forbidden as a health measure against apoplexy."

Newspaper publishers, most of whom were anti-Roosevelt, spewed venom in editorials and editorial cartoons. *Chicago Tribune* publisher Robert McCormick accused the president of setting up a star chamber, the fifteenth- to seventeenth-century English court that has often been a symbol of secretive and illegitimate proceedings.[8] Media mogul William Randolph Hearst dubbed the New Deal "the Raw Deal."

FDR reacted as angrily to such treatment as any president would, but on occasion he could find humor in the insults. His favorite of the anti-FDR cartoons was the image of a little girl who was being scolded by her mother for writing dirty words. The words were his name. When the Washington press corps lampooned him at the correspondents' dinner by presenting a statue of the Egyptian Great Sphinx with his face on it, Roosevelt asked for the figure and took it to Hyde Park.

But the question "Why?" could be asked of FDR *and* his enemies. Why did he defame them so furiously? And why did they hate him so much?

He was changing the rules, and that scares everybody. But the idea that he was a fascist wasn't tenable. Fascists are ultraconservatives, first of all, and he was hardly that. Among their first acts are to destroy democratic institutions. Roosevelt hadn't moved to limit democracy even when many Americans wanted him to. In his attempt to change the Supreme Court's rules of appointment, he went through Congress. In his attempt to oust conservative Democrats, he went to the voters. Hardly the actions of a would-be dictator.

As for his assault on the rich, it was mostly talk. Taxes on the wealthy increased little, if at all. Their fortunes recovered and grew nicely under Roosevelt, much to the ire of his more liberal supporters who complained that he favored the rich. Roosevelt barked like he was going to tear the country's elite apart. But he didn't. He never intended to.

Nevertheless, what he said about the wealthy was hard for them to forgive. He called the most powerful men in America bad names. Their great wealth had heretofore been accompanied by great acclaim, and the greater their wealth, the more admired they were. In their own eyes and the eyes of everyone else, they were the benefactors of America. The job creators. The winners in life's big race. Especially during the 1920s, businessmen were held up as the exemplars of all that was good in America. They were God-fearing, churchgoing men, pillars of their congregations, wise, far-seeing leaders that even the pastors looked to for advice. FDR not only toppled them from their pedestals but he talked of them as if they were scoundrels. He used the Good Book to give his insults godly weight, which many of the wealthy and powerful considered the height of demagoguery.

Some have said the president just liked to stir the pot. Stanley High noticed that FDR loved telling stories about his family that highlighted whatever slightly roguish behavior could be found in that staid Dutch bunch. But maybe there was more to it. Maybe Roosevelt, who seemed to understand the American people so well, was seizing a rare moment to make as great an impact as he could on the nation's consciousness or even what Robert Bellah would call its civil religion. President Wilson had once told his young assistant secretary of the navy, "It is only once in a generation that a people can be lifted above material things. That is why conservative government is in the saddle two-thirds of the time."[9]

Roosevelt may have been hoping that he could alter that formula. Americans often admire the rich and attribute great wisdom to them, which causes them to favor conservative policies that help the rich. The positive side of that tendency is that it dampens envy and encourages stability. The negative side is that Americans will excuse almost as much bad behavior from rich people as feudal subjects would tolerate in a king. Such habits of thought are hard to unseat because Americans believe so fervently that everyone can succeed in America. Even those who ought to know better from their own lives often don't realize they aren't entirely to blame for their misery. More pernicious still, those a bit higher on the scale are quick to believe that the more unfortunate have only themselves to blame.

Roosevelt was already shaking those verities up in frightening ways. He was giving down-and-outers jobs, handing out federal money, restricting how a man could run his own business. It was scary stuff. But to keep those poor wretches he cared so much about moving forward in their own behalf, maybe he realized that he needed to do whatever he could to restructure their thinking. So he pulled those golden calves of his own class off their pedestals.

But those who hated FDR weren't merely making speeches. In what became known as the Bankers' Putsch or Wall Street Putsch, a group of well-heeled veterans approached Major General Smedley Butler claiming to have three million dollars from Wall Street bankers. The money was to organize members of the American Legion as a force that would march on Washington, seize the government, and install the retired general either as a replacement for Roosevelt or as the man who controlled him. But Butler, a two-time Medal of Honor winner, turned them in and testified before a congressional investigative committee in 1934.[10]

That same year the American Liberty League put big money behind an effort to protect the "economy of nature and the plan of Nature's God," property rights and the Constitution. There was no need to specify who was attacking these fundamentals of American life. It was Roosevelt, of course. Liberty League leaders included the du Ponts, Alfred P. Sloan Jr. of General Motors, E. F. Hutton, Dean Acheson, and even Roosevelt's old friend and now enemy, Al Smith, who like so many others had gone over to Wall Street.[11]

But the league's attempts to tie themselves to patriotism and godliness didn't work. Their self-interest was so evident that the New Dealers made a joke of them. Jim Farley, chairman of the Democratic Party, said the American Liberty League ought to be called the "American Cellophane League" because "first, it's a du Pont product and second, you can see right through it."

The president himself couldn't resist having fun at the league's expense. As was so often his custom, he used religious language to sharpen his point. "It had been said that there are two great Commandments—

one is to love God, and the other to love your neighbor," he said soon after the league went into operation. "The two particular tenets of this new organization say you shall love God and then forget your neighbor." The name of the god they worshipped seemed to be "Property," he joked later in off-the-record comments.[12]

The Liberty League misjudged the people's concern with protecting property rights and their ability to see through business propaganda. It never attracted the support it expected, peaking at 124,826 members in 1936. The organization hung together as membership began to decline, but it concentrated on lobbying, press releases, and court fights against the New Deal.[13]

The National Association of Manufacturers also started an anti-Roosevelt campaign, pledging themselves to "serve the purposes of business salvation." Desperate to bring the country back around to their way of thinking, they dedicated half of their income to public relations, raising the budget from $36,000 to $793,043 in three years. They put out press releases, wrote fliers, advertised, set up a speakers' bureau, produced films and radio programs, and established a news service that supplied ready-to-run editorials and news stories to 7,500 local newspapers.[14] Their goal was to tell the story of business the way they saw it. Their primary tactic was to once again appeal to Americans' self-interest.

But their message didn't fly any further than the Liberty League's. During the worst depression the country had ever seen, no-holds-barred business seemed a menace, not the path to salvation.

Judging by his landslide win in the 1936 election, his enemies weren't getting much traction.[15] But they were growing, in numbers and venom. Some of the increase occurred among his fellow Christians. It hadn't begun like that. By the time Roosevelt's New Deal stepped in with aid, churches and their charities were broke. In poorer churches, offerings had dried up to almost nothing, and some of them couldn't even keep their doors open. Priests turned away hungry widows and orphans saying they weren't needy enough. Moonshiners and communists were doing as much as churches, in some communities more, to feed the hungry. The faithful looked to God. When it was Roosevelt who answered, they considered him good enough and God-sent. The *Presbyterian Banner* declared

FDR devout. *Christian Century* titled the president more than a political leader; he was a "religious leader," the publication claimed.

The powerful Federal Council of Churches said of the New Deal: "The measures proposed are of human origin and therefore fallible. But the purposes sought are divine." Southern preachers were equally laudatory. Catholics and Jews were just as supportive, and most of them stuck with him. Detroit's Father Charles Coughlin, whose radio program drew thirty million listeners, said, "The New Deal is Christ's Deal." Later the priest felt that FDR hadn't given him the respect he deserved, and he began to rage that Roosevelt was in league with "godless capitalists, the Jews, communists, international bankers, and plutocrats."[16]

As time went on, more clergy found a lot not to like about FDR and his New Deal. First, the federal government refused to funnel funds through the churches. That drew the ire of the Catholic bishop of Chicago. The Southern Baptist Convention also protested. The Baptists didn't want the money because they thought taking it would violate separation of church and state, but they didn't like the way it was being spent. Jobs ought to be provided by the private sector and charity was best managed by the churches, the Baptists thought.

With what many considered make-work projects and federal handouts given to the worthy and the unworthy alike, the federal government was drastically undermining the country's moral fabric, they believed. When the churches were involved, charity was often paired with judgments about who was and wasn't worthy. That had given churches considerable power in their communities. With the state stepping in, the idea that poverty and even bad behavior were somehow the fault and responsibility of society rather than of each individual got a big boost. Baptists called that meddling in church affairs.

Conservatives weren't the only ones who had a problem. To the more progressive ministers, FDR didn't go far enough. When the magazine *World Tomorrow* took a poll among twenty thousand ministers, 28 percent advocated some form of socialism, with Methodists polling highest at 34 percent. Roosevelt had an opportunity to truly change society, they said, and instead he had served the same old system. Also on the left, religious peace advocates looked with horror at increasing signs that the president they had supported was moving the country toward war.

But convinced he was doing God's work, Roosevelt believed the clergy would be behind him, and so in the fall of 1935, hoping for support that would push his Social Security funding bill through Congress, he sent out more than one hundred thousand letters asking for advice and assessments of the New Deal from ministers, rabbis, and religion scholars, both white and black. "I shall deem it a favor if you will write me about conditions in your community. Tell me where you feel our government can better serve our people," the letter read. It ended with "May I have your counsel and your help? I am leaving on a short vacation but will be back in Washington in a few weeks, and I will deeply appreciate your writing to me."

Clergy replied, some with short notes but many with page after page of reflection and advice. Some ministers even did informal surveys to find out what their communities thought. One man took the letter to a gathering of businessmen to get feedback. Others queried their friends or their congregations.

Many respondents seemed to like a lot about the New Deal. Old-age pensions were among their favorite changes. They wrote stories of starving families who were able to eat again now that their men had jobs. Many praised the president as God-sent, but others were less enthusiastic. They worried that his programs were filled with waste and mismanagement. They saw favoritism and sometimes graft on the local level. They wanted more federal oversight, or they wanted more local control. Some feared that FDR was moving the country toward socialism. They worried that those he was giving work to were loafers, and federal giveaways were having a bad effect on character.

Many evangelicals, especially in the South, had not forgiven him for repealing Prohibition and never would. They had fought hard for the Eighteenth Amendment, and now liquor was back, bringing with it all the old problems. Maybe Prohibition hadn't stopped the flow of booze altogether, but it had hindered it, kept it from being available everywhere. Kids were now drinking more, the pastors complained. Men were squandering their paychecks in bars again. People were being killed by drunk drivers.

Other complaints were more personal. They heard about how Roosevelt didn't manage to attend church every Sunday. They didn't like that. When his children began to divorce their spouses, some pastors didn't like that either. Roosevelt and his missus should have raised their children better and controlled them more, they thought.

The administration paid great attention to the letters, categorizing them into pro, con, and mixed. Many were mixed, some were savagely negative. Responses were so disappointing and would have given so much succor to his opponents that the whole project was scrapped, and the letters were not released.

But FDR didn't give up on the idea that ministers, community leaders, and regular citizens could come together to support the New Deal. So a new plan was made to set up local groups called Good Neighbor Committees that would provide education and support for the New Deal programs—and along the way encourage uncommitted voters to go Democratic. Journalist Stanley High, who had worked as a non-ordained minister and had extensive ties within the religious community, was appointed to lead the effort. Within a few months, committees were operating all over the country. The largest black political gathering ever held to that point took place in Harlem with the sponsorship of the Good Neighbor Committees. African Americans would leave the party of Lincoln in the 1936 election to vote for FDR, and most would never go back.

In the summer of 1939, American businessmen had a new idea for defeating the New Dealers. H. W. Prentis, the fifty-five-year-old head of Pennsylvania's Armstrong Cork Company, posed a question that galvanized the US Chamber of Commerce: Why not turn Roosevelt's tactics against him?

"Economic facts are important, but they will never check the virus of collectivism," said Prentis. "The only antidote is a revival of American patriotism and religious faith." He suggested a public relations campaign that downplayed material wealth, while emphasizing that spiritual values and free enterprise were blessed by God as the American way of life. The idea really took off when James W. Fifield, a tall, handsome Congregational minister with an endearing manner and gangly grace that brought Dick Van Dyke to mind, addressed industrialists gathered at a Waldorf Astoria National Association of Manufacturers convention. The Los Angeles pastor listed Roosevelt's many sins, cast the New Deal as an "encroachment upon American freedoms," and assured his listeners that only business could save the country.

"His audience of executives was stunned," wrote Kruse in *One Nation under God*. "Over the preceding decade, the titans of industry had been told, time and time again, that they were to blame for the nation's downfall." The role of saviors suited them much better. "When he had finished," a journalist noted, rumors reported that the National Association of Manufacturers' applause "could be heard in Hoboken."[17]

Bankrolled by business, Fifield recruited clergymen from around the country during the 1940s and early 1950s to broadcast a theological connection between holiness and capitalism that he called "spiritual mobilization." As has been noted, many ministers had been able to equate wealth with sanctity all on their own. But Fifield brought the idea of Christian capitalism out of the shadows. He gave it respect and spread the idea around. A decade after he began, seventeen thousand ministers were preaching Fifield's gospel, winning cash prizes in sermon contests, and helping convince their communities that the New Deal was evil.

Also, as noted earlier, individual freedom was a crucial link; God gave mankind the freedom to reject the salvation offered by his son, Jesus. Capitalism gave mankind freedom to become rich. Therefore capitalism was a holy economic system. The freer it was, the holier it was. It wasn't a great leap to the idea that any government abridging economic freedom was going against God.

The New Deal's use of government funds to aid the needy was actually stealing from people who earned their money, Fifield's ministers told their followers. The federal government was a false idol that people were depending on and worshipping instead of turning to God, these preachers preached. The Democrats were bearing false witness by promising what they could never deliver, they told congregations all over the country. The anti–New Deal forces were also helped by a growing feeling among Christian fundamentalists that FDR's long dominance of American politics, as well as the rise of Stalin and Hitler, were signs that end times were near.

This marriage of political libertarianism with Christian conservatism was going to grow stronger in the coming decades as other social and religious developments fed into them, including the growth of Christian fundamentalism and its increasing politicization, beginning primarily in the 1970s. Throughout the New Deal, conservative Christians were largely working-class people who stuck with the Democrats no matter what their preachers said. With the election of Eisenhower, that would begin to shift. In the 1980s Fifield's libertarian theologies would begin deciding elections from school boards to the presidency, a development that would continue well into the twenty-first century—and with it FDR's reputation as a man following God would continue to erode.

Franklin D. Roosevelt and British Prime Minister Winston Churchill after a prayer service on the HMS *Prince of Wales* on August 10, 1941.

12

GOD LOVES PEACE/
GOD BLESSES WAR

When Roosevelt took office in 1933 quoting the Prince of Peace, he did not appear to be a man likely to take Americans into war. Pacifists and isolationists had supported him, happy to see that armament manufacturers opposed him. One of Roosevelt's early budget-cutting moves was to decrease the size of the already lean 140,000-member US Army.[1] He not only supported the 1933 Geneva Disarmament Conference, he cabled nations around the world suggesting that all nations enter into nonaggression pacts and limit armaments until all aggressive weapons were eliminated.[2] Hitler withdrew from the conference and the League of Nations.

American isolationism continued strong, as it had for most of US history. A country of immigrants who had left the Old World and fought to get free of its dominion wanted no part of its unending squabbles.

Barely two decades had passed since the United States was pulled into the Great War of 1914–1918, the war that was supposed to end all wars. President Woodrow Wilson had led them into that bloody European mess by promising that they were helping create a world where violent nations would no longer prey on peace-loving people. Clearly such a world had not come into being. Some had come to believe that Germany's aggression during that war had some legitimacy. Others believed the war had benefited no one but the armaments manufacturers. With Europe as messy as ever, World War I began to be referred to as "the war about nothing."

An equally compelling reason to stand clear was that the war had been horrible beyond anything ever experienced. The fifty thousand Americans killed in combat had been a fraction of the casualties.[3] Men who had been gassed returned as invalids. They would never recover. Other men's bodies seemed fine, but their shell-shocked minds were shattered. The peace had been handled so badly that the United States refused to sign the Treaty of Versailles and defied their president by refusing to join the League of Nations.

Roosevelt, who kept a portrait of Wilson in his cabinet room so that his eye often fell on it as he was working on speeches, had watched that great old Christian's heart break and learned from his defeat.[4] FDR had cast some glorious visions of brotherhood and love during the New Deal, and Americans had signed on by the millions. But the time for love talk was over. Images of lions lying down with lambs would never again convince them to send their sons into war. Americans would fight only if their own country was imperiled, and they were a long way from believing that.[5]

By 1935 Europe was sliding toward war. In March, Hitler instituted military conscription. Rebuilding the German army was in open defiance of the Treaty of Versailles. Hitler vowed that he would only use his forces for defense, and no action was taken against him by the international community.

By that time many Americans could clearly see what was coming. Events hardened their attitudes from indifference to war resistance. On April 6, fifty thousand veterans marched for peace in Washington, D.C. Three days later one hundred seventy-five thousand college students staged a one-hour "strike for peace." They demanded that campus Reserve Officers Training Corps programs be scuttled and called for "schools not battleships." On Capitol Hill pacifist oratory rang through Congress.[6] In August Roosevelt signed the Neutrality Act, which placed an embargo on the sale of arms to belligerent nations.

In March of 1936, Nazi troops remilitarized the Rhineland, a borderland between Germany and France. Once again, Hitler had broken terms of the peace agreement. Again, he got away with it.

By 1937, Hitler's military buildup was a massive operation. He was giving tours for important foreigners to admire his progress. Meanwhile Roosevelt continued promising that he would not send Americans to war on foreign soil. Each time he promised, he included the words "on foreign soil."

He was convinced that the United States would not be safe if Nazi aggression continued. If Germany went to war against France and Britain, the United States could not afford to be of no aid. But Americans were not with him. So he decided that he would allow his promise to the voters to work for him. In May of 1937 he persuaded Congress to pass another Neutrality Act that would allow him to sell arms to belligerents if they paid cash. He sold the plan, as he would sell others, with the idea that helping Europe fight its own wars would keep America from having to intervene.

In July, with the Spanish Civil War raging and Hitler egging General Franco on, Roosevelt had his own brainstorm about how to keep peace. He came up with the idea of offering his services to fifty-five nations as a national clearinghouse for international disputes. His deputies, fearing he would be rebuffed, proposed that, instead, he make a major address speaking against the aggression threatening Europe.

In October, FDR gave what came to be known as his Quarantine Speech. Given in Chicago, a hub of isolationist sentiment, the speech was his loudest public sounding of the alarm to date. "War is a contagion, whether it be declared or undeclared," he said, and aggressor nations must be quarantined. "If civilization is to survive, the principles of the Prince of Peace must be restored," he said. The speech, which was well received, proposed no sanctions. When reporters pressed him later on exactly what the United States would do to curb such aggressors, he responded with rare testiness, refusing to put teeth into the threat.

Roosevelt's New Deal had taken the country further to the left than any other president ever had. He did it by making sure Americans were with him. He paid close attention to polls, read letters, and had an astonishing number of conversations. "Franklin always said that no leader should get too far ahead of the people," noted Eleanor.[7] He also put it another way, saying that there was nothing worse for a leader than to look behind him and see that no one was following.

Checking in with the people's opinions had a sacred quality, was a sort of prayer for the president, historian Kenneth Davis believed. Roosevelt's knowledge of what voters were thinking and feeling was uncanny, Stanley High observed. "He is sensitive to the public as some people are sensitive to the weather. There is nothing general about it either. He can break down public opinion section by section. . . . I have heard awestruck Congressmen, with ears flattened from having so long been kept so close to the ground, admit after a conversation with the President that he knew more than they did about the state of mind of their constituents," noted High. Davis believed listening to the voices of the American people was one of the ways FDR thought God communicated with him. The president's reliance on waiting until the people were with him did not go uncriticized. Historian James MacGregor Burns characterized Roosevelt as a "pussyfooting politician" who in his first term "seemed to float almost helplessly on the flood tide of isolationism." Others were even harsher. Clare Boothe Luce said Roosevelt was "the only American president who ever lied us into a war because he did not have the political courage to lead us into it."[8] Luce also mocked him by saying that Hitler had the upraised arm as his salute and FDR had the upraised finger as his, testing the wind to see which way he should go.[9]

Hoover called him a "chameleon on plaid." H. L. Mencken saw the president's attention to public opinion as pure opportunism. He said that if FDR "became convinced tomorrow that coming out for cannibalism would get him the votes he so sorely needs he would begin fattening up a missionary in the White House backyard come Wednesday."[10]

But years after FDR's death, Russian-British philosopher Isaiah Berlin presented an entirely different view that seemed to justify even the president's failure to take earlier action on the war. Roosevelt's "extraordinarily sensitive antennae" allowed him to "to take in minute impressions, to integrate a vast multitude of small, evanescent, unseizable detail," said Berlin, who praised Roosevelt as a "magnificent virtuoso . . . the most benevolent as well as the greatest master of his craft" in modern times.

Roosevelt's keen attention to the ideas and feelings of citizens formed a bond between him and the American people that even the virulent opposition to him and his policies could not break. Despite his failures and faults, voters reelected FDR four times because they had an obscure feeling "that he was on their side, that he wished them well, and that he would do something for them," according to Berlin. "And this feeling gradually spread over the entire civilized world. He became a legendary hero—they themselves did not know quite why—to the indigent and oppressed far beyond the confines of the English-speaking world."[11]

Germany occupied Austria in March of 1938. On September 26, Roosevelt sent Hitler a telegram asking for peace. When Hitler rebuffed his request, he sent a follow-up letter on September 27 again urging peace. In October the führer engineered the worst German pogrom since the Middle Ages. During the rampage, called Kristallnacht or the "night of broken glass," synagogues were torched and homes ransacked. Fifteen hundred Jews were killed and thirty thousand were shipped to concentration camps. The threat Hitler posed was clear to *Time* magazine editors, who named him 1938's Man of the Year, calling him "the greatest threatening force that the democratic, freedom-loving world faces today."[12]

Since peace talk was all that Americans would listen to, Roosevelt continued to speak about peace. He had begun talking of peace from his first days as president, and he would continue through the war, mentioning it at least a hundred fifty times.[13] But now his messages began to be about what was and was not an acceptable kind of peace. That sort of talk sounded like a president at war—or one getting the country ready for a war. As he had in his New Deal speeches, Roosevelt called on biblical images, but now the enemy, instead of money changers in the temple, was those who deny freedoms to others. One of his themes was freedom of religion paired with democracy. In his January 1939 Annual Message to Congress, dictated to his speechwriters himself, Roosevelt explained,

> *Storms from abroad directly challenge three institutions indispensable to Americans, now as always. The first is religion. It is*

*the source of the other two—democracy and international good
faith. . . . Where freedom of religion has been attacked, the attack
has come from sources opposed to democracy. Where democracy
has been overthrown, the spirit of free worship has disappeared.
And where religion and democracy have vanished, good faith
and reason in international affairs have given way to strident
ambition and brute force.*

And then, again, he referred to the Prince of Peace.

*An ordering of society which relegates religion, democracy and
good faith among nations to the background can find no place
within it for the ideals of the Prince of Peace. The United States
rejects such an ordering, and retains its ancient faith.*[14]

That same month, the US State Department turned away the *St. Louis*,
a German passenger ship carrying six hundred German refugees, mostly
Jewish. Roosevelt did not intervene. The ship returned to European
countries that had not yet been attacked by Germans but would later be
conquered. Many of those on the ship died in concentration camps.

In February of 1939, a US bill to admit twenty thousand Jewish refugee children was introduced. It died in committee. In March, Hitler
invaded Czechoslovakia. That spring Roosevelt allowed the French to
place huge orders with the American aircraft industry on a cash-and-
carry basis, as allowed by law. On September 1, 1939, Germany invaded
Poland. On September 3, England and France declared war, honoring
their pledge to protect Poland. Knowing that Roosevelt was helpless
to respond and believing that Americans were a contaminated race of
mongrels, Hitler sneered in 1939, "America is not dangerous to us."[15]

It certainly looked that way. In February of 1940, Roosevelt aroused
the ire of many American Protestants by sending his personal envoy
to Pope Pius XII to try to enlist the pope in making peace and keeping
Mussolini from joining Hitler.[16] In a White House broadcast that was
ostensibly about Christian missionaries, he was still talking peace. And
to the ire of many isolationists he was still defining it as though peace
itself had to meet his standards of holiness.

*Today we seek a moral basis for peace. It cannot be a real peace if
it fails to recognize brotherhood. It cannot be a lasting peace if the
fruit of it is oppression, or starvation, or cruelty, or human life*

dominated by armed camps. It cannot be a sound peace if small nations must live in fear of powerful neighbors. It cannot be a moral peace if freedom from invasion is sold for tribute. It cannot be an intelligent peace if it denies free passage to that knowledge of those ideals which permit men to find common ground. It cannot be a righteous peace if worship of God is denied.[17]

If Hitler heard that speech, he must have sneered again. He didn't care what kind of peace America wanted.

But Roosevelt wouldn't let it alone. In April of 1939, the American president sent another letter to Hitler asking for peace. In response the führer read the letter mockingly at the Reichstag. The audience of German leaders laughed.

"There was something pathetic and yet almost sublime in the way that Roosevelt sent message after message to Hitler and other dictators. Partly, of course, it was for the record; but even more it was an expression of Roosevelt's faith in the ultimate goodness and reasonableness of all men," wrote Burns. "His eternal desire to talk directly to his enemies, whether congressmen or dictators, reflected his confidence in his own persuasiveness and, even more, in the essential ethical rightness of his own position." Only a man "deadly serious and supremely confident" could have spent the time Roosevelt did trying to elevate foreign leaders "who seemed to others to be beyond redemption."[18]

But the American president wasn't quite as helpless as he seemed to Hitler, or as afraid of war as Hitler might have thought. On May 28, FDR called General Motors president Bill Knudsen to ask how American manufacturing could begin making war machines.[19] In early 1940 Congress appropriated billions for a buildup of arms.

In the spring and summer of 1940, France, Belgium, Luxembourg, and the Netherlands fell to German forces. Roosevelt, fearing that an isolationist president might be elected, decided to run for a third term, winning the nomination in July. He sent Eleanor to speak for him at the convention, where his decision was controversial. She told the delegates after his nomination, "This is no ordinary time, no time for weighing anything except what we can do for the country as a whole."[20]

On September 2, 1940, President Roosevelt signed a "Destroyers for Bases" agreement. Under its terms, the United States gave the British more than fifty obsolete destroyers in exchange for ninety-nine-year leases to territory in Newfoundland and the Caribbean, which would be used as US air and naval bases.

On October 29, 1940, FDR held a lottery to decide who would be called up in the first peacetime draft in US history. His advisors had urged him to wait until after the election, but he refused. Sam Rosenman noted that the president wasn't listening to common political wisdom: "Any old time politician would have said [it] could never take place." The big fishbowl and long ladle that had been used during World War I to stir the cobalt capsules containing names of men who would go into battle held a selection of numbers that would decide which men were to be drafted first. The solemn president again talked of keeping the peace. Secretary of War Harold Stimson, blindfolded with a yellow strip of cloth from the covering of the chair used at the signing of the Declaration of Independence, drew the first lottery number. As the number 158 was announced, a scream rang out in the crowded auditorium. Mildred Bell recognized the number as that of her son, twenty-one-year-old Harry Bell, who was to be married the following week.

The next day as Roosevelt, in a rare mood of irritation, traveled by train to Boston to give a speech, he fielded a stream of messages from Democrats fearful that he would lose the election. They implored him to assure American mothers that he would not send their sons to Europe's war. After assuring the mothers and fathers of America that their boys would be well housed and well fed, he said, "I have said this before, but I shall say it again, and again. Your boys are not going to be sent into any foreign wars." His speechwriters included the words "unless attacked" in this speech as they had before, but the president insisted that they be left off.

"It's not necessary. It's implied clearly. If we're attacked it's no longer a foreign war," he argued. That omission would be cited by his enemies many times as proof that he had more warlike intentions than he admitted.[21]

On November 5, he won his third term by a comfortable margin against Wendell Willkie, a businessman who portrayed Roosevelt as president eager for war. In a fireside chat on December 29, 1940, Roosevelt declared the United States would be the "arsenal of democracy" sending armaments and supplies to Great Britain. Before the end of the chat, he indulged in an anger he seldom allowed to show, wrote Rex Tugwell.[22] The Nazis, he said, have "in their background the concentration camp and the servants of God in chains."

"The history of recent years proves that shootings and chains and concentration camps are not simply the transient tools but the very altars of modern dictatorships. They may talk of a 'new order' in the world, but what they have in mind is only a revival of the oldest and the worst tyranny. In that there is no liberty, no religion, no hope."

The apotheosis of FDR's prewar weaving together of war and morality may have been his Four Freedoms speech, delivered in his 1941 State of the Union address on January 6. Roosevelt saw these freedoms as a new bill of rights for the entire world. The first two, freedom of speech and freedom of worship, are guaranteed in the US Constitution. The last two were new: freedom from want and freedom from fear. These freedoms meant to Roosevelt that people everywhere are entitled to basic economic security and life in a country at peace.[23] As he had so many times in the New Deal, the president was casting a grand vision of how life on earth ought to be, but this time he wasn't talking about brotherhood. He was talking about war.

Throughout the speech, he used the four freedoms as values not shared by those seeking domination of the world through conquest and destruction. If the Axis forces won against the Allies, he said America would either be left without friends and conquered also, or be forced into an isolation that it could not survive. The old world where oceans and distance could protect the United States was gone.

"In times like these it is immature—and, incidentally, untrue—for anybody to brag that an unprepared America, single-handed and with one hand tied behind its back, can hold off the whole world . . . ," he said. "As a nation we may take pride in the fact that we are soft-hearted; but we cannot afford to be soft-headed. We must always be wary of those who with sounding brass and a tinkling cymbal preach the 'ism' of appeasement. We must especially beware of that small group of selfish men who would clip the wings of the American eagle in order to feather their own nests."[24]

It was pure Rooseveltian rhetoric: idealistic in concept with homey details and a bit of Bible thrown in to damn his enemies. This scriptural reference from I Corinthians 13:1 was taken completely out of context.

The verse refers to those who "have not charity" as being like "sounding brass and tinkling cymbals," not those who desire to stay out of war. But Roosevelt, had he been challenged, might have said lack of charity toward the world's suffering and Great Britain's valiant fight were at issue.

The Four Freedoms speech was popular, but it didn't convince Americans that they should send their sons to battle. The president, who could always play the long game, may not have expected so much so soon. He was steadily pulling away their certainties and still using their fear of war to soften isolationism. In March of 1941, he instituted the Lend-Lease program, which allowed him to supply Britain with the ships and planes it needed. It was like lending your neighbor a garden hose if his house was on fire, he told Americans in a fireside speech. Once the fire was out, your neighbor would give the hose back.

Then came the summer of 1941. On August 9 Churchill and Roosevelt were to meet face to face for the first time in Placentia Bay off the coast of Newfoundland to discuss the war and draw up the Atlantic Charter, an eight-point agreement that set goals for the postwar world. The British were desperate to have concrete American help. Without it, they might very well lose the war. Having the United States join in a plan for after Britain won the war committed the United States in a way it had never been committed before.

Hoping he would get some assurance of intervention, the British prime minister fretted over every detail of the meetings. In a curious oversight for Roosevelt, freedom of religion was not included in the eight points of the Atlantic Charter. But Churchill, well aware of FDR's religious leanings, planned to stir the president's heart with hymns, prayers, and the faces of young men in uniform.

Arising early on that Saturday, standing on the admiral's bridge of the HMS *Prince of Wales* just after dawn, Churchill looked toward the horizon asking, "Can you see any sign of them yet?"

"You'd have thought Winston was being carried up into the heavens to meet God," said Roosevelt aide Harry Hopkins, who was already aboard the ship.[25] A high point of the meeting was to be a religious service that Churchill had arranged for Sunday morning to elevate Roosevelt's romantic and religious soul. "We have a grand day for a church parade, and I have chosen some grand hymns," Churchill announced before the service. He had selected the three hymns himself and vetted the prayers by having them read to him while he dried after his bath. American and British chaplains would read the prayers from behind a lectern draped with the Union Jack and the Stars and Stripes. Churchill and Roosevelt would sit side by side, with their subordinates standing behind them. Sailors from both sides would stand in ranks beneath the ship's big guns. Before the president arrived, Churchill nervously went about straightening chairs and smoothing a fold in the Union Jack.

As the Royal Marines played "The Star Spangled Banner," Roosevelt, who was determined that he would not use a wheelchair, made his perilous way across the deck to the chairs. The men watching could see that every step caused him pain, but his face was a "calm, carved face, the face of St. George who has trampled the dragon under him," noted one observer. The first hymn with British and Americans sharing hymnals, voices intermingled, floated over the sea:

O God, our help in ages past,
Our hope for years to come,
Our shelter from the stormy blast . . .

Chaplains recited the Anglican General Confession:

Almighty and most merciful Father;
We have erred, and strayed from thy ways like lost sheep.
We have followed too much the devices and desires of our own hearts.
We have offended against thy holy laws. . . .

And then they recited the Lord's Prayer. By the time they began to sing the second hymn, "Onward Christian Soldiers," Churchill was weeping into a handkerchief.

A reading from the book of Joshua included the words: "Be strong and of a good courage; be not afraid: for the Lord thy God is with thee whithersoever thou goest." British writer H. V. Morton was also there and wrote about the scene:

> In the long, frightful panorama of this war, a panorama full of guns and tanks crushing the life out of men, of women and children weeping and of homes blasted into rubble by bombs, there had been no scene like this, a scene, it seemed, from

another world, conceived on lines different from anything known to the pageant-masters of the Axis, a scene rooted in the first principles of European civilization which go back to the figure of Charlemagne kneeling before the Pope on Christmas morning.

The last hymn was "Eternal Father, Strong to Save," traditionally regarded as "The Navy Hymn." "It was a great hour to live," wrote Churchill later. "Nearly half who sung were soon to die." Four months later the *Prince of Wales* was sunk off the coast of Malaya by Japanese bombers.[26]

Churchill's "church parade" touched Roosevelt as deeply as the prime minister hoped it would. He told his son Elliott afterward, "If nothing else happened while we were here, that would have cemented us. Onward Christian Soldiers. We are, and we will go on, with God's help." He later wrote to his cousin Daisy Suckley that as he looked over the men who had so much faith and so many values in common, "it swept across me that here was the only hope, but also the sure hope, of saving the world from measureless degradation."[27] To reporters he called the religious observance "one of the great historic services."

He had been stirred by the service, he had been charmed by Churchill, and he had been roused by Britain's need. He left with Churchill believing the United States might enter the war. But like so many others, Churchill thought Roosevelt was going to do more than he intended. Once he returned home, Roosevelt continued to tell Americans that he was not going to send their sons to war.

Hitler had been careful to avoid attacking American ships. But in October of 1941, the American destroyer USS *Kearney* off the coast of Greenland was summoned to help a British convoy being torpedoed by German U-boats. Although the *Kearney* dropped depth charges and the Germans torpedoed the US ship, it was not sunk. Roosevelt railed against the aggression, but Americans did not clamor for revenge. That fall he announced he had proof of a German "plan to abolish all existing religion—Catholic, Protestant, Mohammedan, Hindu, Buddhist, and Jewish alike. The property of all churches will be seized by the Reich and its puppets. The cross and all other symbols of religion are to be forbidden. The clergy are to be forever liquidated, silenced under penalty of the concentration camps, where even now so many fearless men are being tortured because they have placed God above Hitler." That kind of rhetoric ought to have aroused Americans' war spirit. But it didn't. The plans to abolish religions were fake, which Roosevelt may have known from his World War I experience of British propaganda tactics, but what the Nazis actually were doing was even worse.

On December 6, 1941, Roosevelt made another peace appeal. This time he sent Emperor Hirohito of Japan a cable seeking to avoid war in the Pacific. Japanese were already fighting China and had begun sending troops and ships to South Indo-China. "There is absolutely no thought on the part of the United States of invading Indo-China if every Japanese soldier or sailor were to be withdrawn from there," he wrote.

> I think that we can obtain the same assurance from the Governments of the East Indies, the Governments of Malaya, and the Government of Thailand. I would even undertake to ask for the same assurance on the part of the Government of China. Thus a withdrawal of the Japanese forces from Indo-China would result in the assurance of peace throughout the whole of the South Pacific area.

He ended the letter by writing that both countries "have a sacred duty to restore traditional amity and prevent further death and destruction in the world." At about 9:30 that evening, FDR received word that Japan had landed troops Indochina. He told Harry Hopkins, who was with him in his office, that war was now certain. When Hopkins suggested that it was too bad the United States couldn't strike first instead of waiting for Japan's next move, the president replied, "No, we can't do that. We are a democracy and a peaceful people."

The next morning, December 7, 1941, the attack on Pearl Harbor took the matter out of Roosevelt's hands. On December 8, he asked Congress to declare war on Japan. Hitler honored Germany's commitment to Japan and declared war on the United States. Americans were ready for war now, no more persuading needed.

Eleanor and Franklin D. Roosevelt at the Gubernatorial Inauguration in Albany,
New York, in 1929.

IMAGE COURTESY OF THE FRANKLIN DELANO ROOSEVELT PRESIDENTIAL LIBRARY

13

THE PRESIDENT AND PRIEST

Once the United States entered World War II, Roosevelt left the role of Dr. New Deal, a name he gave himself reminiscent of his days in Warm Springs, when he first began referring to himself jokingly as "Doc." He became Dr. Win the War. In terms of national and international brotherhood, FDR fell short in ways that are still counted against him. He allowed Japanese Americans to be sent to camps, forfeiting their property and businesses. He allowed firebombing of German cities, resulting in tremendous loss of civilian lives. Both those actions continue to tarnish his reputation. Controversy over his lack of action to save Jewish lives continues to this day. He didn't admit as many Jewish refugees as he could have. He didn't bomb Auschwitz or railway lines that carried Jews and others to death camps. Whether his decisions and lack of action were justified or criminally negligent is still disputed.[1]

He termed the Axis alliance an unholy force and cast the war in terms of good and evil so frequently that some accused him of waging holy war. The D-Day prayer he and his daughter Anna wrote has become perhaps the most famous American prayer.[2] He kept freedom of religion front and center when he talked of why the Allies must win the war. He equated American victory with a victory for God. Not surprisingly, Germans did the same. Engraved on Wehrmacht belt buckles during World War II were the words *Gott mit uns*, "God with us." Roosevelt's use of religion during the war was far less novel than his use of it during the New Deal.

⊷═◉═⊷

One White House meeting during the war years provides a glimpse of what Roosevelt's very private faith might have looked like. By 1944, the massive number of atrocities committed by the Nazis was beginning to be known. As the horror mounted, it became clear that this wasn't merely a war of international aggression like so many others. It was a war waged by people so cruelly savage on such a great scale that Western civilization's most basic faith in its own goodness was shaken and would never quite recover.

Hitler's survival-of-the-fittest philosophy when applied to humans as though they were animals in the wild had justified setting up extermination camps where humans could be killed by the tens of thousands each day. German troops had initially shot those whose supposed inferiority meant they should die. But as the Nazis overran Poland and invaded Russia, some five million Jews came within their reach. By 1942, Hitler's Final Solution, which was to clear Europe of Jews, by killing them outright or deporting them to work camps where they would die from starvation and overwork, was being put into effect. As killings went from the hundreds into the thousands, soldiers in the firing squads began to have nervous breakdowns. Execution of such numbers by gunfire simply wasn't practical. Special extermination camps with huge ovens where groups of humans could be gassed and then cremated were the Nazi answer. Having one of the most cultured, civilized countries in the world methodically apply its highly vaunted efficiency to mass murder and unspeakable atrocity caused people everywhere to question what civilization meant, to wonder what humans were capable of.

FDR was among them. He could not understand how so many Germans could be as evil as Hitler convinced them to be. An explanation that satisfied him finally arrived in a way so shrouded in mystery and so utterly unlikely, given FDR's nature, that scholars still puzzle over exactly why it so affected Roosevelt.

On the evening of February 19, 1944, when the Reverend Howard Johnson came for dinner at the White House, World War II was far from over. The siege of Leningrad had ended on January 27, but the D-Day invasion of German-occupied Europe was still three and a half months away. Johnson, twenty-nine years old, served at St. John's Episcopal Church, which is directly across Pennsylvania Avenue from the White House. Johnson received his invitation after Eleanor spoke to a church group. He wrote her a thank-you note saying that he would be happy to help to her in any way possible. She replied with the idea that he might come to dinner with her and the president.

The next day an engraved invitation arrived for him. Such invitations were not unusual. Eleanor had expanded her role as the eyes and ears of the president in ways he didn't always appreciate—for example, by inviting people to dine with them at the White House when he sometimes wanted nothing but a quiet meal. Roosevelt protested the frequent parade of strangers at his dinner table. As in other matters where they did not agree, Eleanor continued to behave as she thought best.

The Reverend Johnson walked over from the church on the night of his invitation. He had been so nervous about the dinner that he consulted a friend about what to wear and how he ought to act. His friend assured him that he would be among a party of about a dozen people and most likely wouldn't attract too much attention. But after presenting his invitation to the White House butler, Johnson was not ushered into a dining room, as he expected. Instead, after taking his hat and coat, the butler led him into the personal quarters of the First Family, down a long hall and to a closed door. When the butler knocked, Johnson heard a voice familiar to millions of Americans call out, "Come in."

To his bewilderment, he entered the president's oval study where the president was waiting, alone. A sterling silver cocktail shaker with a bamboo motif and six matching cups sat on a tray at his desk, along with various types of liquor. Johnson had arrived at what Roosevelt termed "the children's hour," a daily cocktail hour when the president delighted in mixing drinks for himself and guests. Johnson accepted the president's offer of a martini, which Roosevelt mixed without measuring. He prided himself on constantly tinkering with the ingredients in the drinks he served, sometimes adding fruit juice, absinthe, Benedictine, or varying amounts of gin and vermouth. His drinks were invariably and notoriously bad, either because of his experiments or, as many believed, because he only served cheap liquor.

Ill at ease, Johnson politely asked after the president's health. FDR assured him that he was doing fine. Amid their small talk, the president mentioned that he was reading a mystery by British writer Dorothy Sayers. It included scenes from Groton, the prep school Roosevelt and his sons had attended. FDR was especially intrigued by passages about the bells of the chapel ringing, because there had been no such bells when he was a student there.

FDR liked bantering about trivial matters during the children's hour. If Roosevelt had been reading any of the other crime story authors he enjoyed, the conversation might have remained in the light vein that FDR preferred during that time of day, and Roosevelt might have done most of the talking, as per usual. Anything too emotional, serious, or unpleasant was unwelcome at that hour. Faced with a tedious guest or one who might bring up a topic he didn't care to discuss, Roosevelt was adept at telling stories, making jokes, and otherwise eating up the oxygen until time was up, and the visitor was ushered out wondering what exactly happened.

Johnson would hardly have dared to foist his erudite theological opinions on the president without an appropriate opening, and perhaps a second martini. The president rarely had more than a single drink, but he loved encouraging his guests to have just one more. He could be so insistent that Rosenman, who didn't care for alcohol at all, took to pouring his in the potted plants when the president wasn't looking.

Johnson knew, as FDR did not, that Sayers was not only an author of mysteries but also a Christian humanist renowned for her theological writings. "You know, of course, that many moderns like Dorothy Sayers derive from Kierkegaard," Johnson said to the president.

"Who is Kierkegaard?" asked Roosevelt. The president got most of his information from the people he talked to. Admitting he didn't know something caused him no embarrassment at all. Søren Kierkegaard, who wasn't well known in the United States at that time, had lived in Copenhagen during the mid-1800s. Kierkegaard had been recognized mostly among theologians who could read Danish until recently, when his work was translated into English. Often called "the melancholy Dane," Kierkegaard was particularly important to the young priest. His own strong

Christian faith had led him to enter seminary, but while there his faith had faltered. He might have given it up if he hadn't read Kierkegaard's work.

The president's question, of course, was an invitation to expound that Johnson could not possibly resist. The priest described the Dane's philosophy, including man's natural sinfulness and helplessness to reform himself except by the grace and help of God. Kierkegaard believed in original sin, but not in the sense that it was inherited from Adam. Rather, he believed each person was born with this fallen nature and was responsible for it.

Somehow this discussion caused FDR to reflect that he was completely unable to understand a man such as Adolf Hitler. How could anyone do such evil things? Perhaps this question was asked only in a musing sort of way. FDR had possibly asked it rhetorically as he might have many times over the years as reports came in detailing the special horrors Nazis were inflicting on the world. But as chance would have it, this was a question that Johnson had an answer for. The Kierkegaardian answer was a venture into heavy theology, not at all FDR's usual territory. That the president would ever find himself not only listening to a conversation of such deep theological substance, but actively engaged in it, is one part of that night's mystery. The president listened more than he talked that night; he even took notes of books he might want to read.

Kierkegaard believed that proofs of God's existence or meditations on whether God existed were useless. God did not need to be proven by objective facts, and maybe he couldn't be proven to exist by such facts. But that didn't matter because God was a subjective truth already known to each person. The philosopher took from Socrates the idea that humans already know the truth. It is within them all the time, but they aren't aware of what they know. "Thus the ignorant person merely needs to be reminded in order by himself to call to mind what he [already] knows," Kierkegaard wrote. In the Socratic view, "every human being is himself the midpoint, and the whole world focuses only on him because his self-knowledge is God knowledge."

In order to recall what he knows, each person needs a teacher, who may be a wise, learned person or completely ignorant, according to Socrates. All the teacher does is pose some question that opens up this self-knowledge, which is actually God knowledge.

Kierkegaard took this idea in a more theological direction. He believed that only Jesus could open a person to this God knowledge that was within everyone. In order to reach Jesus, a person must come to God "naked and trembling" to ask for forgiveness of sins. The Danish theologian also believed that "faith passionate and sustained—even in the midst of his sins"—is what saves man. Roosevelt, of course, famously believed in the power of faith to save humans—faith of all kinds, in God, in humanity, in the future, in oneself. He also had faith in salvation not merely in heaven but on earth, too.

"Roosevelt already believed, like Kierkegaard himself, that the life of faith was a life of interactions with God's guiding, chiding, accusing, and forgiving Spirit, not one of mystic reverie of an alone with the Alone," wrote John F. Woolverton, professor and former editor of the *Journal of Anglican and Episcopal History*.[3]

A few days after the dinner with Johnson, Roosevelt recommended to Secretary of Labor Frances Perkins that she ought to read Kierkegaard because his writings "would teach you something." "Kierkegaard explains the Nazis to me," Roosevelt said, "as nothing else ever has. I have never been able to make out why people who are obviously human beings could behave like that. They are human, yet they behave like demons." Kierkegaard, he declared, "gives you an understanding of what is in man that makes it possible for these Germans to be so evil. This fellow, Johnson, over at St. John's knows a lot about Kierkegaard and his theories. You'd better read him."

The Dane believed that once a person's own God knowledge is revealed to him, he gains a sense of peace, of security, and release from fear. This description fits every known description of President Roosevelt in even the direst situations he faced—from being the target of an assassin to the collapse of the country's economy to the destruction of the Pacific fleet by the Japanese. He did not flinch. He did not show the agitation that might be expected from any human being.

The converse situation, as described by Kierkegaard, seemed to fit Hitler and his followers. A person who refuses to access this God knowledge is unable to access his own God wisdom and unable to be his own true self. Left without the divine comfort that is available to him, he becomes anxious and fearful. Out of this fear finally comes despair. From despair comes defiance. He begins to feel misused and hangs on to past grievances, which, as they grow larger and larger, give him justification to behave as his truncated nature bids him.

Two parts of the Dane's theology are particularly interesting with regard to Roosevelt. First there is the Kierkegaardian image of a sinner coming naked and trembling before God. As has been noted, FDR was not a tortured soul. Naked and trembling was as far from his style as anything could be. But Roosevelt might have experienced such a moment during his days of paralysis after polio. His despair and sense that God had deserted him were intense. He transcended those feelings, converting his affliction into a test that he was determined to pass. FDR's enthusiastic endorsement of Kierkegaard's ideas would argue that Roosevelt had experienced complete surrender before God, a rather startling image when applied to a man as private, emotionally restrained, and ambitious as Roosevelt.

The second part of Kierkegaard's theology is the idea that this God knowledge unlocks deep truths inside everyone. Kierkegaard never said what the God knowledge inside each person was. Given Roosevelt's reticence to speak of intimate matters and his aversion to too much deep thinking, it's no surprise that in speaking to Perkins, he didn't elaborate on that subject either. But two of the deepest truths that Roosevelt proclaimed and lived stand out as more otherworldly than all the rest. One comes from his Episcopal faith, which taught him that God was incarnate in him and in the world. This idea led him to believe that God had a mission for him, and that the Almighty would help him accomplish that mission. Roosevelt would do his part and God would do his. It's an idea that gives life meaning, sustains optimism about the future, and provides believers with a sense of power beyond what they might have on their own.

The second idea that FDR believed and tried to teach the country is that each group is interconnected with every other group. If one suffers, the others will suffer, too. If one prospers, the others prosper, too. He was showing that the world is of a piece—not an unusual religious idea, but it's more likely to come from monks than politicians. He didn't put it in the kind of philosophical terms Kierkegaard would have. He used the simple language that he generally used, the same language he seemed to think in.

He said it many times. It's worth repeating in the context of Kierkegaard's God knowledge idea because it illustrates so well how brilliant Roosevelt was at putting complex ideas simply. After touring the Dust Bowl in 1936, he presented this idea in one of his fireside chats.

The very existence of the men and women working in the cloth-ing factories of New York, making clothes worn by farmers and their families; of the workers in the steel mills in Pittsburgh, in the automobile factories of Detroit, and in the harvester factories of Illinois, depends upon the farmers' ability to purchase the commodities they produce. In the same way it is the purchasing power of the workers in these factories in the cities that enables them and their wives and children to eat more beef, more pork, more wheat, more corn, more fruit and more dairy products, and to buy more clothing made from cotton, wool and leather. In a physical and a property sense, as well as in a spiritual sense, we are members one of another.

When he says this last sentence, it sounds like nothing more than common sense. Something everybody knows—or could know if they weren't so distracted by greed and self-serving, if they weren't so afraid. "We are members one of another." Most people don't have that view. Some people get glimpses of it, but the glimpses fade and are almost forgotten.

If that is part of God knowledge and if Roosevelt knew it, the riddle of that man so often called the Sphinx would be closer to being solved. During long walks in the woods as a boy, during prayers for his father's survival, during lonely days at Groton, while lying paralyzed, while laughing with those hopeless Warm Springs refugees in their chairs and on their crutches, the God knowledge that is inside all of us might have come to him and stayed with him until it became a part of him that didn't fade away. If the God knowledge that Franklin Roosevelt came to know was "we are members one of another," it would have seemed only reasonable to him that society's laws should reflect that reality.

Perhaps it was that knowledge which caused him to act as he did and made so many people love and trust him. Perhaps knowledge of creation's essential oneness kept him believing that great moral progress was be-ing made. What else but a completely otherworldly vision of life's true meaning would cause this practical politician to proclaim so boldly:

We are beginning to wipe out the line that divides the practical from the ideal; and in so doing we are fashioning an instrument of unimagined power for the establishment of a morally better world. This new understanding undermines the old admiration of worldly success as such. We are beginning to abandon our tolerance of the abuse of power by those who betray for profit the elementary decencies of life. In this process evil things formerly accepted will not be so easily condoned. Hard-headedness will not so easily excuse hardheartedness.

He was wrong, of course. America did not become that place. Those ideals were not earthly.

Washington, Lincoln, and FDR are often named as the country's three greatest presidents. Washington brought the country together. Lincoln divided it and also would not allow it to be divided. Roosevelt was a uniter and a divider to an extraordinary degree. After more than eighty-five years his legacy is still under attack, as are many of the programs he created. The religious underpinnings of his achievements are directly linked to the Judeo-Christian beliefs he held. Those beliefs didn't create God's kingdom on earth, but nor did they perish. Despite all Hitler's efforts, neither did the Jewish people.

Perhaps one of the great Jewish prophets ought to have the last word. "What doth the Lord require of thee, but to do justly, and to love mercy, and to walk humbly with thy God?"[4]

Epilogue

When Franklin Roosevelt died, the *New York Times* declared that in a hundred years people would be thanking God on their knees for him. We're not too far from the hundred-year mark, and that does not seem to be happening. FDR's social welfare programs are still at the center of bitter controversy. In the meantime, much of the developed world has surpassed the United States in providing security for its citizens. The "American dream" is more likely to be fulfilled in a number of other countries, researchers tell us. And American Christianity seems to be dominated by a merger of self-interest and holiness.

From the time of the European discovery of America, the highest ideals and the lowest motives have been in constant tension in the country. As the world is once again being roiled by a new technology that creates new jobs and destroys old ones in ways that no one can foresee, that tension is once again heightened. Violence that threatens the entire world still flares around the world. Religion is often at the heart of the conflict.

The question of right and wrong is as difficult to answer as it ever was.

Anytime researchers look back on a great leader's life, or their own lives for that matter, it's easy to discern patterns that seem to have been created by forces greater than chance. Franklin Roosevelt's life provides a stronger pattern of what might be considered divine interference than many lives.

The question that occurs to many people then and now is: Did God raise up a man to rescue the United States in the Great Depression and to defeat Hitler? Following that line of thinking, we would have to ask, who raised Hitler up? Satan? A punishing God? Or is there no God?

The deeper we go into those questions, the harder it is to find a guide that will help us know right from wrong. Both Hitler and FDR quoted scripture. Millions of people thought Hitler was pure goodness. If we were looking toward success as our gauge, we might agree. Germany, not a very big country, came close to conquering the world.

Ironically, perhaps, considering that Hitler's survival-of-the-fittest philosophy was based on a misuse of science, one gauge of good and evil comes from a scientific idea: that every examination of any idea or result must start by considering the original premise. Hitler's original premise tilted away from love for all of humanity. FDR's tilted toward it. He believed that God expected him to make the world a better place for everybody.

Hitler's premise was that humans are merely animals and must act like animals. Any deviation from the ability to destroy the weak (and those preaching the false doctrine of compassion) would mean doom for all of humanity. FDR's premise was that humans are joined with their creator in making the world a better place, not only for themselves but for each other.

Hitler was talking about how to survive. He took a scientific idea further than was intended. He made a moral injunction out of what was merely a theory of how life on earth developed.

Roosevelt was talking about how to flourish.

The late author David Foster Wallace talked about flourishing during a commencement speech at Kenyon College in 2005. Some of what he said speaks directly to why it matters to know what FDR worshipped. As in everything Wallace pondered, he did a far better job than I can ever do. So here's some of what he said:

> There is no such thing as not worshipping. Everybody worships. The only choice we get is what to worship. And the compelling reason for maybe choosing some sort of god or spiritual-type thing to worship—be it JC or Allah, be it YHWH or the Wiccan Mother Goddess, or the Four Noble Truths, or some inviolable set of ethical principles—is that pretty much anything else you worship will eat you alive. If you worship money and things, if they are where you tap real meaning in life, then you will never have enough, never feel you have enough. It's the truth. Worship your body and beauty and sexual allure and you will always feel ugly. And when time and age start showing, you will die a million deaths before they finally grieve you. On one level, we all know

this stuff already. It's been codified as myths, proverbs, clichés, epigrams, parables; the skeleton of every great story. The whole trick is keeping the truth up front in daily consciousness.

Worship power, you will end up feeling weak and afraid, and you will need ever more power over others to numb you to your own fear. Worship your intellect, be seen as smart, you will end up feeling stupid, a fraud, always on the verge of being found out. But the insidious thing about these forms of worship is not that they're evil or sinful, it's that they're unconscious. They are default settings.

They're the kind of worship you just gradually slip into, day after day, getting more and more selective about what you see and how you measure value without ever being fully aware that that's what you're doing.

And the so-called real world will not discourage you from operating on your default settings, because the so-called real world of men and money and power hums merrily along in a pool of fear and anger and frustration and craving and worship of self. Our own present culture has harnessed these forces in ways that have yielded extraordinary wealth and comfort and personal freedom. The freedom all to be lords of our tiny skull-sized kingdoms, alone at the center of all creation. This kind of freedom has much to recommend it. But of course there are all different kinds of freedom, and the kind that is most precious you will not hear much talk about much in the great outside world of wanting and achieving. . . . The really important kind of freedom involves attention and awareness and discipline, and being able truly to care about other people and to sacrifice for them over and over in myriad petty, unsexy ways every day.

That is real freedom. That is being educated, and understanding how to think. The alternative is unconsciousness, the default setting, the rat race, the constant gnawing sense of having had, and lost, some infinite thing.

I know that this stuff probably doesn't sound fun and breezy or grandly inspirational the way a commencement speech is supposed to sound. What it is, as far as I can see, is the capital-T Truth, with a whole lot of rhetorical niceties stripped away. You are, of course, free to think of it whatever you wish. But please *don't just dismiss it as just some finger-wagging Dr. Laura ser-mon. None of this stuff is really about morality or religion or dogma or big fancy questions of life after death.*

The capital-T Truth is about life BEFORE death.

NOTES

Author's Preface

1. Proverbs 22:6 (King James Version).

2. A few years ago, I rejoined a Baptist church in Dallas, one that recently agreed to admit LGBTQ members with full rights to marry, to be deacons, and to be ordained. That decision caused my church to be ousted from the Texas Baptist General Convention.

Introduction

1. Timothy Snyder, *Black Earth: The Holocaust as History and Warning* (New York: Tim Duggan Books, 2015). Ironically perhaps, both looked to American history for guidance. Snyder points out that Hitler, who grew up reading books about the American West, culled his lessons from the country's shameful actions towards Native Americans: massacres, blankets infected with smallpox virus, and broken treaties.

Hitler, gazing with envy on the vast and fertile lands of the United States, reflected on how settlers seized territory by killing and imprisoning Native Americans who had lived in those lands for centuries. As a result of the land grabs, US farm output was so great even in the midst of the Great Depression that milk was being poured into gutters, fruit was being left to rot in the fields, and so many pigs were being bred that they would eventually be slaughtered and their carcasses buried. Germany, in contrast, didn't have enough crop land to feed its population even when times were good. "Neither the current living space nor that achieved through the restoration of the borders of 1914 permits us to lead a life comparable to that of the American people," according to Hitler. And that was unacceptable.

Germany was in much the same situation as the American settlers had been, Hitler concluded; Germans, a superior race, were unable to gain the farmland they needed because they were locked in by countries filled with inferior people. Poland was such a country, in his reckoning. Taking Darwinian scientific ideas about the survival of the fittest as a political mandate, he determined that Germans ought to wage war on their "inferiors," just as Americans had. Adolf Hitler, *Mein Kampf*, Chapter XI, https://archive.org/stream/MeinKampf _472/ MeinKampf_djvu.txt.

> We ought to remember that during the first period of American colonization numerous Aryans earned their daily livelihood as trappers and hunters, etc., frequently wandering about in large groups with their women and children, their mode of existence very much resembling that of

ordinary nomads. The moment, however, that they grew more numerous and were able to accumulate larger resources, they cleared the land and drove out the aborigines, at the same time establishing settlements which rapidly increased all over the country. . . . But in North America the Teutonic element, which has kept its racial stock pure and did not mix it with any other racial stock, has come to dominate the American Continent and will remain master of it as long as that element does not fall a victim to the habit of adulterating its blood.

2. "The beloved community" is a phrase that was often used by the Reverend Dr. Martin Luther King Jr. to mean a society based on equality, justice, and love for all humans. It's the vision of a world in which hunger, homelessness, and poverty would not be allowed because people would share Earth's bounty. www.huffingtonpost.com/jeffrey-ritterman/the-beloved-community-dr -_b_4583249.html.

3. Thomas H. Greer, *What Roosevelt Thought: The Social and Political Ideas of Franklin D. Roosevelt* (East Lansing: Michigan State University Press, 2000), 3.

4. Hitler, *Mein Kampf*.

5. Eric Metaxas, *Bonhoeffer: Pastor, Martyr, Prophet, Spy: A Righteous Gentile vs. the Third Reich* (Nashville: Thomas Nelson, 2010). Among those he imprisoned and murdered were Christians, pacifists, the mentally and physically disabled, LGBTQ people, Romani, communists, socialists, and Jews.

6. The Twenty-Second Amendment of the US Constitution, ratified by the states in 1951, limited presidential terms to two.

7. William J. Federer, *The Faith of FDR: From President Franklin Delano Roosevelt's Public Papers, 1933–1945* (St. Louis: Amerisearch, 2006).

8. Other presidents had used speechwriters, but he was the first president to use such a large team of them. Many were part of the so-called Brain Trust, a group of mostly university professors he had gathered to advise him before and after his first election. Louis Howe, who had been Roosevelt's closest adviser since his days in the New York State Senate, said people were always asking during the campaign, "Who ghostwrites FDR's speeches for him?"

"There is no actual ghost-writer," he said. "What Franklin does is to take all the data presented to him in a given subject and write it in his own way, incorporating a paragraph here and a paragraph there which has been given to him."

Other writers who worked for Roosevelt back Howe up. Speechwriters Samuel Rosenman, Robert Sherwood, Raymond Moley, and Rexford Tugwell all said the words in his speeches were his, whether written by them or not. Sherwood said that the speechwriters were like ghosts "haunting the White House day and night, until a speech by Franklin D. Roosevelt (and nobody else) has been produced."

The greatest controversy over his speeches came from economist and Columbia University professor Raymond Moley, a key speechwriter for FDR. Years after Roosevelt's death, Moley claimed that he had written the president's first inaugural address, and Roosevelt had copied it over in his own hand so that he could take credit. Moley presented notes taken at the time that seemed to back up his claim. But they aren't definitive proof, to many scholars' minds.

Some people have contended that Roosevelt didn't know enough about scripture to have included as many references to it as were present in his speeches. But facts suggests otherwise. He often did business in the morning while still in bed, next to which a worn copy of the *Episcopal Book of Common Prayer* rested on a white-painted table. Even during the short time that Stanley High was close to Roosevelt, he noticed a book about Jesus's Sermon on the Mount on his bedside table.

Frances Perkins said FDR often read the Bible, referred to it in conversation with her, and could quote passages of it. But even if he never read the Bible while president, Roosevelt had a remarkable memory. During his four years at Groton, he had received doses of scripture, prayer, and sermonizing, not just every day but many times every day.

9. James MacGregor Burns, *Roosevelt: The Lion and the Fox* (San Diego: Harcourt, Brace & World, 1984), 476–77.

10. Jon Meacham, *Franklin and Winston: An Intimate Portrait of an Epic Friendship* (New York: Random House 2003), 119.

1. "Plump, Pink, and Nice"

1. Frank Freidel, *Franklin D. Roosevelt: A Rendezvous with Destiny*, 1st ed. (Boston: Little, Brown, 1990), 6.

2. One of the most famous stories of FDR's childhood dates from when he was five and was taken to the White House to see his father's friend, President Grover Cleveland. Placing his massive hand on Franklin's head, a sad and weary Cleveland said, "My little man. I am making a strange wish for you. It is that you may never be President of the United States." Luckily he did not get his wish. What poor Cleveland found to be such a burden, Franklin would find to be a complete delight. Rita Halle Kleeman, *Gracious Lady: The Life of Sara Delano Roosevelt* (New York: D. Appleton-Century Company, 1935), 146, 150–67.

3. Stanley High, *Roosevelt . . . and Then* (New York: Harper and Brothers, 1937). Universal Digital Library, https://archive.org/details/rooseveltandthen00125imb.

4. Ibid.

5. Kleeman, *Gracious Lady*, 134.

6. Geoffrey C. Ward, *Before the Trumpet: Young Franklin Roosevelt, 1882–1905*, 1st ed. (New York: Harper & Row, 1985), 223.

7. Henry C. Potter, "The Address Delivered at St. Paul's Chapel . . . On the One Hundredth Anniversary of George Washington's Inauguration," April 30, 1889, http://anglicanhistory.org/usa/hcpotter/washington1889.html.

8. William Turner Levy and Cynthia Eagle Russett, *The Extraordinary Mrs. R: A Friend Remembers Eleanor Roosevelt* (New York: John Wiley, 1999), 2.

9. Doug Wead, *The Raising of a President: The Mothers and Fathers of Our Nation's Leaders* (New York: Simon and Schuster, 2005), 387.

10. Ward, *Before the Trumpet*, 155–56.

11. Harvey J. Kaye, *The Fight for the Four Freedoms: What Made FDR and the Greatest Generation Truly Great* (New York: Simon & Schuster, 2014), 36.

2. School Days

1. Sara prided herself on Franklin's ability to act like an adult exhibiting what she called "a kind of kinship with older people." Ward, *Before the Trumpet*, 126.

2. Frank Kintrea, "Old Peabo' and the School," *American Heritage*, November 1980, www.americanheritage.com/content/"old-peabo"-and-school.

3. Richard Bissell, *You Can Always Tell a Harvard Man* (New York: McGraw-Hill, 1962), 162.

4. Ward, *Before the Trumpet*, 199–202.

5. James L. Goodwin, a classmate of FDR's, cited in Bissell, *You Can Always Tell a Harvard Man*, 163.

6. Peabody was born in 1857 and died in 1944, the year before FDR died.

7. Clifford Putney, *Muscular Christianity: Manhood and Sports in Protestant America, 1880–1820* (Cambridge, MA: Harvard University Press, 2003), 107; James McLachlan, *American Boarding Schools: A Historical Study* (New York: Scribner's, 1970), 245–47.

8. Louis Auchincloss, *A Writer's Capital* (Minneapolis: University of Minnesota Press, 1974), https://openlibrary.org/books/OL5440912M/A_writer's_capital.?v=1.

9. Kathleen Dalton, speech at Groton School, *Peabody Press*, April 2015, http://relationsmith.com/grotonschool/14-15/apr15/apr15.html.

10. Frank Davis Ashburn, *Peabody of Groton, a Portrait*, 2nd ed. (New York: Riverside Press, 1967), 104.

11. Ashburn, *Peabody of Groton*, 107.

12. Ibid., 109.

13. Arthur M. Schlesinger Jr., *The Crisis of the Old Order, 1919–1933*, 1st Mariner Books ed., *The Age of Roosevelt*, vol. 1 (Boston: Houghton Mifflin, 2003), 162.

14. Ward, *Before the Trumpet*, 191.

15. S. Warren Sturgis, "The Religious and Missionary Work at Groton," *The Church Militant* 3, no. 3 (April 1900): 6.

16. James W. Fowler, *Stages of Faith: The Psychology of Human Development and the Quest for Meaning* (San Francisco: HarperCollins, 1981), 151–52; Erik Erikson, *Youth, Identity and Crisis* (New York: W. W. Norton & Co., 1994).

17. Meacham, *Franklin and Winston*, 17.

18. Kintrea, "Old Peabo' and the School."

19. Bissell, *You Can Always Tell a Harvard Man*, 171.

20. Morris Dickstein, *Dancing in the Dark: A Cultural History of the Great Depression* (New York: W. W. Norton, 2010), 216–17, cited from T. H. Watkins, *The Great Depression: America in the 1930s* (New York: Back Bay Books/Little, Brown, 2009), 218.

3. Up and Comer

1. Rexford G. Tugwell, *The Democratic Roosevelt: A Biography of Franklin D. Roosevelt* (New York: Doubleday, 1957), 11–12.

2. Frank Freidel, *Franklin D. Roosevelt: The Apprenticeship* (Boston: Little, Brown, 1952), 86.

3. Kenneth S. Davis, *FDR: The New York Years, 1928–1933* (New York: Random House, 1985), 9.

4. Kenneth S. Davis and Marion Dickerman, *Invincible Summer* (New York: Atheneum, 1974), 28.

5. Bissell, *You Can Always Tell a Harvard Man*, 164.

6. Ibid., 164.

7. Jerome Karabel, "It Wasn't So Easy for Roosevelt Either," *New York Times*, July 31, 2005.

8. Alonzo L. Hamby, *Man of Destiny: FDR and the Making of the American Century* (New York: Basic Books, 2015), 15, 23.

9. Hamby, *Man of Destiny*, 21.

10. Doris Kearns Goodwin, *No Ordinary Time: Franklin and Eleanor Roosevelt: The Home Front in World War II* (New York: Simon & Schuster, 1994), 91–97.

11. Burns, *Roosevelt: The Lion and the Fox*, 17.

12. Ward, *Before the Trumpet*, 119.

13. One baby, named after Franklin, died in infancy.

14. Ward, *Before the Trumpet*, 575.

15. James Tobin, *The Man He Became: How FDR Defied Polio to Win the Presidency* (New York: Simon & Schuster, 2013), 13–29.

16. Ibid., 41

17. Frances Perkins, " Reminiscences of Frances Perkins" (1951–55), part 2, 78, in the Oral History Research Office Collection of the Columbia University Libraries (OHRO/CUL), www.columbia.edu/cu/lweb/digital/collections/nny/per kinsf/audio_transcript.html; Kirstin Downey, *The Woman behind the New Deal: The Life of Frances Perkins, FDR's Secretary of Labor and His Moral Conscience* (New York: Doubleday, 2009), 90.

18. Perkins, "Reminiscences," part 2, 463.

19. Ibid., 41.

20. Lela Stiles, *The Man behind Roosevelt: The Story of Louis McHenry Howe* (Cleveland: World Publishing Company, 1954), 82–84. Stiles may have made up the dialogue, or she may have repeated what had been told to her in stories, which were retold many times over the years. But Eleanor, who was among many interviewed for Stiles's book, liked her work well enough to write a recommendation as its preface.

21. Tobin, *The Man He Became*, 126–27.

22. Tugwell, *The Democratic Roosevelt*, 14.

23. Hugh Gregory Gallagher, *FDR's Splendid Deception: The Moving Story of*

Roosevelt's Massive Disability and the Intense Efforts to Conceal It from the Public (Arlington, VA: Vandamere Press, 1999).

24. Gallagher, *FDR's Splendid Deception*, 26; Roger Butterfield, Robert Emmett Ginna, and Robert D. Graff, *FDR* (New York: Harper and Row, 1962), 69.

25. Gallagher, *FDR's Splendid Deception*, 53–63.

26. Perkins, "Reminiscences," part 2, 325.

4. Lead My Sheep

1. Tobin, *The Man He Became*, 210.

2. Ibid., 210–11.

3. Goodwin, *No Ordinary Time*, 118; Gallagher, *FDR's Splendid Deception*, 68–71.

5. "They Will Forget I'm a Cripple"

1. "The Presidency: Bottom," *Time*, March 13, 1933, http://content.time.com/time/subscriber/article/0,33009,745289,00.html.

2. Robert Jabaily, "Bank Holiday of 1933," Federal Reserve Bank of Boston, www.federalreservehistory.org/Events/DetailView/22; George S. Eccles, *The Politics of Banking* (Salt Lake City: University of Utah Press, 1982), 85.

3. Davis W. Houck, *Rhetoric as Currency: Hoover, Roosevelt and the Great Depression* (College Station; Texas A&M University Press, 2001), 163.

4. James A. Farley, *Jim Farley's Story: The Roosevelt Years* (Westport, CT: Greenwood Press, 1984), 36.

5. FDR kept the birthday cards his former headmaster sent him each year. The president-elect, who must have harbored the illusion that his teacher was near to immortal, even specified that Peabody must conduct his funeral service when he died. Not surprisingly, the much older man died first.

6. Jabaily, "Bank Holiday of 1933."

7. Freidel, *A Rendezvous with Destiny*, 90.

8. Adam Cohen, *Nothing to Fear: FDR's Inner Circle and the Hundred Days That Created Modern America* (New York: Penguin Books, 2010), 25.

9. "We Must Act," National Affairs, *Time*, March 13, 1933. http://content.time.com/time/subscriber/article/0,33009,745290,00.html.

10. Gallagher, *FDR's Splendid Deception*, 183.

11. "The Great Humanitarian: Herbert Hoover's Food Relief Efforts," Cornell College, www.cornellcollege.edu/history/courses/stewart/his260-3-2006/01%20one/befr.htm#video.

12. David M. Kennedy, *Freedom from Fear: The American People in Depression and War, 1929–1945* (New York: Oxford University Press, 1999), 91.

13. Kennedy, *Freedom from Fear*, 91.

14. Ibid., 93.

15. "500,000 in Streets Cheer Roosevelt," *New York Times*, March 5, 1933, 1, 2.

16. *New York Times*, March 5, 1933.

17. Gallagher, *FDR's Splendid Deception*, 97.

18. Ibid., 63.

19. "The Boss was superstitious, particularly about the number thirteen and the practice of lighting three cigarettes on a single match," wrote his secretary Grace Tully. "On several occasions I received last-minute summonses to attend a lunch or dinner party because a belated default or a late addition had brought the guest list to thirteen. My first invitation to a Cuff Links Club dinner, held annually on the President's birthday, came about in 1932 when withdrawal of one of the guests left a party of thirteen." Grace G. Tully, *FDR My Boss* (New York: Charles Scribner's Sons, 1949), 22.

20. Mahita Gajanan, "These Are the Bible Verses Past Presidents Have Turned to on Inauguration Day," *Time*, January 19, 2017, http//time.com/4639596/inauguration-day-presidents-bible-passages.

21. Alison Collis Greene, *No Depression in Heaven: The Great Depression, the New Deal, and the Transformation of Religion in the Delta* (New York: Oxford University Press, 2016), 101.

22. Perkins, "Reminiscences," part 4, 26.

6. "A Day of Consecration"

1. Davis W. Houck, *FDR and Fear Itself: The First Inaugural Address* (College Station: Texas A&M University Press, 2002), 102.

2. Rosemary Ostler, "A History of Political Slurs," *Salon*, www.salon.com/2011/09/03/slinging_mud_excerpt_slideshow/slide_show/7.

3. Kaye, *Fight for the Four Freedoms*, 32.

4. Arthur Krock, "Roosevelt Acts to End Bank Crisis," *New York Times*, March 12, 1933, 3.

5. *Time*, March 13, 1933.

6. Franklin D. Roosevelt, First Inaugural Address, March 4, 1933, Miller Center, http://millercenter.org/president/fdroosevelt/speeches/speech-3280.

7. "The Boss, the Dynamo, the Works"

1. Arthur Schlesinger Jr., *The Coming of the New Deal, 1933–1935* (Boston: Houghton Mifflin, 2003), 16.

2. "Action and Action Now: FDR's First 100 Days," a special exhibit publication by the Franklin Delano Roosevelt Library, https://timedotcom.files.wordpress.com/2015/03/actionguide.pdf

3. Leslie H. Fishel Jr., "The Negro in the New Deal Era," *Wisconsin Magazine of History* 48, no. 2 (Winter 1964–1965): 111–26; Elliott Roosevelt, ed., *FDR: His Personal Letters*, vol. 2 (New York: Duell, Sloan, and Pearce, 1950), 1018–19.

4. Houck, *FDR and Fear Itself*, 147.

5. William E. Leuchtenburg, *The White House Looks South: Franklin D. Roosevelt, Harry S. Truman, Lyndon B. Johnson* (Baton Rouge: Louisiana State University Press, 2007), 43.

6. Leuchtenburg, *White House Looks South*, chapter 1.

7. Among them was Erich Ludendorff, who had been at Hitler's side during the Munich Putsch. He wrote to President Paul von Hindenburg: "By appointing Hitler Chancellor of the Reich you have handed over our sacred German Fatherland to one of the greatest demagogues of all time. I prophesy to you this evil man will plunge our Reich into the abyss and will inflict immeasurable woe on our nation. Future generations will curse you in your grave for this action." In less than two months, Dachau, the first of three major concentration camps, was opened outside Munich. It would be used to imprison enemies of the state, including any man who didn't have a visible means of employment.

8. Cohen, *Nothing to Fear*, 72.

9. Schlesinger, *The Coming of the New Deal*, 21.

10. *Boston Herald*, March 6, 1933.

11. Jabaily, "Bank Holiday of 1933."

12. Ibid.

13. *Boston Herald*, March 9, 1933.

14. Letter to the Editor, *New York Times*, March 12, 1933.

15. Jabaily, "Bank Holiday of 1933."

16. *Boston Globe*, March 6, 1933.

17. *Boston Post*, March 10, 1933.

18. *Time*, March 13, 1933.

19. Jabaily, "Bank Holiday of 1933."

20. *New York Times*, March 12, 1933, 57.

21. "Irenee Du Pont Frees Gold Held 20 Years," *New York Times*, March 12, 1933, 62.

22. Cohen, *Nothing to Fear*, 278.

23. Thomas E. Woods, Jr., "The Great Gold Robbery of 1933," Mises Institute, August 13, 2008, https://mises.org/library/great-gold-robbery-1933.

24. "The Presidency: The Roosevelt Week," *Time*, March 20, 1933, 7.

25. William L. Silber, "Why Did FDR's Bank Holiday Succeed?" *Federal Reserve Bank of New York Economic Policy Review*, July 2009, www.newyorkfed.org/media library/media/research/epr/09v15n1/0907silb.pdf.

26. Lawrence W. Levine and Cornelia R. Levine, *The People and the President: America's Conversation with FDR* (Boston: Beacon Press, 2002), 3; Leila A. Sussmann, *Dear FDR: A Study of Political Letter Writing* (Totowa, NJ: Bedminster Press, 1963), 141.

27. Silber, "Why Did FDR's Bank Holiday Succeed?"

28. Levine and Levine, *The People and the President*, 37.

29. Ibid., 6.

30. Ibid., 45.

31. Ibid., 27.

8. "Be Ye Steadfast"

1. Schlesinger, *The Coming of the New Deal*, 33.

2. Goodwin, *No Ordinary Time*, 212–13.

3. Schlesinger, *The Coming of the New Deal*, 45–49.

4. High, *Roosevelt . . . And Then?* https://archive.org/details/rooseveltandthen
00125imbp.

5. Goodwin, *No Ordinary Time,* 204–5, 628–29.

6. Merle Rubin, "A Feminist Portrait of Eleanor Roosevelt," review, *Christian Science Monitor,* May 19, 1992, www.csmonitor.com/1992/0519/19131.html; Bissell, *You Can Always Tell a Harvard Man,* 161.

7. Blanche Wiesen Cook, interview, *American Experience,* www.pbs.org/wgbh/americanexperience/features/interview/eleanor-cook.

8. Perkins, *The Roosevelt I Knew* (New York: Viking Press, 1946), 11–12; Freidel, *The Apprenticeship,* 119.

9. Michael Barone, "Franklin D. Roosevelt: A Protestant Patrician in a Catholic Party," in David B. Woolner and Richard G. Kurial, eds., *FDR, the Vatican and the Roman Catholic Church in America, 1933–1945* (New York: Palgrave, 2003), 5.

10. Perkins, *The Roosevelt I Knew,* 11. At the beginning of the legislative session, a newspaper photographer caught Roosevelt in exactly that stance, wearing a top hat and pince-nez in a photograph that was widely circulated. His head was tossed back, and the expression on his face was disdainful, almost supercilious. "It was the epitome of the stage dandy, the popular 'Van Bibber' character of Richard Harding Davis's stories, and a rank libel upon the flesh-and-blood Roosevelt." Freidel, *The Apprenticeship,* 118.

11. Often referred to as WASPs. The New Deal was the nickname given to the changes in US law that Roosevelt proposed to deal with the Great Depression. Those changes are often credited with setting up a social welfare system to aid Americans when they are unemployed, aged, or otherwise unable to help themselves. Many of those changes were passed during the first one hundred days of the FDR administration, setting a benchmark that caused Americans to focus on every president's first one hundred days. No president since then has accomplished such sweeping change.

12. Roosevelt was the first president to publicly call lynching murder, "a vile form of collective murder." But he refused to support a Republican bill outlawing lynching because he feared losing southern support, which he needed to get his legislation passed. Eleanor was bitterly disappointed. He did instruct the Justice Department to investigate lynching as a civil rights crime. Without a specific law to prosecute, judgments were still hard to secure, but eventually the federal investigations helped end lynching. http://rooseveltinstitute.org/african-americans-and-new-deal-look-back-history/.

13. Hitler's appointments went in the opposite direction. Roosevelt expanded; Hitler contracted. He appointed white men, the whiter the better. Protestant was good, but not too devout. Catholics and Jews would fill concentration camps built specially for them and other "inferiors." People of African descent would not be automatically arrested; Hitler tolerated them if they didn't make trouble and stayed with their own kind. But their mixed-blood children would be sterilized.

14. Page Smith, *Redeeming the Time: A People's History of the 1920s and the New Deal* (New York: McGraw-Hill, 1986), 417–18.

15. Ibid., 417.

16. "Her Life: The Woman behind the New Deal," Frances Perkins Center, http://francesperkinscenter.org/?page_id=574.

17. Ibid.

18. Downey, *The Woman behind the New Deal*, 119–24.

19. Adam Cohen, "Franklin Roosevelt: The First Hundred Days," *Time*, June 24, 2009, http://content.time.com/time/specials/packages/article/0,28804,1906802_1906838_1906979-1,00.html.

20. The National Industrial Recovery Act was later declared unconstitutional by the Supreme Court, but parts of it remained in effect, including a federal guarantee that gave labor the right to strike.

9. "A Christian and a Democrat"

1. Nathan Miller, *An Intimate History* (Garden City, NY: Doubleday, 1983), 314–15.

2. Kaye, *Fight for the Four Freedoms*, 32.

3. Schlesinger, *The Coming of the New Deal*, 37.

4. We find ourselves in a similar time with the advent of the information age. As historian Kenneth Davis observed, the battle between human rights and technology has been one that started in the Stone Age when the first caveman picked up a club. *The Legacy of FDR: A Roosevelt Symposium*, April 20–22, 1997 (Manhattan: Kansas State University), 23.

5. "A New Gilded Age," *America*, October 7, 2013; Jonathan Alter, *The Defining Moment: FDR's Hundred Days and the Triumph of Hope* (New York: Simon & Schuster, 2007), 98.

6. Davis, *FDR as a Biographer's Problem*, 106.

7. Meacham, *Franklin and Winston*, 27.

8. Robert E. Sherwood, *Roosevelt and Hopkins: An Intimate History* (New York: Harper & Brothers, 1948), 9.

9. Franklin D. Roosevelt, "Campaign Address in Sea Girt, NJ, August 27, 1932," American Presidency Project, www.presidency.ucsb.edu/ws /?pid=88395.

10. Ward, *Before the Trumpet*, 1–2.

11. Perkins, *The Roosevelt I Knew*, 64–65.

12. No Catholic had ever been president of the United States. That goal wouldn't be reached until John F. Kennedy won office in 1960.

13. Samuel I. Rosenman and Dorothy Rosenman, *Presidential Style: Some Giants and a Pygmy in the White House* (New York: Harper & Row, 1976), 291–92.

14. Franklin D. Roosevelt, "Radio Address on Brotherhood Day; February 23, 1936," American Presidency Project, www.presidency.ucsb.edu/ws/index.php?pid=15250.

15. Perkins, *The Roosevelt I Knew*, 143.

16. Herbert Hoover had also used the idea of the Golden Rule in international affairs, but it was FDR who made the idea take on a reality that changed how countries felt about the United States. Kennedy, *Freedom from Fear*, 392–93.

17. Roosevelt, "Radio Address on Brotherhood Day."

18. Federer, *The Faith of FDR*, 152.

10. Listening to the Almighty

1. Ibid., 1101.

2. Brands, *Traitor to His Class*, 268; Page Smith, *Redeeming the Time: A People's History of the 1920s and the New Deal* (New York: McGraw-Hill, 1986), 374, 417–18.

3. Kenneth S. Davis, "FDR as a Biographer's Problem," *American Scholar* 52 (Winter 1983/84): 100–8.

4. *Amarillo Daily News*, July 7–12, 1938.

5. "Grasshoppers Are Coming: Farming in the 1930s," Wessels Living History Farm, www.livinghistoryfarm.org/farminginthe30s/pests_02.html.

6. Army National Guard Major Adam Morgan, "In 1937 Colorado National Guard Used Flamethrowers and Explosive against Plague of Locusts," June 9, 2014, www.nationalguard.mil/News/ArticleView/tabid/5563/Article/575751/in-1937-colorado-guard-used-flamethrowers-and-explosives-against-plague-of-locu.aspx.

7. Timothy Egan, *The Worst Hard Time: The Untold Story of Those Who Survived the Dust Bowl* (Boston: Houghton Mifflin Co., 2006), 168; Greene, *No Depression in Heaven*, 35, 60–64.

8. Franklin D. Roosevelt, "Fireside Chat 8: On Farmers and Laborers," September 6, 1936, http://millercenter.org/president/fdroosevelt/speeches/speech-3306.

9. Terry Moore, "Teddy Slept Here, FDR Brought Rain," *Amarillo Globe-News*, February 15, 1999, http://amarillo.com/stories/1999/02/15/new_visits.shtml#.VzzjxGMpLzI).

10. "Dresses Shrank Day FDR Visited," *Victoria Advocate*, July 8, 1990.

11. Grace Tully Archive, Grace Tully Papers, Box 5; Folder: Writings: Unpublished Reminiscences, 1950, Franklin Delano Roosevelt Presidential Library.

12. "Roosevelt to End Campaign in Spurt," *New York Times*, November 5, 1928.

13. John Gunther, *Roosevelt in Retrospect: A Profile in History* (New York: Harper & Row, 1950), 111.

14. Davis, *FDR: The New York Years*, 429–32.

15. Alter, *The Defining Moment*, 176–77.

16. Smith, *Redeeming the Time*, 426. The comment seems to refer to some previous conversation that is never explained in the references to LeHand's words. Perhaps she was referring to the idea that Roosevelt was born under a lucky star.

17. Alexander Feinberg, "Vast Throngs See Roosevelt on Tour," *New York Times*, October 22, 1944, http://query.nytimes.com/mem/archive-free/pdf?res=9C06E0D91038E33BBC4A51DFB667838F659EDE, 35; Gallagher, *FDR's Splendid Deception*, 195.

11. "Judge Me by My Enemies"

1. Alter, *The Defining Moment*, 130.

2. Kennedy, *Freedom from Fear*, 279; *Nation*, January 15, 1936, 60, 65.

3. Gunther, *Roosevelt in Retrospect*, 176.

4. Kintrea, "Old Peabo' and the School."

5. "Franklin Roosevelt at Harvard," *Harvard Magazine*, November 1996, http://harvardmagazine.com/1996/11/frank-roosevelt-at-harvard.

6. Marquis W. Childs, "They Hate Roosevelt," *Harper's*, May 1933; Donald Gibson, *Wealth, Power, and the Crisis of Laissez Faire* (New York: Palgrave/Macmillan, 2011), 10.

7. Leuchtenburg, *The White House Looks South*, 2.

8. Col. Robert McCormick, Subject File, Box 157, President's Secretary's File, Franklin Delano Roosevelt Presidential Library.

9. Freidel, *Rendezvous with Destiny*, 23.

10. Gibson, *Wealth, Power, and the Crisis of Laissez Faire Capitalism*, 106.

11. Ibid., 105–6.

12. Kevin Michael Kruse, *One Nation under God: How Corporate America Invented Christian America* (New York: Basic Books, 2015), 3–5.

13. Gibson, *Wealth, Power, and the Crisis of Laissez Faire Capitalism*, 105.

14. Kruse, *One Nation under God*, 3–4.

15. Roosevelt won the popular vote by 60.8 percent. Only Lyndon Baines Johnson won with a bigger landslide. In 1964, he was elected president by 61 percent of the popular vote.

16. Philip Seib, *Broadcasts from the Blitz: How Edward R. Murrow Helped Lead America into War* (Washington, D.C.: Potomac Books, 2007), 12.

17. Kruse, *One Nation under God*, 6–7.

12. God Loves Peace/God Blesses War

1. Kennedy, *Freedom from Fear*, 388.

2. www.presidency.ucsb.edu/ws/?pid=14643.

3. "America's Wars," US Department of Veterans Affairs, va.gov.

4. Sherwood, *Roosevelt and Hopkins*, 227.

5. Peter Beinart, "Franklin D. Roosevelt: The Price of World Peace," *Time*, June 24, 2009, http://content.time.com/time/specials/packages/article/0,28804,1906802_1906838_1906797,00.html.

6. Kennedy, *Freedom from Fear*, 394.

7. Meacham, *Roosevelt and Churchill*, 43.

8. *New York Times*, October 14, 1944.

9. Roosevelt campaigned in 1944 to prevent her reelection to the US House, publicly calling her "a sharp-tongued glamor girl of forty." *New York Sun*, November 8, 1944.

10. H. L. Mencken, *American Mercury*, March 1936.

11. Isaiah Berlin, "Roosevelt through European Eyes," *Atlantic Monthly*, July 1955, 69.

12. "Adolf Hitler: Man of the Year, 1938," *Time*, January 2, 1939, http://content
.time.com/time/magazine/article/0,9171,760539,00.html.

13. Federer, *The Faith of FDR*, 405.

14. Samuel L. Rosenman, *Working with Roosevelt* (New York: Harper, 1952), 182.

15. Kennedy, *Freedom from Fear*, 393.

16. In turn, the pope repeatedly urged Roosevelt to resist bombing civilian populations and to protect Rome from air attacks. Both their efforts failed. Mussolini did join Hitler, and the Allies firebombed German cities savagely. The central part of Rome was preserved, but other parts of the city were attacked.

17. Michael Fullilove, *Rendezvous with Destiny: How Franklin D. Roosevelt and Five Extraordinary Men Took America into the War and into the World, September 1939–December 1941* (New York: Penguin Press, 2013), 58.

18. Burns, *Roosevelt: The Lion and the Fox*, 76.

19. Arthur Herman, "Arsenal of Democracy," *Detroit News*, January 3, 2013, https://web.archive.org/web/20130828141002/http://www.detroitnews.com/article/20130103/OPINION01/301030336.

20. Goodwin, *No Ordinary Time*, 133.

21. Ibid., 187.

22. Tugwell, *The Democratic Roosevelt*, 561.

23. Sherwood, *Roosevelt and Hopkins*, 266. Hopkins testified to FDR's complete sincerity about those ideals in a conversation with Sherwood.

> You and I are for Roosevelt because he's a great spiritual figure, because he's an idealist, like Wilson, and he's got the guts to drive through against any opposition to realize those ideals. Oh—he sometimes tries to appear tough and cynical and flippant, but that's an act he likes to put on, especially at press conferences. . . . You can see the real Roosevelt when he comes out with something like the Four Freedoms. And don't get that idea that those are just catch phrases. *He believes them!* He believes they can be practically achieved. . . . [I]t's your job and mine—as long as we're around here to keep reminding him that he's unlimited, and that's the way he's got to talk because he's going to act. . . . [H]e knows what he is, even if he doesn't like to admit it to you or me or anybody.

24. Franklin Roosevelt, State of the Union Address; Four Freedoms Speech, January 7, 1941, www.americanrhetoric.com/speeches/fdrthefourfreedoms.htm.

25. Goodwin, *No Ordinary Time*, 264.

26. Winston Churchill, *The Grand Alliance: The Second World War* (New York: Houghton, Mifflin & Co., 1950), 383–84.

27. Meacham, *Franklin and Winston*, 107–16. Much of the description of this day and the quotes comes from Meacham's wonderful rendition of it.

13. The President and Priest

1. In the summer of 1942 the US State Department first heard of Hitler's plan to murder Europe's Jews. Roosevelt set up the War Refugee Board in January of

1944 after Henry Morgenthau informed him of the State Department's lack of action. The *American Experience* account of Morgenthau's involvement is a concise rendition of what happened: www.pbs.org/wgbh/amex/holocaust/peopleevents/ pandeAMEX97.html.

2. Franklin D. Roosevelt: "Prayer on D-Day," June 6, 1944, Gerhard Peters and John T. Woolley, American Presidency Project, www.presidency.ucsb.edu/ ws/?pid=16515.

Almighty God: Our sons, pride of our Nation, this day have set upon a mighty endeavor, a struggle to preserve our Republic, our religion, and our civilization, and to set free a suffering humanity. Lead them straight and true; give strength to their arms, stoutness to their hearts, steadfastness in their faith.

They will need Thy blessings. Their road will be long and hard. For the enemy is strong. He may hurl back our forces. Success may not come with rushing speed, but we shall return again and again; and we know that by Thy grace, and by the righteousness of our cause, our sons will triumph.

They will be sore tried, by night and by day, without rest—until the victory is won. The darkness will be rent by noise and flame. Men's souls will be shaken with the violences of war.

For these men are lately drawn from the ways of peace. They fight not for the lust of conquest. They fight to end conquest. They fight to liberate. They fight to let justice arise, and tolerance and good will among all Thy people. They yearn but for the end of battle, for their return to the haven of home.

Some will never return. Embrace these, Father, and receive them, Thy heroic servants, into Thy kingdom.

And for us at home—fathers, mothers, children, wives, sisters, and brothers of brave men overseas—whose thoughts and prayers are ever with them—help us, Almighty God, to rededicate ourselves in renewed faith in Thee in this hour of great sacrifice.

Many people have urged that I call the Nation into a single day of special prayer. But because the road is long and the desire is great, I ask that our people devote themselves in a continuance of prayer. As we rise to each new day, and again when each day is spent, let words of prayer be on our lips, invoking Thy help to our efforts.

Give us strength, too—strength in our daily tasks, to redouble the contributions we make in the physical and the material support of our armed forces.

And let our hearts be stout, to wait out the long travail, to bear sorrows that may come, to impart our courage unto our sons wheresoever they may be.

And, O Lord, give us Faith. Give us Faith in Thee; Faith in our sons; Faith in each other; Faith in our united crusade. Let not the keenness of our spirit ever be dulled. Let not the impacts of temporary events, of temporal matters of but fleeting moment let not these deter us in our unconquerable purpose.

With Thy blessing, we shall prevail over the unholy forces of our enemy. Help us to conquer the apostles of greed and racial arrogancies. Lead us to the saving of our country, and with our sister Nations into a world unity that will spell a sure peace a peace invulnerable to the schemings of unworthy men. And a peace that will let all of men live in freedom, reaping the just rewards of their honest toil.

Thy will be done, Almighty God.

Amen.

3. John F. Woolverton, "Who Is Kierkegaard? Franklin Roosevelt, Howard Johnson, and Soren Kierkegaard," *Anglican and Episcopal History* 80, no. 1 (March 2011): 1–32. Historical Society of the Episcopal Church, www.jstor.org/stable/42612655.

4. Micah 6:8 (King James Version).

BIBLIOGRAPHY

Adams, Henry H. *Harry Hopkins.* New York: G. P. Putnam's Sons, 1977.

Alonso, Harriet Hyman. *Robert E. Sherwood: The Playwright in Peace and War.* Amherst: University of Massachusetts Press, 2007.

Alter, Jonathan. *The Defining Moment: FDR's Hundred Days and the Triumph of Hope.* New York: Simon & Schuster, 2007.

Asbell, Bernard, and Franklin D. Roosevelt. *The F. D. R. Memoirs.* 1st ed. Garden City, NY: Doubleday, 1973.

Ashburn, Frank Davis. *Peabody of Groton, a Portrait.* 2nd ed. New York: Riverside Press, 1967.

Auchincloss, Louis. *A Writer's Capital.* Minneapolis: University of Minnesota Press, 1974.

Barone, Michael. "Franklin D. Roosevelt: A Protestant Patrician in a Catholic Party." In *FDR, the Vatican and the Roman Catholic Church in America, 1933–1945,* edited by David B. Woolner and Richard G. Kurial. New York: Palgrave, 2003.

Beinart, Peter. "Franklin D. Roosevelt: The Price of World Peace." *Time,* June 24, 2009. http://content.time.com/time/specials/packages/article/0,28804,19068 02 _1906838_1906797,00.html.

Bell, Bernard. "The Religion of FDR." Review of *The Roosevelt I Knew,* by Frances Perkins. *Living Church,* June 1, 1947.

Bellah, Robert N. *The Broken Covenant: American Civil Religion in Time of Trial.* 2nd ed. Chicago: University of Chicago Press, 1992.

Berlin, Isaiah. "Roosevelt through European Eyes." *Atlantic Monthly,* July 1955.

Bess, Michael. *Choices under Fire: Moral Dimensions of World War II.* New York: Vintage Books, 2008.

Bethell, John T. "Frank Roosevelt at Harvard." *Harvard Magazine,* November 1, 1996.

Bingham, Kenneth E. *Groton School Camp: 1893, Squam Lake, N.H.: A History of the First Summer Camp for Underprivileged Boys (the Progressive Era).* Ventura, CA: Binghamus Press, 2009.

Bishop, Jim. *FDR's Last Year: April 1944–1945.* New York: William Morrow and Company, 1974.

Bissell, Richard. *You Can Always Tell a Harvard Man.* Lake Oswego, OR: eNet Press Inc., 1962.

Black, Conrad. *Franklin Delano Roosevelt: Champion of Freedom.* New York: Public Affairs, 2003.

Bottum, J., and David G. Dalin. *The Pius War: Responses to the Critics of Pius XII.* Lanham, MD.: Lexington Books, 2004.

Bradley, James, and Robert Cowley, eds. *What If? 2: Eminent Historians Imagine What Might Have Been*. New York: Berkley Books, 2002.

Brands, H. W. *The Reckless Decade: America in the 1890s*. Chicago: University of Chicago Press, 2002.

———. *Traitor to His Class: The Privileged Life and Radical Presidency of Franklin Delano Roosevelt*. 1st Anchor Books ed. New York: Anchor Books, 2009.

Burns, James MacGregor. *Roosevelt: The Lion and the Fox*. A Harvest Book 57. San Diego: Harcourt, Brace & World, 1984.

———. *Roosevelt: The Soldier of Freedom*. New York: Harcourt Brace Jovanovich, 1970.

Casey, Steven. *Cautious Crusade: Franklin D. Roosevelt, American Public Opinion, and the War against Nazi Germany*. New York: Oxford University Press, 2001.

Chancellor, Edward. *Devil Take the Hindmost: A History of Financial Speculation*. 1st ed. New York: Farrar, Straus and Giroux, 1999.

Childs, Marquis W. "They Hate Roosevelt." *Harper's*, May 1933.

Churchill, Winston. *The Grand Alliance: The Second World War*. New York: Rosetta Books, 2003.

Cohen, Adam. "Franklin Roosevelt: The First Hundred Days." *Time*, June 24, 2009.

———. *Nothing to Fear: FDR's Inner Circle and the Hundred Days That Created Modern America*. New York: Penguin Books, 2010.

Collier, Peter, and David Horowitz. *The Roosevelts: An American Saga*. New York: Simon & Schuster, 1994.

Craig, Lee A. *Josephus Daniels: His Life & Times*. Chapel Hill: University of North Carolina Press, 2013.

Dalton, Kathleen. *Speech at Groton School, April 2015*. Groton, MA: Peabody Press.

Davis, Kenneth S., and Marion Dickerman. *FDR: The Beckoning of Destiny, 1882–1928*. New York: Putnam, 1972.

———. *Invincible Summer: An Intimate Portrait of the Roosevelts, Based on the Recollections of Marion Dickerman*. 1st ed. New York: Atheneum, 1974.

———. "FDR as a Biographer's Problem." *American Scholar* 52 (Winter 1984/1983).

———. *FDR: The New York Years, 1928–1933*. 1st ed. New York: Random House, 1985.

———. *FDR: The New Deal Years, 1933–1937*. 1st ed. New York: Random House, 1986.

———. *FDR: Into the Storm, 1937–1940*. 1st ed. New York: Random House, 1993.

———. *FDR: The War President, 1940–1943*. 1st ed. New York: Random House, 2000.

Desjardins, Mark Denis. "A Muscular Christian in a Secular World." PhD diss., University of Virginia, 1995.

Dickstein, Morris. *Dancing in the Dark: A Cultural History of the Great Depression*. New York: W. W. Norton, 2010.

Dorfman, Joseph. *The Economic Mind in American Civilization*. Vol. 3. New York: Viking Press, 1946.

Downey, Kirstin. *The Woman behind the New Deal: The Life of Frances Perkins, FDR's Secretary of Labor and His Moral Conscience*. New York: Doubleday, 2009.

Dunlop, Richard. *Donovan, America's Master Spy.* New York: Skyhorse Publishing, Inc., 2014.

Eccles, George S. *The Politics of Banking.* Salt Lake City: Graduate School of Business, University of Utah, 1982.

Egan, Timothy. *The Worst Hard Time: The Untold Story of Those Who Survived the Great American Dust Bowl.* Boston: Houghton Mifflin Co., 2006.

Erikson, Erik. *Youth, Identity and Crisis.* New York: W. W. Norton & Co., 1994.

Farley, James A. *Behind the Ballots: The Personal History of a Politician.* New York: Harcourt, Brace and Company, 1938.

———. *Jim Farley's Story: The Roosevelt Years.* Westport, CT: Greenwood Press, 1984.

Federer, William J. *The Faith of FDR: From President Franklin Delano Roosevelt's Public Papers, 1933–1945.* St. Louis: Amerisearch, 2006.

Fenster, J. M. *FDR's Shadow: Louis Howe, the Force That Shaped Franklin and Eleanor Roosevelt.* 1st ed. New York: Palgrave Macmillan, 2009.

Ferdon, Nona Stinson. "Franklin D. Roosevelt: A Psychological Interpretation of His Childhood and Youth." PhD diss., University of Hawaii, 1971.

Fishel, Leslie H. Jr. "The Negro in the New Deal Era." *Wisconsin Magazine of History* 48, no. 2 (Winter 1965/1964): 111–26.

Flynn, John T. *The Roosevelt Myth.* New York: Deven-Adair Co., 1948.

Flynt, Wayne. *Alabama Baptists: Southern Baptists in the Heart of Dixie.* Religion and American Culture. Tuscaloosa: University of Alabama Press, 1998.

Fowler, James W. *Stages of Faith: The Psychology of Human Development and the Quest for Meaning.* 1st ed. San Francisco: Harper & Row, 1981.

Freidel, Frank. *Franklin D. Roosevelt: The Apprenticeship.* Boston: Little, Brown, 1952.

———. *Franklin D. Roosevelt: A Rendezvous with Destiny.* 1st ed. Boston: Little, Brown, 1990.

Fried, Albert. *FDR and His Enemies.* New York: Griffin, 2001.

Fullilove, Michael. *Rendezvous with Destiny: How Franklin D. Roosevelt and Five Extraordinary Men Took America into the War and into the World, September 1939–December 1941.* New York: Penguin Press, 2013.

Gajanan, Mahita. "These Are the Bible Verses That Past Presidents Have Turned to on Inauguration Day." *Time,* January 19, 2017. http//time.com/4639596/inauguration-day-presidents-bible-passages.

Gallagher, Hugh Gregory. *FDR's Splendid Deception: The Moving Story of Roosevelt's Massive Disability and the Intense Efforts to Conceal It from the Public.* Arlington, VA: Vandamere Press, 1999.

Gelderman, Carol W. *All the Presidents' Words: The Bully Pulpit and the Creation of the Virtual Presidency.* New York: Walker and Co., 1997.

Gibson, Donald. *Wealth, Power, and the Crisis of Laissez Faire Capitalism.* 1st ed. New York: Palgrave Macmillan, 2011.

Goldberg, Jonah. *Liberal Fascism: The Secret History of the American Left, from Mussolini to the Politics of Change.* 1st paperback ed. New York: Broadway Books, 2009.

Goldfield, David. *Black, White, and Southern: Race Relations and Southern Culture, 1940 to the Present.* Baton Rouge: Louisiana State University Press, 1991.

Goodwin, Doris Kearns. *No Ordinary Time: Franklin and Eleanor Roosevelt: The Home Front in World War II.* New York: Simon & Schuster, 1994.

Gould, Jean. *A Good Fight: The Story of F.D.R.'s Conquest of Polio.* New York: Dodd, Mead & Co., 1960.

Graff, Robert D., Robert Emmett Ginna, and Roger Butterfield. *FDR.* New York: Harper & Row, 1963.

"The Great Humanitarian: Herbert Hoover's Food Relief Efforts," Cornell College. www.cornellcollege.edu/history/courses/stewart/his260-3-2006/01%20one/befr.htm#video.

Greene, Alison Collis. *No Depression in Heaven: The Great Depression, the New Deal, and the Transformation of Religion in the Delta.* New York: Oxford University Press, 2016.

Greenstein, Fred I., ed. *Leadership in the Modern Presidency.* Cambridge, MA: Harvard University Press, 1988.

Greer, Thomas H. *What Roosevelt Thought: The Social and Political Ideas of Franklin D. Roosevelt.* East Lansing: Michigan State University Press, 2000.

Grower, Calvin W. "The Struggle of Blacks for Leadership Positions in the Civilian Conservation Corps: 1933–1942." *Journal of Negro History* 61, no. 2 (April 1976): 123–35. www.jstor.org/stable/2717266.

Gunther, John. *Roosevelt in Retrospect: A Profile in History.* New York: Harper & Row, 1950.

Gustafson, Merlin, and Terry Rosenberg. "The Faith of FDR." *Presidential Studies Quarterly* 19, no. 3 (Summer 1989), www.jstor.org/stable/40574369.

Hamby, Alonzo L. *Man of Destiny: FDR and the Making of the American Century.* New York: Basic Books, 2015.

Harmon, F. Martin. *The Warm Springs Story: Legacy & Legend.* Macon, GA: Mercer University Press, 2014.

Harrity, Richard, and Ralph G. Martin. *The Human Side of F.D.R.* New York: Duell, Sloan and Pearce, 1960.

Hassett, William D. *Off the Record with F.D.R. 1942–1945.* New Brunswick, NJ: Rutgers University Press, 1958.

Herman, Arthur. "Arsenal of Democracy." *Detroit News,* January 3, 2013. https://web.archive.org/web/20130828141002/http://www.detroitnews.com/article/20130103/OPINION01/301030336.

High, Stanley. Unpublished diary. Franklin Delano Roosevelt Library.

———. *Roosevelt . . . and Then.* New York: Harper and Brothers, 1937.

Hitler, Adolf. *Mein Kampf.* https://archive.org/stream/MeinKampf_472/MeinKampf_djvu.txt.

Hodges, George. *Henry Codman Potter: Seventh Bishop of New York.* New York: Macmillan and Co., 1915.

Houck, Davis W. *FDR and Fear Itself: The First Inaugural Address.* College Station: Texas A&M University Press, 2002.

———. *Rhetoric as Currency: Hoover, Roosevelt and the Great Depression.* College Station: Texas A&M University Press, 2001.

Hughes, Thomas. *Tom Brown's Schooldays.* https://archive.org/details/tombrowns schooloshughgoog.

Isletti, Ronald. "The Moneychangers of the Temple: FDR, American Civil Religion, and the New Deal." *Presidential Studies Quarterly* 26, no. 3 (Summer 1996), www.jstor.org/stable/27551625.

Jabaily, Robert. "Bank Holiday of 1933." Federal Reserve Bank of Boston, www .federalreservehistory.org/Events/DetailView/22.

Jackson, Robert Houghwout, and John Q. Barrett. *That Man: An Insider's Portrait of Franklin D. Roosevelt.* New York: Oxford University Press, 2003.

Jordan, Frederick W. "Between Heaven and Harvard: Protestant Faith and the American Boarding School Experience, 1778–1940." PhD. diss. University of Notre Dame, 2004.

Karabel, Jerome. *The Chosen: The Hidden History of Admission and Exclusion at Harvard, Yale, and Princeton.* Boston: Houghton Mifflin, 2005.

———. "It Wasn't So Easy for Roosevelt Either." *New York Times,* July 31, 2005.

Kaye, Harvey J. *The Fight for the Four Freedoms: What Made FDR and the Greatest Generation Truly Great.* New York: Simon & Schuster, 2014.

Kennedy, David M. *Freedom from Fear: The American People in Depression and War, 1929–1945.* Vol. 9 of *The Oxford History of the United States.* New York: Oxford University Press, 1999.

———. "What the New Deal Did." *Political Science Quarterly* 124, no. 2 (Summer 2009): 251–68, www.jstor.org/stable/25655654.

Kintrea, Frank. "'Old Peabo' and the School." *American Heritage,* November 1980.

Klara, Robert. *FDR's Funeral Train: A Betrayed Widow, a Soviet Spy, and a Presidency in the Balance.* Basingstoke, UK: Palgrave Macmillan, 2011.

Kleeman, Rita Halle. *Gracious Lady: The Life of Sara Delano Roosevelt.* New York: D. Appleton–Century, 1935.

Krock, Arthur. "Roosevelt Acts to End Bank Crisis." *New York Times,* March 12, 1933.

Kruse, Kevin Michael. *One Nation under God: How Corporate America Invented Christian America.* New York: Basic Books, 2015.

The Legacy of FDR: A Roosevelt Symposium. Manhattan: Kansas State University, 1997. https://books.google.com/books?id=dOvqHAAACAAJ.

Leuchtenburg, William E. *Herbert Hoover: The American Presidents Series: The 31st President, 1929–1933.* New York: Macmillan, 2009.

Leuchtenburg, William E., and EBSCOhost. *The White House Looks South: Franklin D. Roosevelt, Harry S. Truman, Lyndon B. Johnson.* Baton Rouge: Louisiana State University Press, 2007. Ebsco (271091).

Levine, Lawrence W., and Cornelia R. Levine. *The People and the President: America's Conversation with FDR*. Boston: Beacon Press, 2002.

Levy, William Turner, and Cynthia Eagle Russett. *The Extraordinary Mrs. R: A Friend Remembers Eleanor Roosevelt*. New York: John Wiley, 1999.

Longmore, Paul K., and David Goldberger. "The League of the Physically Handicapped and the Great Depression: A Case Study in the New Disability History." *Journal of American History* 87, no. 3 (December 2000): 888–922, www.jstor.org/stable/2675276.

Lynd, Robert Staughton, and Helen Merrell Lynd. *Middletown in Transition: A Study in Cultural Conflicts*. A Harvest/HBJ Book. New York: Harcourt Brace Jovanovich, 1982.

McAdams, Dan P. *The Stories We Live By: Personal Myths and the Making of the Self*. New York: Guilford Press, 1997.

McCollister, John. *God and the Oval Office: The Religious Faith of Our 43 Presidents*. Nashville, TN: Thomas Nelson, 2005.

McLachlan, James. *American Boarding Schools: A Historical Study*. New York: Scribner's, 1970.

Meacham, Jon. *American Gospel: God, the Founding Fathers, and the Making of a Nation*. 1st ed. New York: Random House, 2006.

———. *Franklin and Winston: An Intimate Portrait of an Epic Friendship*. 1st ed. New York: Random House, 2003.

Mencken, H. L. *American Mercury*. March 1936.

Metaxas, Eric. *Bonhoeffer: Pastor, Martyr, Prophet, Spy: A Righteous Gentile vs. the Third Reich*. Nashville, TN: Thomas Nelson, 2010.

Meyerson, Harold. "God and the New Deal." *American Prospect*, November 21, 2004.

Miller, Nathan. *An Intimate History*. Garden City, NY: Doubleday, 1983.

Moley, Raymond. *After Seven Years*. New York: Harper & Brothers, 1939.

Myers, Robb. *Life and Love, More Abundantly*. Carmelo, CA: Xulon Press, 2011.

Nolan, Cathal J., ed. *Ethics and Statecraft: The Moral Dimension of International Affairs*. 2nd ed. Humanistic Perspectives on International Relations. Westport, CT: Praeger, 2004.

O'Brien, David J. *American Catholics and Social Reform*. New York: Oxford University Press, 1968.

Ostler, Rosemary. "A History of Political Slurs." *Salon*, www.salon.com/2011/09/03/slinging_mud_excerpt_slideshow/slide_show/7.

Peabody, Endicott. "The Training and Responsibility of Parents." *School Review* 16, no. 5 (May 1908): 281–95, www.jstor.org/stable/1077147.

Perkins, Frances. "Reminiscences of Frances Perkins, 1951–55." Oral History Research Office Collection of the Columbia University Libraries (OHRO/CUL).

———. *The Roosevelt I Knew*. New York: Viking Press, 1946.

Pierard, Richard V., and Robert Dean Linder. *Civil Religion & the Presidency*. Grand Rapids, MI: Academie Books, 1988.

Polk, Andrew. "'Unnecessary and Artificial Divisions: Franklin Roosevelt's Quest for Religious and National Unity Leading Up to the Second World War." *Church History* 82, no. 3 (September 2013): 667–77. doi:10.1017/S0009640713000693.

Potter, Henry C. "Hundredth Anniversary of George Washington's Inauguration." Address delivered at St. Paul's Chapel, New York City, April 30, 1889. http://anglicanhistory.org/usa/hcpotter/washington1889.html.

"The Presidency: Bottom." *Time*, March 13, 1933. http://content.time.com/time/subscriber/article/0,33009,745289,00.html.

"The Presidency: The Roosevelt Week." *Time*, March 20, 1933.

Preston, Andrew. *Sword of the Spirit, Shield of Faith: Religion in American War and Diplomacy*. New York: Knopf, 2012.

Pringle, Henry F. *Theodore Roosevelt*. New York: Konecky & Konecky, 1990.

Putney, Clifford. *Muscular Christianity: Manhood and Sports in Protestant America, 1880–1820*. Cambridge, MA.: Harvard University Press, 2003.

Roll, David L. *The Hopkins Touch: Harry Hopkins and the Forging of the Alliance to Defeat Hitler*. New York: Oxford University Press, 2013.

Roosevelt, Eleanor. *The Autobiography of Eleanor Roosevelt*. New York: DaCapo Press, 1937.

Roosevelt, Elliott, ed. *FDR: His Personal Letters*. Vol. 2. New York: Duell, Sloan, Pearce, 1950.

Roosevelt, Elliott, and James Brough. *The Roosevelts of Hyde Park: An Untold Story*. New York: G. P. Putnam's Sons, 1973.

Roosevelt, Franklin D. "Campaign Address in Sea Girt, NJ; August 27, 1932." American Presidency Project.

———. *The Essential Franklin Delano Roosevelt*. Edited by John Gabriel Hunt. Avenel, NJ: Portland House, 1996.

———. *F.D.R. His Personal Letters 1905–1928*. Edited by Elliott Roosevelt. New York: Duell, Sloan, Pearce, 1948.

———. *F.D.R. His Personal Letters 1928–1945*. Edited by Elliott Roosevelt. New York: Duell, Sloan, Pearce, 1950.

———. *FDR's Fireside Chats*. Edited by Russell D. Buhite and David W. Levy. New York: Penguin Books, 1993.

———. "February 23, 1936." American Presidency Project.

———. "Prayer on D-Day." June 6, 1944. Online by Gerhard Peters and John T. Woolley. American Presidency Project.

Roosevelt, Franklin D., and William J. Federer. *The Faith of FDR: From President Franklin Delano Roosevelt's Public Papers 1933–1945*. St. Louis, MO: Amerisearch, 2006.

Roosevelt, Sara Delano. *My Boy Franklin*. R. Long & R.R. Smith, 1933.

Rosenman, Samuel I. *Working with Roosevelt*. New York: Harper and Brothers, 1952.

Rosenman, Samuel I., and Dorothy Reuben Rosenman. *Presidential Style: Some Giants and a Pygmy in the White House*. 1st ed. A Cass Canfield Book. New York: Harper & Row, 1976.

Roth, Benjamin, James Ledbetter, and Daniel B. Roth. *The Great Depression: A Diary.* New York: PublicAffairs, 2009.

Rubin, Merle. "A Feminist Portrait of Eleanor Roosevelt." Review of *Eleanor Roosevelt,* 3 vols., by Blanche Wiesen Cook. *Christian Science Monitor,* May 19, 1992. www.csmonitor.com/1992/0519/19131.html.

Sandys, Jonathan. *God & Churchill: How the Great Leader's Sense of Divine Destiny Changed His Troubled World and Offers Hope for Ours.* Carol Stream, IL: Tyndale House Publishers, Inc., 2015.

Schlereth, Thomas J. *Victorian America: Transformations in Everyday Life 1876–1915.* Everyday Life in America Series. New York: HarperPerennial, 1992.

Schlesinger, Arthur M. Jr. *The Coming of the New Deal, 1933–1935.* 1st Mariner Books ed. Vol. 2 of *The Age of Roosevelt.* Boston: Houghton Mifflin, 2003.

———. *The Crisis of the Old Order, 1919–1933.* 1st Mariner Books ed. Vol. 1 of *The Age of Roosevelt.* Boston: Houghton Mifflin, 2003.

———. "A Man from Mars." *Atlantic Monthly* (April 1997): 113–18.

Seib, Philip M. *Broadcasts from the Blitz: How Edward R. Murrow Helped Lead America into War.* 1st ed. Washington, DC: Potomac Books, Inc., 2006.

Sherwood, Robert E. *Roosevelt and Hopkins: An Intimate History.* New York: Harper and Brothers, 1948.

Shirer, William L. *Berlin Diary, 1934–1941: The Rise of the Third Reich.* New York: Knopf, 1941.

Shlaes, Amity. *The Forgotten Man: A New History of the Great Depression.* 1st Harper Perennial ed. New York: HarperPerennial, 2008.

Shogan, Robert. *The Double-Edged Sword: How Character Makes and Ruins Presidents, from Washington to Clinton.* Boulder, CO: Westview Press, 1999.

Silber, William L. "Why Did FDR's Bank Holiday Succeed?" *Federal Reserve Bank of New York Economic Policy Review* (July 2009), www.newyorkfed.org/mediali brary/media/research/epr/09v15n1/0907silb.pdf.

Smith, Gary Scott. *Faith and the Presidency: From George Washington to George W. Bush.* New York: Oxford University Press, 2006.

Smith, Jean Edward. *FDR.* New York: Random House, 2007.

Smith, Page. *Redeeming the Time: A People's History of the 1920s and the New Deal.* New York: McGraw-Hill, 1987.

Smith, Wilfred Cantwell. *Faith and Belief: The Difference between Them.* Oxford: Oneworld, 1998.

Snyder, Timothy. *Black Earth: The Holocaust as History and Warning.* New York: Tim Duggan Books, 2015.

Stiles, Lela. *The Man behind Roosevelt: The Story of Louis McHenry Howe.* Cleveland, OH: World Publishing Company, 1954.

Stuckey, Mary E. Review of *The Good Neighbor: Franklin D. Roosevelt and the Rhetoric of American Power* by Allison M. Prasch. *Rhetoric & Public Affairs* 17, no. 3 (Fall 2014): 553–58. doi:10.1353/rap.2014.0030.

Sturgis, S. Warren. "The Religious and Missionary Work at Groton." *Church Militant* 3, no. 3 (April 1900).

Sussmann, Leila A. *Dear FDR: A Study of Political Letter Writing.* Totowa, NJ: Bedminster Press, 1963.

Sutton, M. A. "Was FDR the Antichrist? The Birth of Fundamentalist Anti-Liberalism in a Global Age." *Journal of American History* 98, no. 4 (March 1, 2012): 1052–74. doi:10.1093/jahist/jar565.

Tillich, Paul. *Dynamic of Faith.* San Francisco: HarperOne, 2011.

Tittle, Walter. *Roosevelt as an Artist Saw Him.* New York: Robert M. McBride and Company, 1948.

Tobin, James. *The Man He Became: How FDR Defied Polio to Win the Presidency.* New York: Simon & Schuster, 2013.

Trachtenberg, Alan. *The Incorporation of America: Culture and Society in the Gilded Age.* New York: Hill and Wang, 2007.

Tugwell, Rexford G. *The Democratic Roosevelt: A Biography of Franklin D. Roosevelt.* Garden City, NY: Doubleday & Co., 1957.

Tully, Grace. Archive. Grace Tully Papers, Box 5; Folder: Writings: Unpublished Reminiscences, 1950. Franklin Delano Roosevelt Library.

———. *FDR: My Boss.* New York: Scribner's, 1949.

Waldrep, Christopher. *African Americans Confront Lynching: Strategies of Resistance from the Civil War to the Civil Rights Era.* Rowman and Littlefield, 2008.

Walker, Turnley. *Roosevelt and the Warm Springs Story.* New York: A. A. Wyn, 1953.

Ward, Geoffrey C. *Before the Trumpet: Young Franklin Roosevelt, 1882–1905.* 1st ed. New York: Harper & Row, 1985.

Watkins, T. H. *The Great Depression: America in the 1930s.* New York: Back Bay Books/Little, Brown, 2009.

Wead, Doug. *The Raising of a President: The Mothers and Fathers of Our Nation's Leaders.* New York: Simon & Schuster, 2005.

Weiss, Nancy Joan. *Farewell to the Party of Lincoln: Black Politics in the Age of FDR.* Princeton, NJ: Princeton University Press, 1983.

"We Must Act. National Affairs." *Time*, March 13, 1933. http://content.time.com/time/subscriber/article/0,33009,745290,00.html.

Wharton, Edith. *The Age of Innocence.* Seattle: Amazon Digital Services, 2012. Kindle edition.

Willner, Ann Ruth. *The Spellbinders: Charismatic Political Leadership.* New Haven, CT: Yale University Press, 1984.

Wilson, Mark R. *William Owen Carver's Controversies in the Baptist South.* 1st ed. Baptists: History, Literature, Theology, Hymns. Macon, GA: Mercer University Press, 2010.

Winfield, Betty Houchin. *FDR and the News Media.* Columbia University Press Morningside ed. New York: Columbia University Press, 1994.

Woods, Thomas E. Jr. "The Great Gold Robbery of 1933." Mises Institute, August 13, 2008.

Woolner, David H. "African Americans and the New Deal: A Look Back in History." Blog. Roosevelt Institute, February 5, 2010. http://rooseveltforward.org/african-americans-and-new-deal-look-back-history/.

Woolner, David H., and Richard G. Kurial. FDR, the Vatican and the Roman Catholic Church in America, 1933–1945. The World of the Roosevelts. New York: Palgrave MacMillan, 2010.

Woolverton, John F. "Who Is Kierkegaard? Franklin Roosevelt, Howard Johnson, and Soren Kierkegaard." Anglican and Episcopal History 80, no. I (March 2011). Historical Society of the Episcopal Church. www.jstor.org/stable/42612655.

Wyatt, Timothy. "America's Holy War: FDR, Civil Religion, and the Prelude to War." Memphis Theological Journal 50 (n.d.). http://mtsjournal.memphisseminary.edu/vol-50-1/america-s-holy-war-fdr-civil-religion-and-the-prelude-to-war-by-timothy-wyatt.

Zinn, Howard. A People's History of the United States: 1492–Present. Reprint, New York: HarperPerennial Modern Classics, 2015.

INDEX

Page numbers in italics indicate photographs.